OPERATION MERCURY

Patrick Stephens Limited, a member of the Haynes Publishing Group, has published authoritative, quality books for enthusiasts for more than twenty years. During that time the company has established a reputation as one of the world's leading publishers of books on aviation, maritime, military, model-making, motor cycling, motoring, motor racing, railway and railway modelling subjects. Readers or authors with suggestions for books they would like to see published are invited to write to: The Editorial Director, Patrick Stephens Limited, Sparkford, Nr. Yeovil, Somerset BA22 7JJ.

OPERATION MERCURY

A first-hand account of the fall of Crete in 1941

M.G. COMEAU MM

Patrick Stephens Limited

© William Kimber & Co Ltd 1961, and
M.G. Comeau 1991

First published by William Kimber & Co Ltd in 1961
This revised and expanded edition first published by
Patrick Stephens Limited in 1991

British Library Cataloguing in Publication Data
Comeau, Marcel G.
Operation Mercury: a first-hand account of the fall of
Crete in 1941. – 2nd ed.
1. Crete. World War 2. Air operations
I. Title
940.5421998

ISBN 1-85260-389-5

The Library of Congress no.
90-85976

Patrick Stephens Limited is a member of the Haynes
Publishing Group P.L.C., Sparkford, Nr. Yeovil,
Somerset BA22 7JJ.

Printed in Great Britain
Typesetting by MJL Limited, Hitchin, Hertfordshire.

1 3 5 7 9 10 8 6 4 2

Dedicated to all Royal Air Force personnel who fought
so bravely at Maleme against tremendous odds and
whose gallantry has never been wholly recognized.

Contents

Foreword

by
AIR CHIEF MARSHAL
SIR PHILIP JOUBERT DE LA FERTÉ, KCB CMG DSO
First Commanding Officer, No. 33 Squadron, from
12 January 1916

The average airman is not given to writing about his experiences in war. Hence there does not exist a written record of what the 'erk' himself feels when he is fighting for his life nor of what he can show of heroism, of endurance, and of gaiety in the most daunting circumstances.

It was therefore of the greatest interest to me when, in the course of my researches into the activities of airmen since the early days of flying, I met, on paper, the author of this book. Finding in him that almost non-existent person, the literary erk, I encouraged him in his desire to publish an account of his wartime experiences.

Happily he has fulfilled this task and the record of his days in Greece and Crete is a most worthy addition to the history of the Royal Air Force.

Introduction

The original *Operation Mercury* was first published in 1961. It was the simple story of airmen caught up in the Balkan campaign. In particular, it was an account of the adventures of two squadrons, 11 Squadron (Blenheims) and 33 Squadron (Hurricanes). Most of the stories and anecdotes were derived from notes I had made in 1941 during and immediately after the events described.

Now, fifty years after RAF operations in Greece commenced, my publishers have kindly allowed me the opportunity not only to add to the original script but to include PART II, where I re-examine the Battle of Crete in the light of the wealth of new information now made available.

In order to preserve the 'freshness' of the original account, I have made few alterations to it and then only in the interests of greater accuracy.

Acknowledgements

My grateful thanks are due to Air Chief Marshal Sir Philip Joubert for writing the foreword to the book and for the keen interest and encouragement he has shown since he first saw the script two years ago; to Sir Compton Mackenzie for allowing me to quote from his book *Wind of Freedom* (Chatto and Windus) and to the War History Branch, Department of Internal Affairs, Wellington, New Zealand, whose official histories *Campaign in Greece* (Army Board: Wellington) and *Crete*, by D.M. Davin (Oxford University Press), have helped in much of the background to the book. I am also grateful for their permission to copy troop positions, etc, from the maps therein.

I am indebted to those RAF survivors of the Balkan Campaign who supplied me with much material during 1941 when I first wrote this story and to the more recent help from past members of Number XI Squadron. However, there must be many who do not find their adventures recorded; to those I offer my sincere apologies.

I would like to add that any opinions expressed are entirely my own.

Marcel Comeau
1960

In this new enlarged *Operation Mercury* I am indebted to many Greece and Crete survivors not previously mentioned in the earlier edition, who have kindly taken the trouble to send personal stories, cuttings and photographs.

My thanks go to Squadron Leader W.F.J. Wilson for supplying further details of 33 Squadron history and to Air Vice-Marshal A.C. Dick CB CBE AFC MA FRAeS, chairman of 30 Squadron Association, for his additional information concerning 30 Squadron airmen in Crete which, I hope, will result in the new edition becoming a more balanced account. I am also grateful to his association for the excellent photograph of a 30 Squadron 'short-nose' Blenheim over Albania.

Another prized and rare photograph is of gliders over the Tavronitis bridge; I wish to thank Colonel James E. Mrazek for his help and also the National Soaring Museum, Multi-Media Collection, New York, for allowing me to use it.

Once again, the New Zealand Ministry of Defence, Wellington, have been most helpful in giving me permission to use one of their photographs.

I would like to thank the commanding officers of both XI and 33 Squadrons for their support and assistance.

The book owes much to the skill of Robert Girling, who managed to breathe fresh life into some of my 50-year-old photographs.

Lastly, I am indebted to Gordon Kenward for the excellent way he has redrawn my original maps.

On a point of clarification, throughout the book I refer to 'Palestinians'. In 1941 this term applied to both Arabs and Jews living in Palestine, many of whom were recruited locally to serve on squadrons as aircraft hands.

Marcel Comeau
1991

PART ONE

1
In the Western Desert

There is a RAF Squadron, it's called Thirty-three,
Existing on sand-storms, at Mersa-on-Sea.

We rise every morning, the last star to see,
Then nip away smartly to skive and make tea.

Duff gen is our motto — another move near,
Then we all get blotto on "shandies" and beer.

Far out in the desert, way out in the blue,
Existing on sandstorms at Mersa Matruh.

No 33 Squadron song
(Tune: 'Red sails in the sunset')

The Italian war was already three months old when Ken Eaton and I slung our kitbags out of the desert train and were bounced along a rough track across the khaki wilderness, and up the stony escarpment to Fuka Satellite. The truck dropped us outside a sand-worn airmen's mess hut. Down below lay our new squadron.

No 33 Squadron, a straggling assortment of camouflaged tents, was spread out over a large piece of desert with a score of Hawker Hurricanes standing sentinel over them.

'We are the first squadron to be operating in the Western Desert with Hurricanes,' McKenna, who had taken us under his wing, told us down in 'B'

Flight. 'The Eyeties were ten times as strong as us in the air, but when we swopped our Glads for Hurrybuses they all just belted like the clappers back to Libya. Their CR42 biplane fighters made a good match for the old Gladiator. They can turn on a sixpence, but it doesn't do them much good against a burst in the rear from eight harmonised machine-guns.'

He grinned suddenly and added: 'One Eyetie, shot down by one of our pilots, said: "It should not be permitted that we use the same air." '

We both instinctively liked this bronzed, wiry corporal from Liverpool, with his melodic voice, twinkling blue eyes, and hair bleached the colour of the desert. We were to find out that he was a handy person to have about the place in times of danger.

The closing months of 1940 were stirring times for the Desert Air Force, and 33 Squadron's victories soon topped the fifty mark. 'Deadstick' Dyson, a young 'A' Flight pilot, created an all-time record when he shot down six, possibly seven, Italians with two bursts of firing, the action taking place over our forward troops. He raced into 'B' Flight tent with the news, falling upon his knees in the sand as if in prayer.

'Just shot down six Eyeties,' he gasped. 'Saw three '42s below me escorting six Breda 65s; another two '42s were in front. I cut across their backs with a burst and very nearly piled into three more beneath them. I had time to fire and pull out. When I looked again the sky was full of falling bloody Eyeties.'

The 'B' Flight pilots called him a line-shooting bastard until the Army rang up over the land line.

'Congratulations to the pilot who has just shot down *seven* aircraft,' they said.

One of the Breda 65 bombers had also crashed . . . Five of the six Italians baled out and three of them taken to 64 General Hospital, Cairo. By a remarkable coincidence, the pretty young nursing sister in charge of their ward was none other than Flying Officer Dyson's wife. It would appear that while he shot 'em down, Mrs Dyson patched 'em up!*

Wavell's 'push' started on 8th December 1940. While his little army left-hooked their way through Libya, the Desert Air Force gave the retreating Italians no respite. That first morning the squadron found the coast road west of Bardia congested with Italian transport. Like thunder, they roared down the long columns, lashing them with their fire and leaving a trail of burnt-out trucks in their wake stretching for fifty miles.

'Ping' Newton, the young red-faced Rhodesian who was my pilot, caught two Breda shells to the rear of his armoured plating, and landed trailing yards of fabric behind him.

'Hell, man!' he shouted excitedly, 'You should have seen those Eyetie bastards run!'

Impatient to get back into the air, he was on the verge of tears when Chiefy

---

*This is a rather garbled account of the action as I recall 'Deadstick' Dyson blurting it out in 'B' Flight tent. For a full report see Appendix 3.

Firman convinced him that his aircraft could not be made serviceable so soon. Indeed, it was a wonder that he had brought it home at all. Besides half the fuselage being ripped away and the longerons damaged, the control cables were shredded down to single strands.

All through December the pace did not slacken, with 'B' Flight's Hurricanes ably led by the flight commander, 'Dixie' Dean, always in the thick of it. Besides Ping Newton, his team included the Canadian, Vernon Woodward, Pete Wickham, John Mackie and the Halton-trained 'ex-brat' Flight Sergeant 'Tubby' Cottingham.

For the ground crews it was one continual round of refuelling, re-arming, and repairing, with always more aircraft unserviceable and few replacements.

Because of a shortage of starter trolley accumulators the Merlin engines were hand-started early each morning. Muffled up in greatcoats and scarves against the biting wind, the riggers heaved on the starting handles, while the stars still shone above them, watching the slow-turning propellers creep around, praying for an early response from the cold engines. Much later, in a bath of perspiration, greatcoats discarded, they would begin to hate the engines, the Air Force, and, above all, the fitters huddled in the cockpits. At every turn they called them foul names. The fitters would sit tight, glad to be fitters.

Only after a long time, when the stars had vanished and the sun was spreading crimson fingers of light along the eastern horizon, would an engine burst into a roar, stumble, then pick up again. This was usually 'Silver' Stirling's aircraft and, as a fitter, he was in great demand. By the time all the engines were running it would be morning and the desert sun would be shining under the clouds in a blaze of gold like the Kingdom of Heaven in all its glory.

Sometimes dust storms stopped all flying and blotted out the aerodrome. The wind drove the dust in channels swirling around the tents. Even the hardy desert scarabs sheltered behind the aircraft wheels. Airmen became lost, and sometimes trudged around for hours within a few feet of their tents. They groped their way to the mess and swallowed shandies, the unsurpassed remedy against the choking dust which penetrated everywhere.

The mess was the centre of squadron life. In the evenings, with trestle tables awash with Stella beer, its wooden walls echoed to raucous airmen's voices lustily chanting the 'Boat songs', whose origins lay in the distant past. Song followed song in time-honoured sequence, and nightly a tall, rangy transport driver would climb a table to sing the RAF striptease solo, peeling off a garment at each verse:

> This old shirt of mine, the inside is quite fine,
> But the outside has seen some story weather.
> So I'll cast this shirt aside, for I mean to travel wide.
> Roll on the SS *Tora Peechi*.

The grinning erks always joined in the chorus and, at the appropriate moment, sloshed beer over him.

'B' Flight had a lucky escape one evening when a Wellington bomber, operating from Fuka Satellite, burst into flames shortly after take-off. It completed a tight circuit and was abandoned by the crew directly it touched down again. Blazing like an incendiary, the bombed-up Wellington trundled the length of the aerodrome at eighty miles an hour, passing like a ball of fire clean through 'B' Flight tents before its hydraulics gave out and the wheels folded up. Despite exploding ammunition, dozens of coloured flares, and the bomb-load blowing up, by a miracle no one was hurt. The Wellington's geodetic skeleton remained as a prominent landmark on top of Fuka escarpment until the war ended.

Meanwhile, with the exception of small tough pockets of *Fascisti* troops, the mass of Italians still retreated, and Wavell's 'push', started as a five-day raid, became a victorious campaign. Soon unescorted Italian prisoners, only too pleased to be captured, were walking back eagerly to the prison camps. Many, left to their own devices, pestered the life out of east-bound trucks trying to thumb lifts towards Alexandria. Some, mistaken for Palestinians, lived for weeks on various RAF squadrons, turning up at mealtimes and disappearing at night.

Right from the start our motor-transport drivers had spent much of their time in the forward areas. They would return with their trucks laden with carboys of Chianti, which was ladled out by the mugful in the mess at night. In the early days, before the Italians had revealed themselves as being so harmless, a 33 Squadron driver had a gruelling experience when one evening his empty Chevrolet was stopped by the Army and loaded with prisoners until it bulged. When darkness fell he was still driving along the deserted coast road, eyeing the rifle in his cab and praying that he would not have to use it. Suddenly there was a loud explosion. As he braked hard the Italians swarmed over the side, rushed the cab, and sent him flying. Heavy spanners and wrenches were snatched from his tool-box. Belatedly he found his rifle, but by that time the truck had been jacked up, a punctured wheel removed, the spare wheel fixed on in its place, and the tools returned to their box. Briskly clambering into the back again, the Italians politely requested him to drive on.

Just before Christmas Flight Sergeant Salmon, a fitter from Servicing Section, took a party forward to the Italian aerodrome at Monistir. Ken Eaton went with them. For the remainder at Fuka Satellite, Christmas was a wild affair. There were plenty of Italian weapons to try out. Ping Newton disgraced himself by shooting holes through the flight tent with an ancient carbine. The motor-transport section went to Christmas dinner dressed as Italian generals, resplendent in white satins and red sashes.

Highlight of the festivities was the sight of two very drunk Fleet Air Arm officers being chased by the CO in a staff car. Reaching a Swordfish in the nick of time, they started up and bounced unsteadily across the aerodrome, with the staff car in hot pursuit. With one main-plane scraping the ground, the old biplane became airborne, climbed dangerously, and then, to our mixed horror and amusement, dived down upon the frustrated CO, rear gun blazing. As the Swordfish stall-turned for another run at the target, the staff car, dodging a liberal spray of bullets, swung around sharply and made off at great speed. In his haste the CO ran two wheels down a slit trench, but managed to scramble to safety before the next onslaught. Shortly afterwards the air-craft disappeared in the general direction of Fuka Main, and no one seems to have ever found out what happened to it.

A biting, blinding, dust storm was blowing when we moved back to base. The Hurricanes had preceded us, the pilots taking off on their gyro instruments, flying blind into the swirling murk. Our overloaded Chevs, weighed down with Flight equipment, pilots' kit, airmen's kit, and erks clinging precariously on top, groped their way through the darkness towards the coast road.

Known as the 'switchback', the one track to the Delta was already notorious for its bad camber and uneven surface. Red-eyed with stinging grit, our driver strived to hold the swaying vehicle on the right course. The Chancelight, hooked behind us, rolled and pitched like a destroyer in a storm, a sort of trailer-borne searchlight.

We saw ourselves as conquering heroes when we drove into Amrya on the Alex-Cairo road.

'Make way for the Talata Talatines!' we all but shouted. Like most squadrons we carried an immense pride within us: pride in our pilots' achievements, and in our own participation in the squadron's history.

On the following day the Monistir detachment returned in triumph, headed by Jeffers, one of the squadron's old sweats, driving a heavy Italian Lancia. They had been in the wars. Chiefy Salmon, walking ahead to guide them over an unmarked minefield, had waved Jeffers over a mine. It blew up under the Lancia's tail, blowing out some heavy planking but causing no casualties among Eaton and the other airmen in the back.

I was pleased to see Eaton again. We had joined the RAF at the same time and had become close friends back in England. A good-looking dark-haired Londoner, Ken Eaton gave the impression at first acquaintance of being irresponsible — even shallow-natured — but those who got to know him better found him to be the kindest, most generous, most thoughtful of mortals. He was a natural target for hard-up erks.

Now he was back again richer by a kit-bag full of Italian .44s, which he hoped to sell at a pound a time among the new arrivals at base. He said that some of the sights in the forward area were pretty grim: Italians killed in bed, dead women in a strafed mobile brothel, men on field punishment retrieving hands, legs, arms and feet to make up complete sets for burial.

Moved to Ismailia, there was a growing conviction within the squadron that we were going to Greece. When we re-sprayed the aircraft with dark-earth-and-green camouflage we were certain of it.

About this time Eaton and I struck up a friendship with 'Piggy' Swain, a likeable corporal from No 112 Squadron who had just returned from Greece on a repair job. He had been stationed there since the beginning of December, and he soon excited our imagination with stories of the epic air battles fought over Albania against the Italian CR42s. He spoke of the cruel weather in the cold mountains, and of the wonderful welcome given by the warm-hearted Greeks. Ken and I knew that by hook or by crook we must get to Greece.

When we bolted ungainly long-range tanks beneath the Hurricanes we thought we were on our way at last. But disillusionment came the following morning in the shape of a scruffy-looking orderly-room wallah ambling down the road towards me and singing the Egyptian National Anthem — a somewhat ribald version — at the top of his voice.

'You're posted, Lofty,' he shouted.

I froze: 'Posted? Where to for Pete's sake?'

'Seventy OTU over the other side of the 'drome, mate. They're off to Kenya.'

Without collecting my kit, I walked blindly down to the hangars and pulled up a chock to contemplate my misfortune. It was some time later that I became aware of an aircraft landing. It was an old OTU Wellesley, which was making its final approach impervious to a barrage of red flares shooting across its nose. Making no attempt to lower its undercarriage, the old bomber sailed majestically nearer. Then, like a gigantic tin can, it hit the concrete runway, rattling and clattering to a halt. I stood up, dismayed, and decided there and then that I was not returning to Flying Training Command. I would go to Greece even if I had to go as a stowaway. . .

2
Greece to Paramythia

To Valona, to Valona,
Every morning just at nine,
Same old kites and same old squadron,
Same old target, same old time.

North of Corfu dawn is breaking
And the sun begins to shine.
Macchi-hundreds and G-fifties
Waiting for us dead on time.

Do four runs up says the CO
And make every bomb a hit.
If you do you'll go to heaven
If you don't you're in the grit.

On the way back, same old fighters
And the gravy's running low.
How I wish I could see Larissa
Through the snow-storm down below.

How I wish I were in Athens
Drinking cognacs by the score
And I need not ever go back
To Valona any more.

Bomber Squadron song (Greece),
to the tune of 'Clementine'
Attributed to 30 Squadron

Deafening applause greeted the squadron trucks in the streets of Athens. Waving girls packed the wrought-iron balconies. Excited children running alongside, chopped the air aggressively with their hands shouted fiercely: 'Mussolini!' Old greybeards standing on the pavements clapped and called: 'Bravo! Bravo!' A continuous rain of myrtle leaves and flower petals fell into the backs of the vehicles.

We leant over the sides of the Chevs and waved back, some of us self-consciously; others like Ken Eaton, making the most of the occasion, saluting and bowing to the sea of happy faces. The Greeks returned the salutes with outstretched arms giving us their recently revived ancient greeting — a cross between a Fascist salute and an RAF rude gesture.

Ahead of us the morning sun shone above the Acropolis painting with contrasts of light and shade the pentelicon marble of the Parthenon. It was all breathtaking. The sun's warmth which filled the air had entered the hearts of the people of Athens.

To the Greeks we appeared as loyal friends who had come to their aid at a time when we were ourselves down on our luck. More than that we were the *Aeroporos*. At one time the Italians had ranged the Greek countryside machine-gunning women and children in the isolated villages. This despicable practice had ceased with the arrival of the RAF fighter squadrons.

By October 1940, the indignation against the Italians smouldering in the hearts of the Greek people had become a flame of patriotism when their northern frontier was invaded. Lacking equipment, guns, and transport, the Greek soldiers had hurled themselves recklessly at the invaders. Outnumbered and fighting a modern mechanised army, they had scaled the Pindus heights to grapple with the astonished enemy. Even old women and children had hauled ammunition up the snow-swept peaks to maintain the soldiers of Hellas. Four months had now passed and Mussolini's proud divisions were crumbling. The Greeks were giving chase but, with everything thrown into their struggle, it was going to be a race against time; no nation could withstand such a pace for long.

Eleusis, our destination, stood some twenty miles outside Athens and near the beautiful bay bearing its name. In those waters 2,350 years earlier the Athenian nation, taking to their ships, had fought the world's first great sea battle when they defeated the combined forces under Darius the Persian and saved the Western world from Asian domination.

Here our Hurricanes kept company with the assorted aircraft of the Royal Hellenic Air Force. Potez 63s stood in line with Battles, Henschels, Dorniers and a few Blenheims. The fighters were Polish PZLs, obsolete high-winged monoplanes, bought by the Greeks in exchange for tobacco. Despite a phenomenal rate of climb they were slow and had little endurance. That they shot down the much faster modern Savoia-Marchetti 79s was a tribute to the greater skill of their Greek pilots.

The Hurricanes were soon in action escorting Blenheims over Albania. Our pilots, flying over the wild and rugged mountain peaks barely out of the grip of winter, began to appreciate the hazards which the bomber boys had been experiencing throughout the past four months.

First to arrive had been 30 Squadron with their short-nosed Mk 1 Blenheims. Six days after the Italians invaded Greece they were in action over Albania. One flight was bombers, the other two fighters, with bomb-carriers replaced by four fixed Brownings. Throughout November 1940 they had fought the air war over Albania alone until joined by 84 and 211 Blenheim Squadrons. The long winter had passed but, even now, with spring on the way, the mountains were still claiming more of our aircraft than the Regia Aeronautica.

Unnecessarily long distances between the aerodromes and the Albanian border halved our Hurricanes' operational time and, in so doing, made their task doubly difficult. There were several landing grounds in the north but the Greeks had been cautious in allowing the RAF to use them for fear of upsetting the Germans. It was hard to reconcile their temerity against the Italians with this timorousness towards the Nazis.

To a limited extent the country had economic ties with the latter. Even the Royal Hellenic Air Force Junkers still went to Germany for their major overhauls. Germany was a dictatorship and so was Greece, howbeit a very mild one, and Prince Paul led the Greek youth in a movement outwardly similar to its German counterpart. With such a lead from their government it was not to be wondered at that many ill-informed peasants were pro-German to the extent that, in the weeks to come when black-crossed Stukas were blasting their homes, they would argue stubbornly:

'They are *Italianos*, not *Germanos*! Perhaps *Italianos* are using German aeroplanes?'

I was not destined to see the Acropolis at close quarters although 33 Squadron remained in the Athens area for several weeks. It was while eating a slap-up meal on my one and only pass to the city that the waiter placed before me a small bottle of colourless liquid labelled 'Ouzo'. Mistaking this for table water I filled a glass and drank deeply. It tasted pleasantly of aniseed and I felt no ill effects until I had finished the meal, paid my bill, and walked out into the sunshine. I then fell flat upon my face.

The next twenty-four hours became a hazy nightmare. At times I awoke from my stupor long enough to appreciate that I was in the most unlikely situations, including at one time conducting a large Greek orchestra. I seemed to spend my time drinking from larger and yet even larger glasses. Everywhere were smiling, friendly Greeks, one of whom took me back to Eleusis but refused payment.

By noon the following day I awoke. My head was splitting and I had an insatiable thirst. Draining my water-bottle I immediately passed out until the following morning. Then, feeling very ill, I dragged my unwilling body down to the aerodrome.

Chiefy Firman was waiting for me with a nasty gleam in his eye.

'Pack your kit and bring it here in half an hour,' he snapped. 'You're off to Albania.'

Skirting the mountains the twin-engined Vickers Valentia, known affection-
ately as the 'Flying Pig', landed in the glacial valley called Paramythia. It
had been a ghastly trip with the ancient biplane buffeting its way through
the snow-clad, jagged, precipices of the Pindus range, each peak seeming
higher than than we could ever climb. Just when the crash had appeared inevitable, we had hit down-currents, dropping hundreds of feet like a plummet.
It had not been the best cure for a hangover . . .

Set under sheer mountain cliffs the muddy landing ground at Paramythia
was almost inaccessible by road. From where we stood a narrow winding
track like a thread of white cotton climbed steeply in coils to the distant village high up the hillside where tiny white houses clung for dear life to the
hard, unyielding rock. A mountain stream, cascading from above, ran down
the only street, crossing and recrossing the road at several places. Higher
up and to the right, mountain bears sheltered in a dark cavern under the snow-
covered summit. It was to this cave that the intrepid Greeks had smuggled
their valuables when the Italians overran the frontier.

We spent our first night in the village. Awakened by the distant tinkling
of goat-bells, I looked out over the valley towards the majestic snow-covered
peaks of the Pindus range and knew why the Greeks had named this place
Paramythia — more than a myth. The whole countryside seemed to be
peopled with Olympian creatures. Nymphs besported themselves in the woods
and cold watersheds. Gods were fleeting through the sky changing the
destinies of mortals and I wondered what part they would play in the struggle
ahead.

Far down below an aero-engine spluttered into life as some modern Achilles
prepared himself for battle. My reverie broken, I hurried to the aerodrome.

Along the edge of the landing-ground, in a line either side of five mud-
bespattered Hurricanes, a handful of RAF Gladiators and Greek PZLs stood
at readiness. The Hurricanes and half of the Gladiators belonged to 112 Squadron. Whisked off to aid the Greeks last November while in the middle of
converting to eight-gun fighters, they had arrived with the two sorts of aircraft. The remainder of the Gladiators came from 80 Squadron, bitter rivals
of No 33.

These two squadrons, 112 and 80, were the veterans of the Albanian war.
Often and hard had they fought against the Regia Aeronautica. Always outnumbered, they had come back for more so often that their opponents now
seldom ventured over the border.

The rivalry between 33 and 80 had been of long standing. The former, with
many years of overseas service behind them, had naturally resented these new-
comers to the Middle East challenging their supremacy. On the other hand
the latter, bringing with them an overdose of squadron pride, had made it
plain that they played second fiddle to no one. At Heluan in Egypt when the
two had come together these simmering jealousies had erupted into constant
free fights. Incidentally, the Air Force, either blind to the friction or choosing to ignore it, took away the 'C' Flights of both squadrons and formed from
them a new fighter squadron — No 274. One can well imagine the lack of

co-operation prevalent in this offspring of 33 and 80 for months to come —
but that is another story.

Scoring had been equal in the Western Desert. Then 33 won a lucky break
when 80 pulled out to re-equip with Hurricanes while they, receiving their
new aircraft without leaving the desert, continued to add to their victories.
It was to be a short-lived advantage. Eighty, like 112, transferred to Greece
before the change-over could be effected, were soon in action again — still
with their old Gladiators. Based at Yannina, holding the front alone at one
time, they had already shot down over fifty Italians.

Now the two detachments at Paramythia eyed each other with suspicion,
keeping an uneasy truce. When our flight of Hurricanes flew in we gloated
inwardly at the thought of the scores our pilots were bound to knock up. The
Glads didn't stand a chance by comparison! But it was an attitude difficult
to maintain. On such a small landing-ground with such limited supplies we
were forced to share oxygen bottles, food, and the one and only vehicle on
the aerodrome: an old saloon car used for transporting oil, dope, petrol, and
tired airmen. Although 80 Squadron repeated to us how good they were each
day, they were kind in lending us tools and equipment without which we could
not operate. Under these circumstances the rivalry died a natural death —
but that was before 28th February. For by sunset on that glorious day fighters
from Paramythia, in full view of the jubilant Greek forward troops, gave the
Italians such a beating that the whole Greek nation paid homage to the Royal
Air Force. For No 33 Squadron, too, it was a day to remember. . .

Information had leaked out from Italian sources that a mass attack was due
to be made over the Greek lines. Large numbers of bombers with fighter escort
were to be expected.

Great excitement prevailed at Paramythia. I sat on Ping Newton's wing waiting for the moment to start up. Already Gladiators, looking vicious and pur-
poseful, were airborne. We watched them circle the narrow valley in a climbing
turn. Close behind, the little PZLs, bouncing across the grass, tore off the
deck, lifting like rockets. Then 112's Hurricanes were away and, last of all,
our flight led by a new flight commander. For a while the valley was filled
with the sound of fighters and then was quiet again.

Time dragged as we waited. The erks sprawled upon the damp turf or pulled
up a chock and gossiped with 80 Squadron airmen. This, we thought, was
the start of a new era of co-operation. . .

A Gladiator was in trouble. We could hear the engine running and missing
like a bag of nails before it throttled back and the biplane lost height rapidly,
one wing held down spilling the air for a quick landing. It touched on three
points and rolled over the rough grass towards us. The fitters and armourers
crowded around, dragging petrol and ammunition boxes.

'Shot down two 42s!' someone shouted across to us.

Two more Gladiators over the hills side-slipped into a landing with the wind
singing through their flying-wires and blackened gun-channels. The erks of
112 and 80 were really bustling now. Then the new arrivals were roaring away
again. An airman with a string of spanners tied around his middle and carry-

ing a roll of fabric tore past:

'That makes three more!' he panted.

By now the circuit was crowded with aircraft. PZLs, Gladiators, and 112's Hurricanes were all trying to get down in the fastest time with the little PZLs landing down-wind, up-wind, and cross-wind in their excitement. Some machines taxied to their flights, battle scarred; one bi-plane with fabric-ripped wings and a flat tyre, another displaying bullet holes in an irregular line along the length of its fuselage. Aircraft were being re-fuelled, re-armed, and patched up. Some were taking off again.

As each pilot added his score to the mounting total of victories, the ground-crews became even more jubilant. When the final count had been made the incredible fact emerged that the small band of fighters from Paramythia had accounted for no less than 28 Italians with another 27 probables — all for no loss to themselves. A possible total of over 50 enemy aircraft had been shot out of the sky! It was the greatest loss to be suffered by the Italians in one engagement throughout the war.

'Where the hell are our Hurricanes?' growled a 33 Squadron armourer. All the other fighters were now down. Then there were our boys overhead — five together and the weaver way behind.

I went to meet Newton as he landed. He stood on one brake for me to swing him around and then cut his engine. Never before had I seen him looking more dejected. Over the wild, foreign terrain the flight had become hope-lessly lost. They had never got near the battle. Only Ping Newton had fired his guns — and that at a split-second view of a biplane before it disappeared among the clouds.

To complete the squadron's degradation an 80 Squadron pilot came across to complain that he had been shot up by a Hurricane ...

Soon afterwards, we heard that 33 Squadron were about to move north to Larissa. We welcomed the Greek Junkers 52 transport which flew in a few days later to return us to Eleusis.

3
Larissa and Almyros

We come from Legs Eleven, we're a shower of rotten skates.
We never pay the long-due rents, we seldom pay the rates,
But from the Nile to Singapore we've left our empty crates,
Lined out in rows and rows and rows.

The beer! The beer! You'll get no lemons here,
The beer! The beer! From Alex to Kashmir.
So bring your lovely barrels out and lay them down right here,
Lay them out in rows and rows and rows.

Our officers are pilots of the very highest class,
Famous from Karachi way up to the Kohat pass,
They never use their undercarts — just lob them on the grass,
Lob 'em down in rows and rows and rows.

The kites! The kites! The darlings of the Flights,
The kites! The kites! The fitter's joys and lights,
Just wheel them into 'Servicing', we'll put them all to rights,
And wheel them out in rows and rows and rows.

Our aircrews they just sit around in deck-chairs in the shade,
They seldom do a 'recco' and they never do a raid,
But every Friday fortnight when it's Squadron Pay Parade,
They're surging round in rows and rows and rows.

Air Obs! Air Obs! To get their hard-earned bobs,

AGs! AGs! They're milling round in threes,
Then back to the mess you chaps and lounge beneath the trees,
And get blind drunk in rows and rows and rows.

11 Squadron song
(Tune: 'Marching thro' Georgia')

L arissa, ancient city of Achilles, now became 33 Squadron's new home.
 The town, lying in the plain of Thessaly, looked north to a distant wall
of mountains crowned by Mount Olympus. Italian bombers had been main-
taining daily attacks upon the close-packed houses and a violent earthquake
early on 1st March — the night following the Paramythia victory — had succeeded in destroying wherever they had failed. Now, reduced to a rubble-
heap, even the buildings left standing menaced the debris-littered streets with
collapsed balconies and cracked walls.

Greeks lived a troglodyte existence among the ruins. After the earthquake,
casualties had been heavy but especially in the main square where hundreds
of terrified women and children running there for refuge had been buried when
the surrounding buildings collapsed inwards upon them. Tremors, but on a
smaller scale, still shook the town and the neighbouring villages from time
to time and were to last for several days after our arrival; Italian bombing
however, callously continued regardless of the earthquake, ceased abruptly
with the coming of the Hurricanes.

On 5th March, homeless Greeks picking their way through the rubble stopped
to listen and then to point excitedly. Low on the horizon, in squadron formation, the sturdy humped-back fighters of No 33 roared towards Larissa at full
throttle. They pulled up over the town and once more swooped past the now
wildly cheering Greeks. The 'Greccos' went mad. It was the morale-lifter
they had long awaited. What to the erks had been just a beat-up was to them
a dramatic climax to a week of terror. Their faith in our pilots was touching.
All over Greece, weeks afterwards, Greeks would waylay airmen with a tap
on the shoulder and: 'Mister–Larissa–Hurricanos!' Then with a hand they
would carve the air while making their own free interpretation of the sound
of a diving Hurricane.

On the aerodrome we found the Blenheims of 11[1] Squadron. By the time
33 had arrived they were already seasoned campaigners. As with other bomber squadrons, most of their losses so far had been due to cloud, icing, and
mountains. Only a few days before our arrival, of ten machines sent to
Paramythia only one arrived — and that one did a belly-landing due to an
iced-up undercarriage. One Blenheim which crashed into the mountains was
carrying its groundcrews. Of the six occupants, three were killed and three
injured. The injured had been rescued by the Greeks and brought back on
mule-back.

Steel girders and walls of brick fell among the airmen's beds during the
earthquake but, by miraculous good fortune, no one was injured. Rescue squads

[1]Although the squadron now uses Roman numerals for XI Squadron, and both were used during the war, I have kept to the more usual Arabic figures for wartime references.

went into the town and helped to dig out the buried townsfolk.

Shortly after arriving at Larissa, 33 Squadron changed commanding officers. The new CO, Squadron Leader St John Pattle, DFC, was destined to emerge the central figure in the air fighting over Greece.

Unlike many commanding officers, Pattle did not need to enter the squadron hangar through the side door, for the prowess of this young South African had already become a legend. As a fighter his cool use of brains as well as flying skill had won him 23 credited victories, but that was not all. He was a great tactician. In the past, under his leadership, Gladiator pilots had flown into action so confident in his clear-cut theories on aerial combat that time after time they had pulled off the impossible. Many stories were circulating concerning his deeds and although some may have been exaggerations it is probably true to say that no more perfect flyer evolved from the last war.

It had been said that he always nursed the younger, unblooded pilots, leading them right up to their target before slipping to one side so that they could register their first 'kill'. Most airmen believed that his unclaimed victories totalled many more than those credited to him for, besides being a tenacious fighter, he was the most modest of men — always trying to evade the limelight.

A master at deflection shooting, several of his victories were said to be 90-degree shots. There was a story of the newly arrived Gladiator pilot who scoffed at the idea of anyone shooting down an enemy fighter from right-angles. Pattle had immediately taken the cynic over the front, singled out a G50 — because of its open cockpit — and put his theory into practice there and then.

The day he took over 33 Squadron was a day to remember. Standing before the pilots he quietly apologised for his lack of Hurricane experience. Coming from a Gladiator squadron, he had only flown a Hurricane once before.

'Perhaps one of you fellows would like to take me up and show me the ropes,' he said.

With little hesitation they all chose 'Ping' Newton — the man with such a natural aptitude for flying that he had first soloed after only one and a half hour's instruction. If he was not the best flier on the squadron he was in any case certainly the maddest. The display took place right overhead. The new CO was on trial and every airman craned his neck to watch.

'Pattle's bound to come off second best,' they said.

The Hurricane had bags of power all right, but no buoyancy like the Gladiator. You couldn't fly 'by the seat of your pants' in a Hurricane. The erks could not have been more wrong.

Three times he placed Ping Newton on his tail and always within seconds, the Rhodesian found his CO's aircraft reflecting in his mirror — positioned for an easy kill. The roles were reversed and Newton, throwing his Hurricane about the sky, tried everything in the book, blacking out constantly with the violence of the quick direction changes. But he had as little success in shaking off the Hurricane tucked behind his tail as did Sinbad with the Old Man of the Sea.

On the ground again Pattle once more assumed his quiet, modest character. From pilots and groundcrews alike he generated respect and affection.
'Ginty' Smith, the shock-ginger-headed Irish rigger from 'B' Flight, put all
our feelings in a nut-shell when he said:
'Be Jasus, but 'twould be an honour to do Jankers for the dear man.'

The war went well during those early March days and as our pilots' success
continued to mount the erks, for a little while at least, spent a carefree existence feasting each evening in the neighbouring villages. With such a favourable
rate of exchange a whole sheep roasted on a spit in the middle of the main
street cost a mere few coppers per head. The villagers would gather around
toasting the airmen's health, laughing, and singing. Poor they were but there
were no bounds to their hospitality, as a party of 33 Squadron groundcrew
discovered to their embarassment one evening.
In one little earthquake-shattered village the ouzo and the retsina had been
doing the rounds for an hour or more. Already the airmen and Greeks were
linking arms and drinking to 'Victory' and 'Long Life'. As was customary
everyone broke into the anti-Mussolini song of derision which commenced:
'With a leer upon our lips . . .' and which by then had a more vulgar RAF
version. Song was following song when out of the blue 'B' Flight armourer,
Jack Weatherby, insisted upon singing 'I once had a heart Margarita . . .'
The effect was astounding. Every Greek immediately leapt to his feet and
engaged his nearest neighbour in earnest conversation. The whole village ges-
ticulated and talked at once. Above the general hub-hub of voices, the word
'Margarita' arose repeatedly. Amused village women, with their large head-
scarves thrown back over their shoulders, crowed around Weatherby.
'Thelis Margarita?' they asked.
The puzzled armourer was leaning back in his chair: 'What in the name
of blazes is going on!' he said, turning to the other erks for some sort of explanation.
Two gendarmes elbowed their way to the front of the crowd to stare at the
airmen, thumbs stuck authoritatively in their belts.
'Ti thelis?' they demanded.
'Margarita?' asked Weatherby unhappily.
That did it. Motioned to his feet he was immediately marched off through
the village. With the remainder of the community, men, women and children,
the rest of the airmen followed behind in procession fully expecting to see
him thrown in the local lock-up.
A shuttered house on the village outskirts engulfed the trio in its shadow.
As they disappeared inside, the erks ran up to the building and charged through
the front door like a rugger pack. Intent upon an early rescue they took the
stairs two at a time. Unexpectedly finding themselves in a lady's bedroom
they pulled up suddenly. In a large double bed lay two young women sleeping.
The gendarmes shook them awake and pointed to the astonished Weatherby.
Waving an arm towards the bed like a conjuror who has produced two rabbits

from one hat, one smiling gendarme turned to him and announced: *'Horisti, Margarita!'*

Unwittingly Weatherby had asked for a prostitute . . .

The lives these simple friendly villagers lived were as uncomplicated as their emotions. They hated the Italians for attacking them; they loved the British for coming to their aid. It was as simple as that. One evening I went with some 11 Squadron airmen to another favourite little village in the hills. The tavern was packed. The old men had formed a circle around us leaning on their crooks. Behind them crowded row upon row of friendly Greeks while women and children crammed the open windows from the outside. They seemed fascinated by our every movement.

Jock McQueen, one of our number, had been one of the survivors of the Blenheim which crashed on the way to Paramythia. He still walked with difficulty on his bandaged leg. This leg intrigued the Greeks who pleaded with us to hear the story. It was simply impossible not to 'line-shoot' to these people. So, with the aid of a French-speaking Greek soldier, I commenced the tale something like this:

'One day it was decided to send many *Inglisi* aeroplanes to bomb the cowardly Italians.'

Thunderous applause greeted this statement.

'The *Inglisi* aeroplanes, heavy with bombs, flew away from Larissa. They flew towards Albania.'

Fresh applause.

'They flew high and it was cold. There were many black clouds. Ice covered the *aeroplanos.*'

A hushed silence fell throughout the tavern. The old men lowered their eyes.

'The *aeróplano* of my friend' — I pointed to McQueen — 'fell from the skies. It fell upon the hard rock of the mountain. Some *Inglisi* were killed.'

The tavern wept. Amid tears the Greeks cried out: *'Pau, pau, pau!'*, meaning 'Dear, dear, dear!'

'But,' I ended triumphantly, 'some *Inglisi* were alive and came back to fight the *Italianos*! My friend has returned to fight the *Italianos*!'

My words were drowned in the mighty cheer which followed as, happy once more, they surged round Jock shaking his hand and patting his leg.

There was an incredible sequel to this episode. Another airman named St Ruth thought it fun to jump up, strike his chest, and shout: 'Me *Grecco*!'

To renewed cheering he took a proffered crook from a goatherd and stared round the room with mock ferocity until his eye fell upon his tent-mate, McQueen.

'Him — *Italiano*!' he sneered.

McQueen, rising to a chorus of jeers and cat-calls, hobbled out to join St Ruth in mock battle. There was a deal of argument with the Greeks before they would even lend him a crook with which to defend himself. Eventually, however, suitably armed, the combat commenced. Every stroke dealt by St Ruth was loudly applauded; all defensive moves by the crippled McQueen were noisily booed. When he obligingly stretched out on the floor St Ruth was able to place a foot upon his stomach and strike a 'Big-game hunter' posture.

The mass of wildly cheering Greeks surged forward, scooped St Ruth on to their shoulders, and marched round the tavern singing and waving their arms. Their hero of an hour previous lay under their feet and it required all our energy to save him from being trampled to death.

Soon after this, 11 Squadron left the aerodrome to 33's Hurricanes and took the dusty road south-eastwards to the Greek Air force landing-ground at Almyros in the Bay of Volos. I accompanied them.

Any regrets that I may have had in leaving 33 Squadron were to some extent offset by the immediate realisation that 11 was not just another squadron. Coincidence had thrown together an unusual collection of outstanding personalities. The Adjutant, a lovable character, ran squadron affairs in the laissez-faire manner of a colonial administrator. Much of his work fell upon the capable shoulders of an LAC fitter called Duff. Despite his brogue and his unprepossessing appearance, he was an organizing genius with a filing-cabinet brain.

Between these two extremes of personality there existed a hard core of talented individuals including artists, authors, repertory actors, and several tough guys, two at least of whom had fought in the Spanish Civil War. Many had been with 11 Squadron for several years and served the squadron with a pride which had become almost reverence. I got the impression that Eleven was more than a squadron; it was an exclusive club.

Almyros landing-ground lay on the eastern edge of the plain of Thessaly. At one end of the field stood four Greek Battles and an Avro 504K. The Battles were to fly off to Albania each morning, rain or shine, dropping supplies for the forward troops. At first, 11 Squadron's Blenheims confined their activities to daily reconnaissance along the northern frontiers.

Picturesque coastal boats called *benzinas* started landing petrol and bombs for us at Almyros jetty. Because Almyros village with its retsina taverns stood equidistant from jetty and landing-ground, the collection of these two essentials became a coveted job among the erks. As the trucks always paused at the village for refreshments, whichever direction they were travelling, it was a jolly crowd who returned to camp at the end of each day.

The happiest weeks of my life were spent at Almyros. I had been given charge of a hundred or so women, recruited to construct a dispersal road for the Blenheims. These women, who all came from nearby Exinopolis, an ugly village built on the grid system, were refugees from the Turkish War of 1923. Regardless of their ages, which ranged between 16 and 60, they all rushed at the job with a vigour and stamina that at first was frightening to watch. Flailing the ground with shovels and adzes, and with their head-scarves wrapped around their mouths, each sweating girl appeared determined to dig more ground than her neighbour.

I started by giving them a daily target of so many yards to clear but, as they invariably worked to achieve double whatever distance I set, I soon left them to their own devices.

And as they worked they sang; sad songs, gay songs, always in that harsh but intriguing harmony peculiar to the Greeks. Sometimes their singing took a religious turn and the sound would carry across the rolling plain as from the open doorway of a church; other songs followed the pattern of the modern Greek love songs with the words always variations of saying *I love you.*

My function was to issue instructions in French to their woman foreman but as they had a far better idea of what they were doing than I, and as the woman invariably answered me with a helpless gesture and 'I understand but I have forgotten much' I found it easier to leave everything to 'Madame' who was a capable leader if a poor linguist.

We paid them a few shillings a week for their toil. They considered us generous. Most Greeks lived in poverty, but the lot of the refugee was the worst. Each morning they would bring enormous bouquets of flowers to us to show their appreciation.

At night Exinopolis village made us most welcome, although any preconceived ideas we may have had towards furthering our acquaintanceship with the girls was quashed from the word go by the strict chaperoning customs of rural Greece. Instead, their menfolk took it upon themselves to entertain us royally in the local tavern. One night they would allow us to pay for the drinks, the next evening insisting forcibly in buying everything from their meagre resources. It was a united village enterprise. Every family in the settlement clubbed together to raise the money which to them represented a large sum and to us a handful of coppers.

One evening when I had taken more than my share of retsina, my hosts, fearing for my safe return to camp, informed Madame who led me to her two-roomed house and bedded me down for the night. To my chagrin I awoke the following morning to find myself in an iron bed — obviously the only one in the house — while Madame, her husband and six children slept on the mud floor around me.

And so the honeymoon continued. For nearly a month 11 Squadron enjoyed themselves among the hospitable Greeks where eggs came by the bucket-load and stewed octopus with beans could be eaten nightly in Almyros village.

Wing Commander Stevens, the CO — a good-looking friendly man with twinkling eyes known universally as 'Long John' — came up to see the girls one day. He immediately showed concern over the state of my shoes — large sizes in footwear being unobtainable in Greece — but solved the problem by giving me a pair of his own. This incidentally enabled me to prefix any discussion on squadron affairs with:

'Well, if I was in the CO's shoes — as of course I am...'

He also gave me *carte blanche* to travel to Volos whenever I liked to search for shoes of our mutual measurements.

It was on one of these trips to Volos that I first made the acquantaince of Kishkey the motor-transport driver whose recent adventure on this Almyros-Volos road had earned for him the prefix 'Killer'. He had been returning to the aerodrome with stores when, while taking a blind corner with his eyes upon the sharp drop to his left, there was a sudden jolt and a yell from behind. Braking quickly he ran back from the Chevrolet to be met with a torrent of abuse from an aged peasant who sat by the roadside clutching upturned wicker panniers and surrounded by hundreds of smashed eggs. Some feet away a donkey lay as if pole-axed. His humane instincts aroused, Kishkey ignored the gesticulating Greek and made straight for the donkey. Only a feebly twitching hind leg indicated that life had not left the wretched animal.

Filled with remorse he drew his revolver, placed a foot upon the creature's head, and fired all six chambers. This act drew even louder cries from the old man.

Unable to comprehend, Kishkey loaded him on to the Chev and took him to Almyros and the squadron interpreter, through whom he eventually received adequate payment for his loss. The bewildered Greek related how Kishkey's truck had merely tipped him off-balance but, when he had asked for compensation for his smashed eggs, the young *Inglisi* had brushed him aside, walked up to his innocently sleeping donkey and blown its brains out.

4
Blitzkrieg

On 6th April Hitler marched into Yugoslavia. Twenty infantry divisions, seven armoured divisions, and 1,200 front-line aircraft strong, the Germans crumbled the Yugoslav horse-drawn opposition, gutted Belgrade, and burst through the Monastir Gap into Greece. Simultaneously a second arm thrust through Eastern Macedonia towards Salonika.

With the Germans holding the once-neutral Yugoslav frontier and the vital pass at Monastir, the original defence arrangements could no longer apply. The small Allied force guarding the eastern approaches was unable to straddle the width of Greece along its present line. While New Zealanders along the right flank made a fighting withdrawal to the Olympus range, Greeks, Australians, and Imperial forces, together with a New Zealand machine-gun battalion, held on grimly to the hill slopes overlooking Monastir. Here for three long days they took their deadly toll of German armour.

Throughout the first day enemy motor cyclists, each with a sidecar machine-gunner, were bowled down like ninepins by accurate machine-gun fire from the hills and the non-stop British artillery fire. Nor did the shelling cease when darkness fell. At night the sky was ablaze with gun-flashes from both sides, bursting shells, and vicious streams of red tracer. A snow-storm blanketed the hills towards dawn and the battle raged through a wall of swirling snow. Strong parties of German infantry, moved to the front by troop-carriers, stormed the slopes under a hail of bullets from the tough Aussie defenders only to retreat, leaving behind mounds of their comrades dead and frozen;

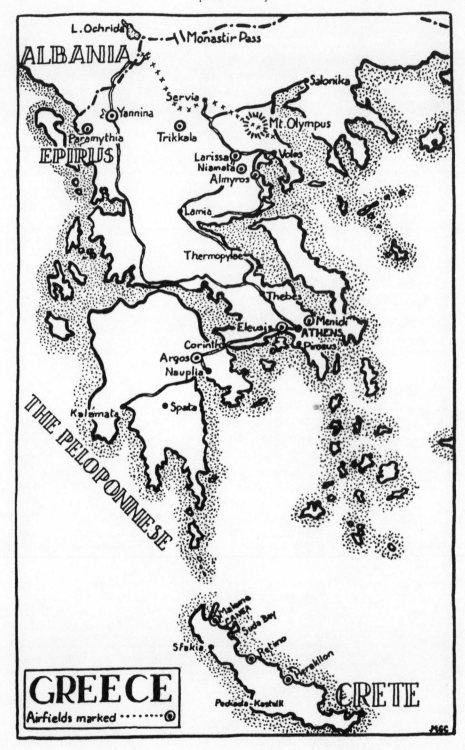

black patches upon the white snow.

By the third day the full force of the German armour was felt. Over 400 tanks had been mustered for the assault. JU87 dive-bombers screamed down upon the defenders in vertical dives, unloading their bombs among the trenches with deadly accuracy. But the tanks crashing through the centre positions came under fire from gunners of the Royal Horse Artillery who engaged them over open sights and repelled every attack.

Meanwhile the east flank of the line had been established by now with the New Zealanders holding the Olympus passes. It was the turn of the Australians and Greeks to fall back and shorten the line and their withdrawal was covered by the British 1st Armoured Brigade.

Already the Germans were renewing their attacks through the three gateways leading into Greece. Now their central thrust drove deep towards the new positions at Portas Pass and a clear road to Larissa and the plain of Thessaly. Rather than give up more ground, Greek Mountain Guards armed with rifles attempted to stay the advancing armour and died heroically in the path of the Germans. They held up the advance for a few hours but nothing halted the invaders for long until they ran head-on into the 19th Brigade of Australians and the 4th New Zealand Infantry Brigade holding their new positions around Servia and Portas Pass. Here, below them, on 14th April the Aussies watched the build-up of enemy forces all day. A shuttle-service of JU52 troop-carrier aircraft had landed load after load of German infantry on the Kozane plain to the north while overhead black-crossed planes had bombed and strafed their positions non-stop. The skies had never cleared of hostile aircraft.

On 15th April, when the expected assault commenced, it was mounted by an enemy still slow to appreciate the fighting calibre of the 'wild Aussies' and their quieter but nonetheless determined New Zealand 'cobbers'. The lesson they had still to learn cost them dearly. With foolhardy confidence they moved up towards the defences and were slaughtered. Despite heavy shelling and mortar fire as well as the inevitable dive-bombing, the Australians threw back one sustained attack after another. By the end of the day hundreds of Germans had been killed and several hundred more taken prisoner.

The ground attacks ceased but shell-fire from both sides flashed through a night sky already criss-crossed with tracer streams and ack-ack directed against RAF Blenheims unloading their bombs among enemy troop concentrations north of the passes.

To the east, 5th New Zealand Infantry Brigade had already joined battle with the German armour advancing upon Olympus from Salonika. Here, around the passes, fierce fighting ensued in the swirling mists and rain-washed forests but, although the positions were penetrated in some places with parties of German machine-gunners firing on the defenders from the rear, the line was soon restored.

Maoris, directed solely by the tell-tale clanging of cow bells strung between defences, advanced upon the intruders with fixed bayonets in sinister silence. Only when their fearsome shadows, made more terrifying by billowing gas-capes, loomed out of the clouds like demons from hell, did they yell their spine-chilling *hakas* and strike down the invaders.

All along the line from Servia to the coast the defenders massacred the Germans until they must have wondered how much more in men and machines the enemy was prepared to sacrifice. For once in its history it seemed as if the invincible Wehrmacht had been halted.

At first, the RAF also were hitting the enemy with considerable success. Pattle's Hurricanes, wading into a flock of 30 Me109s over Eastern Macedonia, shot five down without loss. The vital bridge over the river Vardar at Veles was destroyed by Wellington bombers of 70 Squadron. Wellingtons blasted the railway station at Sofia, the Bulgarian capital, and blew up an ammunition train. Bristol Blenheims, with little fighter protection, roamed far and wide bombing German troop concentrations, tanks, vehicles, and key roads and railways along the path of the invading armies. Sometimes cloudy weather made it difficult to find the targets but it also protected the aerodromes from attack. No 11 Squadron's Blenheims found the road to Monastir packed tight with German mechanised units. They dropped their bombs and, wheeling in formation, watched as the whole floor of the pass seemed to rise into the air from the force of the explosions. Dawn found them over the same target again, then back in time to make another raid by mid-day. A fourth raid mounted that afternoon was only cancelled because of deteriorating weather.

Every available aircraft was thrown into the struggle. Groundcrews worked the clock round to keep them flying. There were plenty of the Luftwaffe in the air too, but most of them had been directed to aid the Wehrmacht in their attempt to batter through the grimly-held Servia-Olympus line. The Regia Aeronautica, however, appeared to have been scared away by Pattle's Hurricanes and the only recorded operation carried out was by a solitary aircraft which machine-gunned a flock of sheep in the undefended Peloponnese.

RAF losses were light at first — but it was too good to last. On 13th April, Greek Easter Sunday, six Blenheims from 211 Squadron, just back from an unescorted raid on the road north of Lake Ochrida, took off again for the Monastir Gap. This time Me109s found them and shot them all down. Under sustained dive-bombing attacks the Anzac defences still blocked the German advance but elsewhere a new stage in the battle had been reached.

It was upon the Greek sector that the German threat was greatest. The stout-hearted Greek soldiers were fighting enemy tanks with little else but antiquated rifles of half a dozen varying bores and with little ammunition to use. Cavalry units faced the Germans with nothing but their sabres. Even before the battle for the passes commenced it had been obvious that Greek courage alone could not hold back a powerful armoured thrust west of the Australian defences. A further withdrawal a hundred miles south to a new line at Thermopylae had been decided upon to save the whole Allied force from German encirclement and annihilation. Not only was this to sacrifice the greater part of the Greek mainland but the victorious little Greek army in Albania would have to be left to its own devices.

At Almyros we listened uneasily to the distant gun-fire and searched the skies for signs of the Luftwaffe who had so far left us in peace.

Late one afternoon, an 11 Squadron Chev moving out of Volos swerved suddenly to the roadside when a flight of cannon-firing Messerschmitts screamed low overhead, diving on the shipping in Volos harbour. The erks lay in a ditch and then drove hot-foot back to Almyros. But neither this news nor the appearance of several German 'Shufti-kites' flying over the aerodrome on the following day deterred the squadron from preparing for another night raid in conjunction with 70 Squadron's Wellingtons.

That night the Olympus defenders were able to watch British bombers unloading their explosives among the Panzers down below. The raid was a great success but, six hours later, while the tired crews were discussing the damage they had caused, the Luftwaffe were already moving in to the attack.

That morning German bombers and fighters swept down upon the Thessalian plain like a swarm of locusts, a hundred or more in serried waves. Forty-two bombers droned over Larissa. Hanging on their wingtips or high above flew yellow-nosed fighters and fighter-bombers, weaving and turning. Smaller groups detached from the main force scoured the countryside like Zulu impis thirsting for blood.

They pounced upon newly-arrived 113 Squadron's Blenheims over the hill from us at Niamata, roared with blazing guns down the line of parked aircraft, then came back three more times, killing groundcrews and wrecking every single Blenheim. At Almyros we watched the black columns of smoke rising from stricken Niamata and hastily scrambled all serviceable aircraft to a safer area.

Another enemy force, skirting the mountain crags, hurtled down the steep-sided Paramythia valley. The aerodrome was thick with twin-engined Yugoslav aircraft, only recently landed. Wings alight with the flickering flames from their guns they swept, crackling like a forest fire, through the defile, damaging or destroying every one of the 44 machines below them. In a trench near the inferno of smoking transports and exploding petrol tanks, Piggy Swain, the airman who had befriended us in Egypt and excited our imagination about Greece, lay dead.

At Larissa there had been no warning. Twenty Messerschmitts swept across the aerodrome as three Hurricanes, led by Flight Lieutenant Mackie, were taking off. The erks, abandoning starter trolleys and racing for shelter, turned in time to see Pilot Officer Cheetham's aircraft destroyed at once. Mackie, already hit by cannon fire from half a dozen fighters, suffered the same fate. As he became airborne he was killed, his aircraft crashing nearby.

In the third fighter sat a young unblooded sergeant named Genders but called 'Chico' because of his pink baby-face. Arriving on the desert in the middle of Wavell's push, his non-smoking, non-drinking, non-blaspheming habits, coupled with his youthful appearance, had immediately labelled him as 'odd'. He had been allowed to make very few operational flights although, fresh from OTU on Hurricanes, he had put in more hours on that machine than the rest of the flight put together. On the ground the erks had made use of

him — taxi-ing aircraft between Flights. Now his chance had arrived — and
what a chance! One solitary fighter challenging a sky thick with Germans,
swirling overhead like migrating birds.

As his wheels came up, he skidded away from the strafing Messerschmitts
. . . held the nose down, gaining speed . . . then climbed at full throttle towards
the mass of Germans. The 109s, surprised, scattered — but not before Genders
had sent a long burst into one of them. The fighter fell out of the sky and
disappeared from view. Now the solitary Hurricane was being hit from all
directions. An aileron disintegrated with a burst of cannon fire. Undaunted,
Genders kept the machine flying with harsh kicks on the rudder-bar. Airmen
down below, rifle-potting at the passing Messerschmitts, paused with bated
breath to watch the stricken Hurricane. Forced to make flat, clumsy turns,
and by now out of ammunition, Genders was a dead duck. Flying through
the smoke clouds rising from the bomb-straddled town, a fresh formation of
fighters crossed the aerodrome, heading east. Ignoring his pursuers, Genders
dragged the Hurricane's nose around and chased after them in a dive. His
audacity paid, for the Messerschmitts did not stay to fight.

Suddenly the skies cleared of aircraft and a very proud baby-faced sergeant
pilot coaxed his crippled Hurricane in to land and receive the acclamations
of the squadron.

Meanwhile, 33 Squadron airmen who had maintained a steady barrage of
small-arms fire from gun-pits and trenches throughout the raid, were well
rewarded. One Me109 pilot, a fire-eating major, caught a volley through his
engine and into his legs. Part of one calf shot away, he sat in a welter of blood.
Unable to reach his base, he joined the Larissa circuit in a blind fury and
prepared to land. But, to show his displeasure, he held his thumb tight on
the firing button. With blazing guns he turned in on his final approach, nor
did he cease firing until the Messerschmitt skidded to a wheels-up halt. Anger
still unabated, the Nazi jumped from the cockpit and danced around his aircraft, swearing and fist waving — stamping his wounded leg up and down.
But the pain came afterwards, and he was crying and whimpering by the time
they took him to the sick bay.

Events were moving fast. Air Vice-Marshal D'Albiac, who had witnessed
the Larissa raid, ordered the squadrons back to Athens. In any case the Army
were leaving all Greece north of Thermopylae to the tender mercy of the
invaders. To avoid jamming the roads with refugees, secrecy was imperative.

It was nearly a disaster, therefore, when the Hurricane pilot with withdrawal
instructions for 11 Squadron lost his bearings over Almyros that evening, dropping the vital cannister a few miles away upon a new aerodrome still under
construction. By first light on the next day the searching erks found the area
covered with men, women, and steam-rollers, but luckily the cannister was
retrieved from their midst unopened, thus saving a minor catastrophe.
Nevertheless, catastrophe was rapidly approaching these warm-hearted people, and we could do nothing to warn them of it.

Withdrawal began that evening. Within half an hour of receiving marching
orders, the squadron trucks started to pull out. Hammers and axes were turned

upon anything we could not take; tents were fired with petrol. Only a small demolition party stayed to blow up the petrol and bombs so laboriously collected from the caiques over the past weeks. Colquhoun, an armourer, salvaged a motor-cycle which was being hammered to pieces. Although he had never driven one before, he managed to ride it all the way to Athens over the perilous mountain roads.

The destruction of the squadron tractors proved no problem to the nimble-minded Kimber, a corporal fitter with an inherent flair for improvisation. His plan was to start them up, lash open their throttles, and then jump clear at the last moment, leaving them to smash over the edge of a nearby vertical-sided hollow.

The plan worked in parts. Kimber and the willing helpers from Servicing Section successfully leapt from the fast-moving line of vehicles just before they disappeared from view. But instead of smashing, the tractors roared down the near side of the hollow, raced across the grassy floor, climbed the farther vertical cliff, and thundered in formation across the plain at full throttle until they became receding black dots upon the distant horizon.

From Yannina and Paramythia, Larissa, Niamata, and Almyros, convoys of RAF trucks converged upon Athens. No longer opposed, the Luftwaffe and Regia Aeronautica found easy targets along the roads, jammed in many places with south-bound vehicles and north-bound Greek army pack-mules, ox-carts, ancient lorries, converted taxi-cabs, and even omnibuses. Along rock-strewn cliff edges and in the open country, dive-bombers, Dorniers, and Savoia Marchettis bombed mercilessly. Men clearing the road of smouldering wrecks were scythed down by the low-flying Messerschmitt fighters and the vicious little CR42s.

Signs of the chaos of retreat were everywhere: dumped tools, stores, and kit, stalled or burnt-out trucks, a chancelight which had left the road to remain perched unbelievably half-way up a mountain . . . a charabanc full of Yugoslav soldiers overturned in a ditch. There was a Chev blocking the road balanced delicately over a sheer drop, with its front half out in space, and the driver clambering to safety and yelling to those in the back:

'Don't jump off till I'm out, for Christ's sake!'

The bulk of 11 Squadron had a lucky passage, although part of the convoy was strafed by Messerschmitts. That first evening the loaded trucks drove off into the dusk, following the rugged rock-strewn coast through Stylis and on to Lamia by morning. Junkers dive-bombers had visited Lamia before us and had left the town a shambles. Apprehensively the airmen searched the overcast skies, because now the road stretched long and straight across the plain and over the Sperkheios River to the shelter of the mountains and Thermopylae. Sirens sounded as the trucks nosed out of the town. Pressing their feet hard down on the floorboards, the drivers sent the Chevs rocking and swaying along the road as the first Stukas appeared. There was no cover. The erks behind hung on grimly to the slatted sides. But the Germans ignored them and continued the task of flattening the pretty little town once more.

By the following night, they had driven along a road like a continuous Big

Dipper reaching Thebes — by this time out of petrol. There were frantic hours of searching in the blackout before a local garage proprietor came to their aid. Refuelled, the squadron set off the next morning to join the main stream of traffic, passing through Daphne, with its rhododendron blooms pouring over the hills like a sea of blood, and on towards the aerodrome at Menidi, 20 miles from Athens.

Meanwhile, back at Almyros, in a tent some distance from the landing-ground, armourers Bob Halstead, Chris Lawton, Lawrence Wheatley, 'Smudger' Smith, Turner-Bishop and 'Skesh' Scarlet, together with an electrician, Fred Archer, had slept on, unaware of the sudden exodus of the rest of the squadron.

When they peered out of the tent doorway the following morning they could scarcely believe their eyes! The demolition squad had fired the tents with Very pistols and the whole valley was filled with a huge cloud of black smoke from 80,000 gallons of burning petrol.

Still not fully comprehending, they made their way to the deserted cook-house tent and breakfasted like kings on tinned pineapple which they discovered in a zinc bath. Having no opener for a crate of Libby's milk they solved the problem by shooting a few cans with their .38 revolvers and holding the dripping milk over the bath. Afterwards, strolling in leisurely fashion towards the aerodrome, they intercepted some Greeks who were making off with a bomb trolley.

'Why do you want this trolley?' one of them asked. 'The Germans are already in Volos and will be here by ten this morning!' It was already nearly nine!

Only stopping to grab a few items, the airmen made for the road to the south as fast as their legs could carry them. As they departed, five Ju88s and three Me109s circled the aerodrome and then flew off to Almyros jetty to bomb and strafe a small merchantman.

In Almyros village they joined a straggle of wounded Greek soldiers with blood-soaked bandages. Others sprawled in horse-drawn carts, some moaning with pain. They finally overtook this depressing column and, led by 'Lofty' Halstead, forged on alone.

By the time the main 11 Squadron convoy had reached Lamia, the armourers had been missed and a telephone call was immediately put in to Menidi. Two Blenheims took off at once. They flew over the party of airmen, now two hours away, and landed in a pall of black smoke on an aerodrome covered with salvaging Greeks. As the German occupation was, by then, an hour over-due, some of Prince Paul's young fascists, wearing black shirts, mistook the pilots for Germans and approached them giving them the Nazi salute. Finding no stranded airmen and with Germans only minutes away the Blenheims quickly headed back to Menidi.

Bob Halstead's party walked all that day and, at night, slept on the floor of an empty house. The following morning they came across the Lascar crew of the bombed cargo ship at Almyros. With reverence they were carrying the body of their aged skipper, killed in the attack.

A further day of walking followed when, eventually, the airmen were fortunate enough to be picked up by a New Zealand Army truck and taken to Athens.

5
Menidi, the Battle of Athens and Evacuation

We once lived in Elysian fields, as everybody knows,
Till one day came Hurricanos with a yellow nose
And Uncle Goering's little lads lashed out their daily dose,
Line astern in rows and rows and rows.*

They dived, they looped, they never seemed to shirk,
We dug, deep down, and said, 'Gawd bless the work!'
They put the fear of you know what up every single erk
Who grovelled there in rows and rows and rows.

11 Squadron song
(Tune — 'Marching thro' Georgia')

The permanent Greek Air Force base at Menidi, set among Attica's purple hills, boasted hangars, tarmac, and some modern trimmings. It had been in use by our bomber squadrons ever since Italy invaded Greece. A Fieseler Storch, like a greenhouse with wings, perched among a collection of Greek Dorniers and Junkers along the hangar aprons. No 84 Squadron's

*Of all the wild rumours circulated by both British and Germans during the Balkan campaign, none was more universally believed by every airman than that Reichmarschall Goering had created a crack unit of fighter aces, trained to oppose the RAF in Greece and recognisable by their yellow spinners. The fact that most German aircraft attacking the Greek aerodromes had their spinners (the boss in the centre of the propeller blades) painted yellow gave confirmation to the rumour.

Blenheims occupied the far edge of the aerodrome. Veterans of the winter campaign, 84 were moving out shortly and leaving 11 Squadron some of their aircraft.

For the erks of 11 Squadron who had arrived late on 17th April there was little rest. Dog-tired and hungry, they were hauled out of bed at three in the morning to service the Blenheims for yet another raid. Two of the Blenheims failed to return.

That afternoon our old friend the Vickers Valentia flew in. The ancient biplane had smashed its tail unit shortly after flying us to Paramythia, but an old Chippy-rigger, a permanent member of the crew, had now fashioned a completely new one from the limited resources at his disposal. Using the skill of his dying trade, and taking several weeks, the job had only just been completed. We watched him as he walked around and around the aircraft, inspecting with a critical eye, and always returning with pride to examine his workmanship on the tail.

But his triumph was to be of short duration. During breakfast the following morning the distant whine of diving aircraft cut across the airmen's noisy chatter. 'Wimpy' Wymer, an old Gladiator man, said with authority: 'Glads'.

Then everyone scattered for cover as a string of Messerschmitt 109s roared across the aerodrome and down the line of Blenheims with guns alight. Airmen raced towards the landing-ground. Already a cloud of smoke hung like a black pillar in the morning air.

'Bloody wars!' yelled Wymer. 'They've hit the "Pig"!'

Like a Viking funeral pyre, the Valentia stood blazing. Crackling flames leaping skyward were devouring the doped fabric and, in the intense heat, already leaving a gaunt skeleton of twisted struts and bays.

On the roadside nearby sat the old Chippy-rigger, with the tears rolling down his cheeks. Ironically, only his tail unit did not burn.

Half an hour later, while ground crews ruefully examined the damaged Blenheims, a high-flying 'Shufti-kite' framed the aerodrome in the broad white loop of its contrail. Manning trenches and gun-pits, the erks waited, ready for anything. On the far side of the aerodrome, 'Silver' Stirling, the fair-headed ex-33 Squadron fitter, along with some others, hastily improvised with a Vickers 'K' machine-gun grabbed from a shot-up Blenheim turret. Belted ammunition lay on the grass in long lines ready for use. They had not long to wait.

A large number of aircraft was approaching from the east. At the same time a Blenheim appeared suddenly on the circuit. It was going to be a close thing. Followed by scores of anxious eyes it won the race with seconds to spare and rolled up to the hangar apron in front of me. 'Lucky' Hudson, the Australian pilot and only occupant, was in the act of climbing out when a horde of Me110s came shooting over the woods. He gave them a calculated look of contempt, shouldered his parachute, and walked with deliberate steps towards the hangars.

Preceded by a terrified assortment of stray dogs racing across the landing-ground, the 110 destroyers hit Menidi. Bellies scraping the grass, they flashed

past as if propelled by the rhythmic thumping of their cannons. Suddenly the
aerodrome was alight with Bofors and small-arms fire. A Greek Junkers burst
into flames on the hangar apron. A Blenheim collapsed suddenly on a broken
oleo. The noise was terrific.

So low were the Messerschmitts flying that a nearby Bofors sent a burst
into another Bofors across the aerodrome, killing the officer in charge. Then
they were diving back for a second run in. Stirling's 'K' gun fired in fits and
starts, the cordite-smudged erks frantically feeding in fresh belts of ammunition. Out in the open a bunch of eight Aussie soldiers having a late breakfast
alternated between taking mouthfuls of tinned sausage and rifle-potting the
passing aircraft.

A dozen columns of smoke arose among the Blenheims. Paddy Duff, enraged
at seeing 11 Squadron aircraft destroyed piecemeal, wrenched an 84 Squadron Lewis machine-gun from its mounting and, like a man berserk, advanced
down the centre of the aerodrome firing from the waist at the oncoming fighter-
bombers. By a miracle he was not hit.

For my part, whenever I followed a 110 in my rifle sights, Hudson's Blenheim got in the way. After the raid I discovered two holes through the rudder
which no German had made.

Meanwhile, at Eleusis, 33 Squadron had been fighting on against overwhelming
odds and their losses soon began to mount. Next to lose his life was Flight
Lieutenant Holman, a Rhodesian ex-policeman with nine victories to his credit.
The villagers where he fell placed his body in their lying in state coffin with
'Britis Pattriot' written on silk collarette across his chest.

The following day Flight Lieutenant Harry Starrett (6 confirmed kills) was
lost. In a valiant attempt to save his badly shot-up Hurricane, he attempted
a landing. Trailing smoke as he touched down, the aircraft skidded to a halt
and burst into flames. Although rescued from his burning machine, he died
in hospital shortly afterwards.

No 33 Squadron, now joined by pilots from 208 and 80 Squadrons, still
battled on aggressively against an enemy who daily appeared to grow in
strength.

On 19th April, at about the same time that Menidi was under attack from
Me110s, the early patrol of Hurricanes landed at Eleusis and was being hastily
refuelled. Jock Fraser from 'B' Flight, sitting on a mainplane to carry out
a quick turn-around inspection, was busy removing the HT battery when he
heard the sudden whine of diving aircraft. Looking up he saw about a score
of Me109s with yellow spinners hurtling down towards him, wings alight.
Hurling himself to the ground he instinctively ran towards the oncoming
aircraft.

In a bedlam of machine-gun fire and cannon the Hurricanes were hit again
and again and, by the time Fraser had reached the nearest trench, the German fighters had swept around the perimeter and returned for another strafing run before departing. Five of 33's precious Hurricanes had been badly
damaged; Jock Fraser's aircraft had a large hole through the battery tray . . .

Surveying the dismal scene, Chiefy Salmon, stalwart among squadron engineers, ordered the five wrecked aircraft to be moved into a hangar.

Throughout that day and all through the night teams of airmen laboured, stripping engines, transferring mainplanes, riveting, repairing and patching.

Tug Wilson, a wireless operator, worked alongside Tommy Yeomans, electrician, and two airframe riggers, re-wiring lights, reflector gun-sights and undercarriage circuits. Chiefy Salmon had visualised that, by cannibalising, three good aircraft could be made out of the wrecks and, to this purpose, he bullied and cajoled the willing erks, often plunging into the work himself.

The airmen slaved on at a feverish pace and, by first light, had produced three reconstructed Hawker Hurricanes ready for testing! It had been a miracle!

As dawn broke, some of the repair teams staggered to their beds and collapsed, others had gone with Tug Wilson for an early breakfast, but had barely sat down when the air-raid siren sounded. Racing outside they stared at the sky and at a white condensation trail noose over the aerodrome. A Me110 was making a leisurely reconnaissance.

Shortly afterwards came the deadly vamping drone as a Staffel of JU87B Stuka dive-bombers approached. They formed a circle over the hangar containing the Hurricanes and, one by one dived down, sirens screaming, dive-brakes extended.

Each pilot released his 1,100 lb bomb load before pulling away, blacked out by negative G. Brickwork fell in clouds of dust and sheets of twisted metal hurled in every direction as fire and black smoke engulfed the building.

As the bombing commenced, airmen had dived for cover but they need not have bothered. The Stukas looked for no other targets. When they departed, they left behind a wrecked hangar and three burnt-out Hurricanes.

At the time, the leaked information was thought to have been the work of Fifth Columnists. However, it was later discovered that, from the time the Germans entered Larissa, they controlled the national telephone system. Even while the RAF were operating near Athens every telephone call had been monitored.

Three more raids on Greek Easter Sunday were broken up by the remaining Hurricanes. Battling it out against overwhelming odds, the pilots of 208 and 80 Squadrons flew as a team with 33 Squadron under the inspired leadership of Squadron Leader Pat Pattle. There was no room for petty squadron rivalry now. Every pilot was a survivor and a veteran. Only the day before, this small band had defeated every attempt by large enemy forces to reach Athen's two exposed aerodromes — shooting down eight for no loss. But there were too many Germans. In the afternoon the final battle was to take place. Sir Compton Mackenzie describes the ensuing action in his book *Wind of Freedom* (Chatto and Windus):

That Sunday, the last 15 Hurricanes gathered on Eleusis from 33 Squadron which had been at Larissa, 80 Squadron which had been at Yannina, and 208 Squadron fought over Athens from dawn to dusk. Some of those 15 Hurricanes would have been marked 'Unserviceable' in less desperate circumstances, but they all flew that day. In the afternoon a number of Stukas protected by Messerschmitt 109s and 110s came over to bomb the Piraeus as they had been bombing it, first by night and, since the almost complete destruction of the RAF Squadrons, by day also, ever since 6th April. There were more than a hundred of them. Squadron Leader M. T. St John Pattle, DFC, a young South African who had 30 enemy aircraft to his score, led those 15 Hurricanes into that cloud-flecked azure which has canopied some of the supreme scenes of history. Three of the barbarians he shot down, and then while he was shooting a 110 off the tail of another Hurricane his own was attacked by two 110s. His aircraft broke up in mid-air and he crashed down into the waters of the Bay of Eleusis; but both the 110s that shot him down were themselves shot down after him. What was mortal of Squadron Leader Pattle came to rest in waters consecrated to Liberty, and the Barbarians plunged where so many other Barbarians, they more civilized enemies of Liberty, had been plunged nearly 2,500 years ago. Twenty-two of them were exterminated on Hitler's birthday, and of the 15 Hurricanes eight were left to carry on the fight against at least 800 of the enemy.

WO Tubby Cottingham had destroyed two fighters when his own aircraft was suddenly raked by cannon-fire at close range. Squadron Leader Pattle, leaving his own tail unguarded, had gone to his aid and shot the Me110 from his tail before his own aircraft was attacked by two other Messerschmitts and seen to break up.

Cottingham, shot through the knee, his aircraft out of control, baled out and landed in the Bay about 500 yards from his Hurricane. Local fishermen brought him ashore, wheeling him on a handcart which they had decorated with a string of fish, brought to the surface when his 'plane had struck the water.

When Pattle, the 'Perfect Knight' of aerial combat, fell that day the RAF lost their top-scoring pilot of World War Two. No one knows his exact score. Officially it is 34 but most agree that it was 40-plus. Records were lost during the campaign. They were victories gained over hostile terrain, mostly in a Gladiator, against odds few Battle of Britain pilots had to encounter. That fateful day he was a sick man and went into combat with a high temperature, the only reason any enemy could have bested him.

The end was near. Blenheims that had survived the day's attacks were already flying out some of the 'key' men. A Maltese-crossed Dornier flew in that evening with half of the Yugoslav Government. Its occupants, surviving the blitz upon Paramythia on 15th April and two more heavy bombing and strafing attacks while their aircraft underwent repairs, did not take kindly to the volume of small-arms fire which now greeted them from trigger-happy erks at Menidi. The aircraft circled the aerodrome for a full half-hour, kept aloft by airmen pot-shooters. When it eventually landed and discharged its voluble cargo of irate, fist-brandishing Yugoslavs, the erks made themselves scarce.

Next day the Greek army in Epirus surrendered. Refusing to give up the positions won from the Italians, they were cut off from the rest of Greece by the speed of the German advance.

Throughout the day the Luftwaffe pounded both of the Athens aerodromes. At Eleusis, while a few of 208 Squadron's Lysanders made tracks for safety, 33's groundcrews were hard at it effecting all possible repairs to the battle-racked Hurricanes. Bombs hit a bowser standing among the aircraft during one raid, and Aircraftman Banks quickly leapt towards the flaming vehicle and drove it clear of the Hurricanes.

Messerschmitt fighters over Menidi put on an aerobatic display which would have drawn a crowd in times of peace. Yellow-nosed 109s skimmed around the perimeter, making daisy-cutting turns, chasing stray airmen down the trenches, and firing at everything and everybody. Twice forming line-astern they roared flat-out across the grass towards the hangars, stood on one wing, and sped like letters through a letter-box through the gap between the sheds. Messerschmitts appeared suddenly from below hedges, among tents, and round hangar corners. Airmen in tree-tops and trenches, firing at them, stood in half-admiration of their flying skill.

Sneaking out in between the raids, a few Blenheims still made their escape. The remaining wrecks were smashed up further. It was time to go.

Once more the overloaded trucks were on the move, bearing remnants of half a dozen squadrons southwards. Already the few flyable Hurricanes had left Eleusis for Argos, a Greek landing field in the Peloponnese; without their protection the airmen anxiously scanned the skies. Kimber had fitted a Lewis machine-gun into the back of his Chev and I a Vickers 'K', but neither of us relished the idea of facing strafing Messerschmitts from the open back of a truck.

Soon we were driving through Athens, and I could not help but contrast our previous triumphant entry into this fair city with this sad departure along its deserted streets. I could not lose the lump in my throat. A chilly breeze was blowing. A few old men at one corner turned as we passed by. They still clapped their hands with great dignity and called 'Bravo!' after us. A tall blonde waved from the shadows near the city outskirts. For the Greeks this was the final test. They knew that we were leaving them to the Germans. They had every excuse for throwing a few bricks. Instead, they called their sad adieux as each truck drew level as if to say: 'Thank you for coming to our aid. We know you have done your best.'

I cannot imagine this happening in any other capital in the world.

At the same time the main convoy of trucks crammed with 33 Squadron erks was also heading south from Eleusis. Armourer Jock Kennedy, who rashly told an officer that he could drive, was given a Chevrolet and instructed to take it to Argos in the Peloponnese. Together with his compatriot Jock Fraser, and with little real understanding of the vehicle, he set off alone, almost immediately taking the wrong road.

They had journeyed along a rough track for ten bumpy miles when a formation of Stukas droned overhead and commenced to attack a nearby target.

They swerved under some trees and switched off the engine.

Afterwards, no matter how they tried, they could not get the engine re-started. Eventually, one of a friendly crowd of Greek spectators offered to fetch his mechanic friend from another village. He set off at a trot. The airmen waited a long time and had nearly given up all hope when he returned on a bicycle with another Greek who straight away commenced to examine the faulty engine.

Along with the crowd of men, women and children the two Scots looked on, fascinated as one by one engine parts were removed. The carburettor was taken off, stripped and cleaned. When everything had been re-assembled the engine was tried and, much to the ecstatic delight of the mechanic and the assembled crowd, roared into life. Even in adversity the Greek people could not do enough for them!

After more adventures, on a journey constantly interrupted by German air-craft, the two airmen reached their destination and reported to the MT officer that they had brought vehicle number x.

'But you can't have done!' came the astonished reply. 'That vehicle could not be repaired in time so we sabotaged it, putting it permanently out of action so that Jerry could never use it!'

Meanwhile, our long convoy had turned towards the Corinth isthmus, that narrow neck of land which joins the Peloponnese to the Greek mainland. The cliff road, reputed to be the worst in Europe, followed the coastline. Behind us Piraeus, the port of Athens, which was under a heavy dive-bombing attack, suddenly threw up a sheet of red flame as a petrol ship exploded. Stukas were active everywhere, diving on the shipping. Even small Greek caiques and *benzinas* were not escaping the onslaught and, as we crawled southwards nose to tail, we watched them at their devil's work below us as from a cinema bal-cony. Whenever they looked too menacing the Chevs halted and Kimber and I would unload our machine-guns to some vantage point among the boulders. Near Corinth Kimber had a narrow shave while under a strafing attack from Me109s. He was firing at them from one end of a small stone bridge when an unlucky burst of cannon fire struck the parapet and collapsed half of the bridge at his side.

Eventually darkness fell and the Luftwaffe left us in peace. The long line of trucks crawled onwards, halting at endless traffic blocks along a road already liberally strewn with the depressing charred remains of the less fortunate. Driving without lights, walking-pace speed at times, tempers ran high. A Pales-tinian driver, who switched his headlights on had one of the lamps promptly shot out. Slow to learn, half an hour later he switched on the remaining one, and that too was shattered in the same manner.

Fears that the vital bridge across the canal had been blocked by bombing proved groundless. The line of transports passed the red glow of burning ship-ping in the Bay of Corinth, and were soon driving on through the darkness towards Argos.

Here, under wet trees in a thicket near the landing-ground, the tired, kit-less airmen rested the night. Half of 33 Squadron slept in the thicket, the remainder being among the Hurricanes on the aerodrome across the fields. Almost at once I bumped into Ken Eaton. We still had six fighters ready for take-off over there, Ken said. There had been seven, but the Greeks had brought one of them down with their two Bofor guns. Comforted by the proximity of the Hurricanes, the tired erks spread themselves out on the damp grass and slept the sleep of the just.

Perhaps sleeping with less assurance that night were the five airmen left behind among the cannon-shattered wrecks at Menidi. Neither were they reassured when on the following morning the Luftwaffe put on their biggest show ever, attacking the aerodrome for 70 minutes non-stop.

In between the raids which followed, the three aircraftmen, Les Robinson, Fred Archer, and 'Porky' Blyth, together with Corporal Dicky Dickenson and a Chiefy, started examining the wrecked Blenheims with the desperate intention of making one of them serviceable and trying their hand at flying it off. Their final choice was a 'short-nose' which seemed in better shape than the rest — relatively speaking. She stood on the far side of the aerodrome full of bullet holes, cockpit hood jammed open, turret also jammed, cockpit instruments missing or shot through, port engine cowlings missing, and engines leaking oil. The aircraft had a lopsided stance, like a drunk, because of a flat main wheel.

At this point a pilot appeared from nowhere. He had been shot down and had just walked all the way back to base.

'Do what you can for this old wreck,' he said. 'I'll try getting it into the air.'

They worked on the short-nose throughout the day, cannibalising parts from other Blenheim wrecks. By late afternoon the six of them considered that the machine stood a sporting chance of getting airborne. They all climbed in: Porky Blyth in the turret, Fred Archer in the bomb-well, Chiefy and Dickenson squeezed in amidships, and Robinson in the perspex nose complete with course instructions and colours of the day.

With vibrating engines the Blenheim trundled unsteadily into its take-off run, missed a large hoarding at one end of the field by inches, and charged through the air a few feet from the ground. There was an air raid over Piraeus. Fortunately unobserved, they flapped along at sea-level with engines at full power but still not gaining height. There was a deal of commotion among the shipping, and Robinson thought it prudent to fire the colours of the day at a nearby destroyer. He received a very fine burst of naval ack-ack in return, and a barrage of abuse from the pilot for firing the wrong colours.

There was no compass, but by the sun and by map-reading the numerous islands they somehow covered the hundred miles to Crete. One engine was by now overheating alarmingly. Hurriedly searching for somewhere flat, by good luck they spotted the strip at Heraklion, and flew straight in — downwind. To their consternation there was a steamroller chugging serenely up the runway right in their path. When the lady driver looked up she dropped everything and jumped clear.

The short-nose swerved as it hit the ground. Missing the steamroller by inches, it swung off the runway and churned through a mass of shrubbery and tall grass. At the same time a procession of German bombers flew down the strip.

Behind the rocks, to where they had hastily retired, the erks congratulated each other upon their escape, and then they were all suddenly struck by the same thought — not one of them had the faintest idea whether there had been enough petrol for the trip. *It was the one item they had never checked.*

Meanwhile, before an audience of airmen in the thicket nearby, the Luftwaffe fell upon Argos and played out the last act in the Greek tragedy. From early morning onwards the sky above the clouds had been stiff with Germans. Nevertheless, not only did five replacements land from Crete unopposed but two Hurricanes set off on offensive patrolling. Battle-climbing their way upwards they become swallowed up in a grey quilt of clouds at 1,500 feet just before the first Messerschmitts dived down. Spitting fire, the 109s hit the strip at 400 miles an hour, cutting down the Bofors crew almost before they had a chance to fire. A Hurricane, hit by cannon-shell, roared across the landing-field, caught in a ditch, and flipped over on its back. Four more Hurricanes, quickly airborne, disappeared from view, but most of the remaining fighters were destroyed on the ground before their pilots could reach them. Nearby, a handful of Greek Avro trainers folded up in flames.

Followed by Eaton and Stirling, Kimber and I had lugged our machine-guns away from the wood, setting them up with feverish haste in a field by the aerodrome. There was a 208 Squadron Lysander, airborne, skimming the trees with its wheels barely fifty yards away with a diving 109 on its tail. Hugging the ground the 'Lizzy' flew past us, its parasol wing and squat body already ripped by the strings of tracers hacking into the aircraft like golden chisels. Neither fire from our machine-guns nor the desperate burst of .303 from the rear-gunner could alter the course of events. As the pilot threw his machine towards the protection of a tree-lined gully, a burst at point-blank range from the fighter sent it crashing into the hill-side.

For the remainder of the day Argos remained under attack. With both Bofors silenced, the Germans had it all their own way. We could only watch as Messerschmitts and Dorniers strafed and bombed the aerodrome and the olive-groves where airmen sheltered. The raiding reached a crescendo when, during the afternoon, a procession of Me110s fell out of the clouds one by one and roared across the plain. We counted 40 of them. They strafed the aerodrome for nearly an hour, flying slowly at reduced speed, nose to tail, in one low continuous circle. They blasted every wreck again and again, and then turned their guns upon the groundcrews among the olives. As each Messerchmitt passed low overhead, we opened fire on its oil-bespattered outline. Kimber caught one machine, lower than the others, with a burst. We could see the tracers smacking into its starboard engine. Then Silver Stirling was hopping about the field in delight and yelling: 'By Christ! We've hit it!' The machine left the formation and made off towards the north, trailing a long pennant of smoke.

Next morning Stirling had thrown himself on the ground as another Messerschmitt, leaving the circuit to investigate, bore down upon us. A line of cannon shells lashed the ground between our two guns, and then the aircraft was banking over the thicket. Beneath the trees several hundred airmen and soldiers held their breath, well aware of the fearful havoc a salvo of bombs coul. make among the packed men and vehicles. But the fighter-bombers had stayed long enough, and soon they were receding dots on the horizon. It was heartbreaking to take stock of the damage they had caused. By the end of the day all the Greek trainers, the Lysander and remaining Hurricanes had been destroyed. The aircraft in the air had made no contact with the Luftwaffe and headed for Crete.

The Hurricanes had departed, but there was still another day of trials ahead for the exhausted airmen who during the night had moved by trucks among the foothills between Argos and Nauplia port. Miserably cold after two blanketless nights in the open, they faced another hectic 12 hours at the mercy of the Luftwaffe, who now ruled the skies above.

For the Air Force drivers there was no rest at all that night. Along with some Army drivers they had taken their 'Chevs' to a distant cliff edge, drained the engines, and ran them until they seized up before pushing them over the side. Kimber, who had gone with them, was walking back towards the hills alone when in the darkness he stumbled across two exhausted Australians staggering among the boulders. They were carrying a third Australian with them. The man had both feet blown off while helping to wreck a tank which had run out of fuel with no more of the correct sort available.

Kimber left them along the cliff while he made a long search for a stretcher with which he eventually returned to help transport the injured man back to his unit.

By dawn, formations of Junkers, Dorniers, Heinkels, and Messerschmitts were everywhere, attacking shipping or soaring overhead pattern-bombing. Bombs fell across the troop-packed hillside hurling earth and rock splinters skywards, killing and maiming airmen and soldiers. Dorniers descended upon the thicket by Argos aerodrome and left it a charred and leafless wilderness. Someone had tipped them off. Fortunately their bombs were wasted; the woods had been cleared the night before.

Blenheim pilots from 11 and 30 Squadrons were still ferrying key men to Crete. The pilots, flying alone, in an area dominated by the Luftwaffe, never knew what they might encounter on their return.

No 30 Squadron successfully rescued a group of 33 Squadron airmen left behind at Eleusis. Without kit, eight of them, including Colin France, 33's cheerful telephonist, had crammed like sardines into a 'short nose' and reached Maleme.

The departure of the Hurricanes made matters worse for soon the Regia Aeronautica were taking a hand. 'Lucky' Hudson, the Australian, returning from Crete was bounced by four CR42s. Realising the Blenheim had no rear gunner, the Italians made a series of quarter attacks without danger to themselves. Bullets hit the bomber from all sides and although Hudson, reputed to be the first man to roll a Blenheim, tried every evasive manoeuvre he could not shake them off. Eventually his shattered aircraft splashed into the sea.

However, true to his 'Lucky' reputation, two supply ships heading for Nauplia appeared; one of them, an ammunition ship, fished him out of the water. The Australian barely had time to dry himself before the vessels were set upon by a large formation of German dive-bombers. Forming their notorious 'circle of death', the Stukas peeled off one by one to bomb the defenceless merchantmen.

By the time they had reached Nauplia, both ships had received direct hits; the ammunition ship was ablaze, taking water and listing heavily. There were many casualties. Together with some of the surviving crew, Hudson dived over the side just before the vessel exploded in one of war's biggest bangs to date, shattering the Greek houses all around the harbour.

Rendered nearly unconscious by the blast, the Australian was soon swimming for his life as the Germans, having exhausted their bombs, came down low over the water, machine-gunning the survivors as they tried to reach the shore.

The smouldering hulks of the two supply ships left a pall of black smoke over the harbour. From the foothills of Nauplia we had witnessed the Stuka attack but at the time we did not connect the incident with 'Lucky' Hudson, who had reached us later and sat quietly upon a rock with an airman's tunic draped over his shoulders . . .

Meanwhile, Chiefy Salmon and his Group 1 tradesmen from 33 Squadron were ordered to fly to Crete and organise the reception for any Hurricanes that might land there. Together with some high-ranking officers they boarded a Short Sunderland flying-boat lying at anchor but no sooner were they seated when a score of Messerschmitt 109s came diving, line-abreast, across the harbour.

The huge flying-boat was a sitting target. Back and forth the fighters flew with cannons blazing, hitting the smouldering wrecks again and again, climbing over the town and returning for a further onslaught.

Those in the defenceless Sunderland crossed their fingers and prayed. Recording the incident afterwards, Chiefy Salmon wrote: 'The Captain of the aircraft and his co-pilot maintained an unflustered calm; my airmen sat very still but some of the senior officers panicked and others gave orders because they felt they had to, on the principle of never mind what you do but *do* something!'

After the raid the Sunderland took off for Crete. How so large a target was missed by the Germans remains a mystery.

Despite setbacks, the evacuation of the airmen in the hills went according to plan. That evening they marched the six miles to the port. Last-minute orders were given as they set out.

'You are to maintain ranks regardless of bombing or strafing. If anyone is hit it will be up to the man next in line to get him to the beach. If anyone is hit and falls out, he must be left behind. On no account must ranks be broken.'

'It's enough to wipe the silly grin off anyone's face,' said Kimber, who had rejoined us.

Pathetic, silent groups of civilians stood among the bomb-crumbled outskirts of the town. A few smiled sadly as the long line of airmen passed, but here and there black-shirted youths of Prince Paul's Youth Movement, wearing Sam Brownes, gave the Fascist salute and mocked the passing British. It was hard not to break ranks and retaliate. In the dusk the Greeks were laying out lines of dead bodies, victims of earlier bombing and strafing — crumpled bundles of flesh and rag, men, women and children. Someone in a large house lit a lamp as we passed — a simultaneous volley of rifle shots from airmen and Australians in the town extinguished the light.

Further into the town Australians in the best of humour stood in trucks handing out tins of bully beef and peaches to a growing crowd. The Greeks jostled around the Aussies with outstretched arms and all but blocked the road. There was still fighting ahead for these tough soldiers before they embarked.

As night fell, the waters of Nauplia Bay glowed a rosy pink from the flickering flames of the still-burning merchantman. A Short Sunderland flyingboat, like a surfaced sea monster, rode at anchor silhouetted against the glow. Troops stood patiently in rows at the water's edge and waited. Motor-barges, low and black, chugged from the shores into the night. For a moment the glow from the harbour illuminated the huddled soldiers and airmen in each craft, painting them with a pastel pink before they disappeared into the blackness like a Grand Finale with each player making his bow before the footlights.

In next to no time I found myself scrambling aboard the already bombscarred assault ship *Glenearn*. A cheery word from a merchant seaman and a mug of steaming hot cocoa was thrust into my hand before I descended with a crowd of airmen and soldiers below decks.

Down in the dark, stuffy, leaking, bilge-washed hold a crowd of dispirited and bomb-happy troops panicked as the first bombs started falling with the dawn after we had been several hours under way. The explosions alongside, sledge-hammering the underwater plating like direct hits, sent a wave of claustrophobia through the hold. Suddenly the companionway became blocked with screaming, sweating soldiers fighting for a foot-hold. But those who reached the tight-jammed exposed decks were soon trying to force their way down below once again to escape the attacking Junkers, who had by now come down low to rake the decks with cannon and machine-gun fire.

After a while the Germans called it a day, but not before four Ju88s had been shot out of the sky by some accurate firing from the cruiser *Phoebe*, who was escorting us. The plucky *Glenearn* was not to keep her luck for long. On her very next trip she was so badly bombed that it was a miracle that she kept afloat. She had to be towed back to Crete and then to Egypt. Also not so fortunate was the next load of troops to leave Nauplia. Seven hundred of them aboard a Dutch transport, the *Slamat*, had the little ship bombed and sunk under them. Two destroyers succeeded in picking up most of the survivors, but were themselves both bombed and sunk later on in the day. Only 42 sailors and eight soldiers were saved; 900 men were lost.

Back on the *Glenearn* we were soon limping past the ruined hulk of HMS *York*, sunk previously by Italian frogmen, and into the natural anchorage of Suda Bay, Crete. For most of the airmen on board it meant a quick return to Egypt, but for a few it was only the beginning of a far more violent chapter in their lives; for some of these it was to be the final chapter.

6
Crete: the Luftwaffe discovers Maleme

With the collapse of Greece, Crete had suddenly gained in importance. Overnight this backwater in Middle East strategy had become both a front-line base and Britain's last foothold in Europe. For the Germans, its neutralisation or capture was now essential to protect Axis shipping in the Aegean and to prevent British bombers using the island as a base from which to bomb the valuable oilfields of Roumania. Securing Crete would be tantamount to driving the British Fleet out of Eastern Mediterranean waters. It would also be the first stepping-stone towards Cyprus and the Egyptian Delta. Already a cut-and-dried plan for an air assault upon Crete was before Hitler: the suggested date — 18th May, 1941.

To the British, even by the beginning of May, this was no secret. Besides useful information passed on by our Greek friends, air reconnaissance reported the rapid build up of troop-carriers and sea transports in southern Greece. A remarkably accurate appreciation* of the nature of the impending assault

*In hindsight the appreciation of the impending assault no longer appears so 'remarkable' since the post-war revelation that the British possessed 'Top Secret' Ultra, the machine able to decode German high grade secret messages. Three people in the Middle East, Admiral Cunningham, General Wavell and General Freyberg had advance knowledge of every detail in the German Invasion plan. However, Ultra was a tricky secret to keep. To act too obviously upon the information received might cause suspicion and result in the code being altered. By the same token, General Freyberg dared not position his forces too accurately in case the Germans suspected the truth. Sworn to secrecy, he had no way of communicating the certainty of forthcoming assaults on the airfields to his commanders.

and the likely target areas was circulated. Acting upon these assumptions, the defence of the island was planned.

Before the loss of Greece, Crete had been garrisoned by a small holding force concentrated, in the main, around the Suda Bay fleet anchorage. Air protection had been given by the Fleet Air Arm and, in the later stages, by the RAF operating from three small landing-strips hacked out of the narrow coastal plain. The mountainous nature of the remainder of Crete not only dictated the positions of these aerodromes but also limited their size. It was now necessary to extend the island's defences to safeguard these three vulnerable areas.

The airfields, connected by the one and only road, all possessed the barest facilities. Even if more fighters were made available, the landing-grounds would have been too small to hold them.

Maleme, a Fleet Air Arm base, was little more than a reclaimed stretch of sandy beach; Heraklion not much bigger; and Rethymnon was a small field. A fourth aerodrome, inland from Heraklion at Padiada Kastelli, was still under construction. It could not now be incorporated into the general defence system and had to be rendered unserviceable.

The only available troops to defend these areas were the battle-weary, decimated battalions of Anzacs which had been arriving from southern Greece throughout the last week in April. They had come in destroyers, merchantmen, caiques, and even water-logged rowboats. All were now without kit, many without weapons — some units did not possess a single rifle between them. Ammunition was short, so were spades. Trenches were being scraped out with tin hats. Machine-guns which had been rescued were without tripods or spare ammunition-pans.

Because of a serious shortage of transport, many of these soldiers, exhausted as they were, had to foot-slog it to their new positions from Suda Bay. It was 30 miles to Rethymnon, 65 miles to Heraklion. No wonder, therefore, that many with only too vivid memories of the continuous dive-bombing they had endured, were bitter and blamed the RAF for their present predicament. Airmen passing them along the hard dusty road were met with a torrent of abuse.

'RA bloody-F!' catcalled the soldiers. 'Rare As Bloody Fairies!'

It was a hard pill to swallow.

One day a party of exhausted Aussies rowed their waterlogged craft into the Venetian harbour at Canea; yet another heroic escape made by a group of men who, too late for evacuation in Greece, still refused to surrender to the Germans! They brought with them four sacks of mail which had been standing on Kalamata jetty. However, when three turned out to be for the RAF, the enraged Aussies dumped them into the water.

By the middle of May the defences had started to take shape; Australians held Rethymnon and Heraklion, New Zealanders covered the 20 miles of coast running east from Maleme and including Canea, the Cretan capital. With the exception of detachments of airmen on the three airfields, 100 men working two radar stations, and 130 men around Suda Bay, most of the RAF groundcrews had been flown back to Egypt.

Not intending to miss the final show, when the RAF started evacuating I had given 11 Squadron the slip. No 33 Squadron's fighters were still operating somewhere on the island, and I had set out to find them. Burwell, a dependable if rather morose 'A' Flight airman, had come with me. He had no ties with 33 Squadron, but the adventure had appealed to him.

Searching for the squadron we drew a blank at Rethymnon — deserted except for one dejected-looking Gladiator facing the road — and again at Heraklion, 35 miles farther on, where 112 Squadron was in possession. Third time lucky, we doubled back along the coast through Canea towards the extreme west of the island, and found the squadron at Maleme.

Maleme aerodrome was wedged between sea and road. To the south the ground, bare of cover except for a small vineyard, rose to the base of Kavkazia Hill, 340 feet high. To the west lay the River Tavronitis.

No 805 Squadron, Fleet Air Arm, the original occupants, had been flying their Fulmars, Gladiators, and Brewster Buffalos from the aerodrome in defence of Suda Bay throughout the Greek campaign and were almost played out. Underpowered, undergunned, and slow, the Buffalos now stood in an untidy row by the shore. All were 'write-offs'. Only one Fulmar and a Gladiator now remained to be maintained by 50 groundcrew billeted east of Kavkazia Hill at Maleme village.

Kavkazia Hill, wooded to the north, scrub-covered to the south, dominated the area inland from the aerodrome and offered good defensive possibilities, but the broad, stony bed of the Tavronitis, with the water at that time of the year reduced to a mere trickle, was a harder proposition. With much dead ground around the river mouth, its defence required more men than were available and only the Iron Bridge which carried the road across was adequately guarded. South of the road, in an olive grove along the river bank, lay the tents of 30 and 33 Squadrons.

With 14 Fighter-Blenheims, 30 Squadron had been sent to Maleme in the middle of April to protect the sea lanes and subsequently to give cover for the evacuations from Greece. All serviceable Blenheims had by now returned to Egypt, but some hundred ground staff were still waiting to be flown out.

No 33 Squadron's airmen, on the other hand, were needed to keep our remaining fighters flying — together with 112 Squadron at Heraklion. After seeing away the remaining Hurricanes at Argos landing-ground, they had crammed into Chevs and retreated under constant German air attacks to the most southern tip of the Greek mainland. From here at Kalamata, where hundreds of British troops were to be trapped by the speed of the German advance, they were brought to Crete by Short Sunderland. They had arrived at Maleme without a change of clothing, bedding, or even eating utensils. A few blankets were borrowed, but there were no ground-sheets for protection against the damp ground. The men were sleeping upon duck-boards; the slats, too widely spaced for comfort, pinched at the intersections, and waffle-scarred the sleepers.

All my friends were there: McKenna, Eaton, Tubby Dixon, Sturgess, Ginty

Smith, and Paddy Rennie, the thick-set Irish ACH who now ran the cook-house tent as he had run the bar at Fuka Satellite. All were in good spirits despite the many inconveniences, but the threat of imminent invasion — apparent to every man on the island — had produced an atmosphere all of its own. A mad game of 'Shoot' had commenced in a stone hut among the trees. It was to develop into a marathon game which lasted out our stay at Maleme. Already a mountain of drachma notes covered a corner of the hut — too large a sum for any single erk to 'shoot'. When the money they could not spend ran out, the players substituted IOUs for banknotes.

Over the doorway of the hut someone had chalked: THE ISLE OF DOOM. Bob Bartlett, who played an accordion at squadron parties, wandered about with a solemn countenance and a twinkling eye, wailing:

'We are all doomed men!'

Some men had rifles, and there were a few Italian carbines and revolvers about, but the aerodrome, with eight Bofors and one RAF Lewis machine-gun, was still inadequately protected. The Bofors were badly sited — most of them, standing on flat patches of sand, could not have been more vulnerable to air attack. The Marines who manned them used no form of protection or camouflage. They came under a different command, and the fault could not be remedied. With courageous stubbornness they insisted upon being as near as possible to the aircraft they had been sent to preserve, resisting all entreaties from the New Zealanders to move them. The New Zealanders, whose job it was to defend the aerodrome from land attack, remained in conceal-ment and took no active part in protecting the landing-ground until the inva-sion took place.

Where the aerodrome lay beneath the road-level four aircraft pens had been constructed out of sandbags and earth-filled petrol drums. The RAF Lewis machine-gun perched above the first pen in its own sandbagged emplacement. It was in a suicidal position, but had been placed there ready, in the event of invasion, to ignite by tracers a nearby petrol dump. By the time I arrived, Ken Eaton had taken possession. Across the road from him was a second gun-pit with a good mounting — but the gun was a dummy one carved out of wood.

Eight Hurricanes had been gathered together at Maleme, four with 80 Squad-ron pilots who had stayed on to take their turn (as did the spare Fleet Air Arm officers). As soon as the aircraft arrived they had been in action main-taining protective patrols over the evacuation routes and, after the end of April, the Suda Bay area. There were no spares to keep the Hurricanes flying. The only tools were in two boxes which Chiefy Salmon had managed to salvage from Greece. Nevertheless, the worn-out aircraft stayed airborne, and soon found the enemy.

Ju88s and Stukas were making increasingly heavier raids on the shipping in Suda Bay. Here, on 3rd May, Flying Officer Woods and Sergeant Genders — both labelled 'Chico' and both by now veterans — waded through a forma-tion of 24 Ju88s; Woods shot down one confirmed and damaged a second, while Genders damaged four. The next day Woods and Flying Officer Noel-

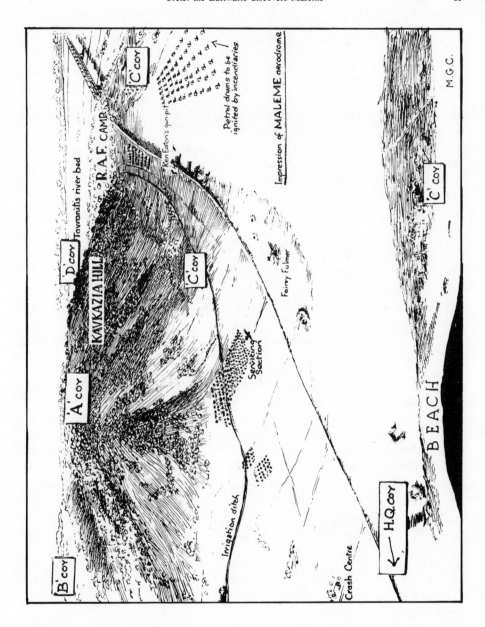

Johnson accounted for four more of them.

But by now the strain on the pilots, who had been fighting almost daily since the German attack upon Greece, was considerable, and on the evening of 12th May six of them were relieved by replacement pilots flown in from Egypt and led by the new CO, Squadron Leader Howell.

So far the Germans had left Maleme alone, but that evening the village and the aerodrome perimeter were bombed and strafed by Junker 88s, who returned at dawn the next morning to bomb the already unserviceable Blenheims 30 Squadron had left behind on the airfield. The erks hurried their breakfasts, and made for the landing-ground. This, it seemed, was not going to be just another day.

In his gun-pit Ken Eaton stood like a personal bodyguard over the three Hurricanes with their pilots already in the cockpits and the erks hanging on their wingtips.

There was a whine and a roar and 30 Me109s flashed out of the sun. The air crackled with their exploding cannon shells. The erks were racing for cover followed by a fusillade of bullets as Sergeants Ripsher and Reynish trundled their Hurricanes along the strip at a desperate full throttle, Sutton harnesses flapping, nothing fastened up. The Messerschmitts shot overhead, while the two men sat with their backs to the oncoming fighters, fighting to gain height, struggling to gain a little more speed out of the lumbering Mark Is as they lifted their undercarriages . . .

Half a dozen Messerschmitts were flying straight down the strip as Squadron Leader Howell in the third Hurricane opened his throttle. Eaton in his gunpit hung on to the Lewis, blazing wildly at them. Yet another wave of aircraft skimmed the beach. There were so many Messerschmitts it was impossible to keep track of them. Everything was yellow tracer and crackling cannon, thumping Bofors and rifle shots. One-o-nines swept past the CO on either side before he was airborne. Others came in on his starboard quarter just as he came 'unstuck'. Two Germans flashing past his nose left him their slipstream. The Hurricane dropped violently in the bumpy air, then, miraculously unscathed, carried on. It kept low and headed for the protection of the hills.

To the east Sergeant Reynish was holding his machine in a vertical bank with three Messerschmitts trying to turn inside him. He was more than a match for them. Then he was on the tail of one of them; the 109 turned slowly on its back out of control, and dived into the hills. But by now there were 12 Messerschmitts in pursuit of the Hurricane, and they all disappeared from view over the hills.

German fighters were diving low over the landing-strip, shooting up the scrap-heap of Brewster Buffalos along the coast. Eaton, with a fresh pan of ammunition, gave them a long burst. Then Sergeant Ripsher came out of nowhere above the enemy aircraft as they flew out to sea. He shot one of them out of the formation, and it hit the water with a mighty splash. But more fighters were tailing the lone Hurricane. Ripsher was twisting and turning desperately to try to shake them off. Too near the ground to manoeuvre freely, he headed back towards the aerodrome. Fighter after fighter poured shells into his stricken machine — but he still kept flying.

Eaton and the Bofors crews were pumping up everything they had at the pursuing 109s while Sergeant Ripsher lowered wheels and flaps, attempting a landing. But, as he hovered over the shore on his final approach, an unlucky string of Bofors shells smacked into him, killing him instantly.

The Messerschmitts kept at it non-stop for half an hour or more. There was no sign of the CO or Sergeant Reynish — and little hope for them.

Then the skies cleared over Maleme. By the road a replacement Hurricane was on fire and the one remaining Fleet Air Arm Fulmar burnt fiercely on the ground. A mushroom of black smoke hung over the sea-shore where the Brewster Buffalos stood. All who had witnessed it were badly shaken by Ripsher's dramatic death. A trickle of men were making their way towards one of the gun-sites on the far side of the aerodrome. Tempers were high and a first-class row was brewing between the gunners, their officers, and the New Zealanders, with whom they were already out of favour because of their badly sited guns. The outcome was a new directive to the gunners not to open fire until prior orders had been received from an officer. As there were few officers, this was both impractical and stupid. When a smaller number of Messerschmitts renewed the attack shortly afterwards, no one was handy to give orders and the Bofors remained silent.

Three and a half hours after he had taken off, Squadron Leader Howell brought his Hurricane back to Maleme. We were amazed to see him, and the erks all tumbled down the bank to swing his aircraft into the pen to refuel it. He had hugged the deck upon take-off until he had cleared the combat area. Then, climbing to a good height, he had found himself up-sun from two 109s who were returning to Greece. He tagged on to them, keeping in their blind spot, and flew out to sea with them for a while. Then he shot down the nearest one and damaged the other. Running short of fuel he had landed at Rethymnon. No other Hurricane had reached Maleme — anyway, he had seen a Hurricane in flames out to sea, which must have been Sergeant Reynish . . .

Late that afternoon, as the air chilled and the shadows lengthened, the aerodrome lay quiet beneath the Lewis-gun emplacement. Ken Eaton, red-eyed and smoke-blackened, hung wearily over his parapet watching with amused interest the activities of Ginger Stone, a fitter from 'B' Flight, who had salvaged two Browning guns from a wrecked aircraft and was busy scratching a hole in the aerodrome itself in which to fit up his 'contraption'. Yards of belted ammunition stretched out on either side of him like twisted tyre tracks. The only other airman on the strip was a Palestinian called Hess. He stood in a pen next to the CO's Hurricane polishing the petrol bowser. The remainder of the airmen had wandered back to their tents. There were no aircraft to repair. One Hurricane left.

Hess, a quiet, elderly man, whose greying hairs added to his dignified bearing, hated the Nazis, at whose hands he and his family had suffered greatly. As self-appointed 'Bowser King' he had remained in his pen, surrounded by thousands of gallons of 100-octane petrol, throughout the day.

After each raid he had immediately started his pump engine in case it should be needed. For some reason it had become a comforting sound to listen out for. He was to remain almost constantly on duty throughout the following week. I never even saw him eating. He was no fool, and we knew that he had great courage. One chance incendiary bullet and he would have been trapped in a blaze of petrol — the bowser blocking his only exit.

Eaton and I slithered down the sandy bank and walked with Ginger Stone past the solitary Hurricane to join Hess.

Suddenly, half a dozen Messerschmitts had skirted the hills and roared low over our heads. Tracers knifed the darkening sky. Not waiting for orders, a solitary Bofors sent a chance clip of shells in their general direction.

'Well flake me! Look at that!' Ginger Stone was gazing skywards.

One of the 109s had exploded, and broad strips of fabric like bunting, hung above us. The tail-less fighter careered out of control into the sea, with the remainder high-tailing it for Greece. The mottled green cloth floated slowly to earth and draped itself across the bowser.

For us, contrary to popular definition, war was rapidly becoming 'short periods of boredom interspersed with long periods of action'.

Right *The author, eighteen years old.*

Below *Mersa Matruh. The Gladiators of 'A' Flight, 33 Squadron, were changed for Hurricanes while still operational in the Desert. 80 Squadron had no time and went to Greece with Gladiators. 112 Squadron, caught while changing, arrived in Greece with both Gladiators and Hurricanes.*

Bottom *CR42 shot down by 33 Squadron, 1940.* (Author)

Left *33 Squadron — an Italian pilot being interrogated. The only common language is Spanish, known to the Palestinian who can speak no English. He translates into Yiddish to another Palestinian who then translates into English.* (Author)

Below *33 Squadron on the move.* (Author)

Right *Corporal Harry McKenna, 'B' Flight.* (Author)

Far right *Vernon Woodward, DFC and bar, second highest scorer for Canada, with 21 aircraft destroyed.*

Below right *30 Squadron over Albania.* (30 Squadron Association)

Above *A 211 Squadron Blenheim takes off from Paramythia.*

Below *A Blenheim returns from a raid, Greece.*

Above right *After the Larissa earthquake. 11 Squadron airmen rescue their kit.*

Right *A Vickers Valentia, taking a 33 Squadron detachment to Paramythia.*

Below right *A Greek Ju52 at Paramythia, recently returned from major servicing in Germany.*

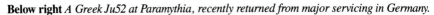

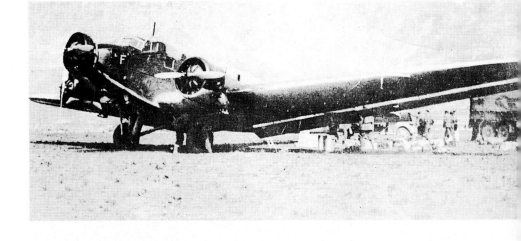

Left *Squadron Leader Marmaduke E. St John Pattle DFC and bar, top-scoring RAF pilot in World War II.* (by kind permission of Unwin Hyman Ltd)

Below *33 Squadron at Larissa, together for the last time. L to R, standing: PO S. F. Winsland, PO R. D. Dunscombe, PO C. A. C. Cheetham, FO P. R. W. Wickham, FO D. T. Moir, FO H. J. Starrett. Sitting: FO E. J. Woods, FO F. S. Holman, Flt Lt A. M. Young, FO V. C. Woodward, Sqdn Ldr M. St J. Pattle DFC, Flt Lt E. H. Dean, Flt Lt J. M. Littler, Flt Lt G. Rumsey, PO A. R. Butcher.* (by kind permission of Unwin Hyman Ltd)

Bottom *Almyros: Greek girls make a road for the Blenheims.*

Right *Larissa: Sgt 'Chico' Genders. One Hurricane against the Luftwaffe.* (by kind permission of Unwin Hyman Ltd)

Below *Larissa: An Me109 shot down by ground-fire. 'Ping' Newton is standing on the wing.* (by kind permission of Unwin Hyman Ltd)

Above *'Chiefy' Salmon (on the right) examines cannon-shell damage.* (Author)

Above *'Lofty' Halstead, 11 Squadron. Left behind at Almyros.*

Below *The chaos of retreat: 11 Squadron.*

7
Maleme: Prelude to Invasion

O peration Mercury, the German plan to occupy Crete, was proceeding fairly well, although transport difficulties had now put back the proposed invasion date to 20th May. General Kurt Student, GOC 11 Air Corps, had 22,750 men already assembled in southern Greece. Of these, 10,000 paratroops and 750 glider-troops were to take part in the initial assault; 5,000 to be flown in. At his disposal was a vast armada of three-engine Junker transports — 700 of them, as well as some 80 gliders. Each glider was capable of lifting a dozen or more men. The remaining 7,000 men were to go by sea in two flotillas, which included destroyers, steamers, torpedo boats, minesweepers, speedboats, and a large fleet of caiques. Only with the seaborne troops were the Germans scraping the bottom of the barrel.

Air protection for the operation was to be given by General Freiherr von Richthofen's 8 Air Corps — 650 aircraft strong and including three groups of Dornier 17s, two groups of Junkers 88s, one group of Heinkel 111s, three group of Junkers 87 dive-bombers, and two reconnaissance units. Fighter cover was to be provided by 180 Me110s and Me109s. It was going to be quite a party.

The main assault was to fall upon Maleme, with smaller groups of paratroops dispersed along the coast to contain Heraklion, Rethymnon, Suda, and other strategic points until the aerodrome at Maleme had been occupied and airborne troops flown in. Canea, ten miles east of Maleme, was planned to fall on the first day. Primary targets for his Assault Regiment of glider-troops were to be Kavkazia Hill and the RAF tented camp.

It was to be the day long-awaited by Student and his men to show the world this revolutionary way of making war. The paratroops and glider men were the very elite of his hand-picked soldiers. Many were fanatical Nazis, but many were well-educated and, as events showed, were not the ruthless killers we had been led to believe. All possessed an *esprit de corps* born out of the supreme confidence they all shared in their invincibility. Perhaps it was a pity that Student was unaware of the old Japanese proverb which runs: 'It is difficult to be strong and not rash'.

If, at Maleme, we had known more fully what was in store for us, we would have given an even bigger welcome to the two infantry tanks which arrived late on the evening of 14th May and were hidden in the north-east corner of Kavkazia Hill. Both had seen long service in the Western Desert and were minus a few parts, but, nevertheless, their arrival was encouraging.

But with the renewed attacks upon the aerodrome the next morning, there was little time for contemplation. In one raid the Navy Gladiator, attempting to take off and engage the milling Germans above, turned over. It became the target for every Messerschmitt in the vicinity, but an ex-motor mechanic New Zealander dashed from cover and rescued the pilot.

To avoid exposing too many men to the attacks of strafing fighters, the CO had arranged a 24 hour stand down from duty on a roster system. It gave some of the erks an opportunity to wander off into the hills and relax for a while, but men like Eaton, Stone, Hess and McKenna ignored the arrangement. If 'Jerries' were pasting their 'drome they felt entitled to hit back. Their reward came sooner than they expected.

By the next morning we could muster four Hurricanes; two more-or-less airworthy and two replacements flown in the previous day. They were soon taking off and heading east, three flown by Fleet Air Arm pilots, followed a little while afterwards by Squadron Leader Howell in the fourth.

Already the Luftwaffe was abroad. From Greece wave after wave of Ju88s, Me110s, and Ju87 dive-bombers were heading towards much-blitzed Suda Bay under a top cover of fighters. They droned past the sea-shore in a swarm — out of range. The airmen, listening to the distant crump-crump of exploding bombs and the booming of naval ack-ack, kept a watchful eye on the sky. Time after time the Messerschmitts had surprised them — hiding in the glare of the sun. Today would be the same, and they wanted to be ready for them. Bofors crews struggled to repair their damaged guns. Ken Eaton stood behind his Lewis. Ginger Stone lay awkwardly in his shallow pit with his 'contraption', surrounded by ammunition belts. Some erks carried rifles, but others had only their Italian carbines, untrustworthy and made in the year dot. They were loaded with British ammunition of a slightly larger size. This had been tried out in Greece. Most times the rifle fired but occasionally the barrrel split like a peeled banana. All were praying that if the Germans came their arrival would not coincide with the return of the Hurricanes.

'Look!' shouted little Tubby Dixon. 'There they are!'

He was pointing out to sea. Then everyone saw the group of swift-flying specks heading towards the 'drome. They moved quickly. Every eye watched them. Every gun was loaded and ready.

There were six of them, and judging from their unprecedented behaviour they must have considered themselves to be invisible from the landing-ground. For some minutes they continued circling behind Theodhoroi Island to the right of the aerodrome. The airmen began wondering if they were going to be attacked after all. Why the German leader had not come out of the sun in the good old foolproof manner no one will ever know! When the Messerschmitts finally emerged from their hiding place, every gun lay trained upon them. Their path towards the aerodrome was followed through a hundred gun-sights.

Not a shot until the aircraft crossed the coast. Then the whole perimeter flickered and crashed with the defenders' rapid fire. In a flash the leading Messerschmitt was swinging back towards the open sea, trailing a plume of black smoke — the pilot desperately trying to lift his machine from the water. The next two fighters crashed along the beach, channelling up cascades of sand. Trailing smoke, the three remaining attackers dived for the distant horizon. It is doubtful if any reached their base in Greece. According to some airmen, two out of three fell into the sea.

The two pilots along the beach were alive and both subsequently made prisoner. One who had landed near Platanias was in tears. The good Cretan housewives, first on the scene, had yanked him out of his cockpit and beaten him up. The village ladies had stolen his engagement ring, he complained to the MO. His finger had been hacked off with a carving-knife, and he brandished the bloody stump as he spoke. Wiping away the tears, he explained that his grief was not at the loss of his finger but because he wanted the ring back. It had been a present from his fiancee.

Meanwhile, Squadron Leader Howell had been taking on the Luftwaffe single-handed. After shooting down a Ju52 troop-carrier in flames over the sea, he had climbed towards the main enemy concentration, sailed past a mass of Me110s, and then scattered a flock of Junkers dive-bombers. Ignoring the German fighter umbrella above him he had singled out the nearest Stuka and shot it into the water. He was proving a worthy successor to Pattle. When he had landed he was delighted to hear how the raiders had been repulsed before they could fire a single shot.

We had lost two of the other three Hurricanes, and the third came down at Rethymnon, shot to pieces, but the Fleet Air Arm pilots had accounted for six Germans between them.

To make the day complete, who should breeze into Maleme, but Sergeant Reynish, back from the dead. He had baled out of his flaming Hurricane over the sea, swum for several hours, and had finally been fished out of the water by the Cretans.

That evening I returned to the camp, lifted my tent flap, walked in, and fell full length over a large Victorian hip-bath, a grimy, rusty, iron relic of another age. Fed up with sleeping on duck-boards, a diminutive Irish corporal had salvaged this monstrosity from a village rubbish dump to use as a bed. But

once found, the problem remained — how to get it home? From the dump
to the camp was a long journey, the bath weighed a ton, and Paddy was no
Samson. There had seemed only one solution. After a long struggle he positioned it upon the bank so that he was able to crawl inside like a hermit crab,
and then charged blindly through the undergrowth.

Farther down the bank stood a New Zealand sentry, guarding the camp
approaches with one of the eight Tommy guns his company possessed. Each
day had brought its fresh crop of invasion rumours — Heraklion had been
captured — paratroopers had seized Suda Bay, et cetera, et cetera — and so
it was natural for him to assume that the aerodrome was being attacked and
that he was being run down by a light tank. The crashing and metallic clanging drew nearer. There was just time for two hasty shouts of:

'Halt or I fire!'

Then he dived for cover and opened up with his gun ...

What happened next is easy to imagine. Like the subterranean roar of the
legendary bull which holds Crete between its horns, Paddy's bellow, magnified by the iron dome around him, rumbled across the hill.

But while we tossed and turned that night, the little Irish corporal lay snugly
curled up in his new bed, looking like a leprechaun, at peace with the world.

The attacks continued as usual the following day and despite the efforts
of Chiefy Salmon and his repair gang we were unable to operate. As it was,
working under almost constant air attack, they and their two small tool boxes
had worked miracles. Now there was little more they could do. So, in between
raids, Chiefy was now instructing his men in the art of catapult shooting.
Weapons had been assembled and an old Duty Flight yellow disc stuck up
for target practice. The other erks watched with interest.

'I suppose they think they can stop the flakers with catapults,' someone
remarked, but Chiefy knew what he was doing.

Morale was so high at that moment I really think they would have tried
even that.

From early morning on Sunday, 18th May, we could hear the distant skies
thunder as wave after wave of dive-bombers, Ju88s and Heinkel 111s escorted
by Messerschmitts massed over the shipping in Suda Bay and the Cretan capital, Canea.

At Suda, the sky was blotched with sudden black patches as the British
ack-ack defence hurled everything they had at the diving Stukas. Nineteen-
year-old Gunner Ted Telling* blazed away with his Naval pom-poms as each
Junkers came into range, as he had now been doing for many days. The Bay
was turbulent with the water-spouts of near-misses and covered with a haze
of smoke coming from burning shipping, victims of earlier attacks. At the
same time large formations of Heinkels droned over Canea, pattern-bombing
as they went. Sticks of explosives fell among the tall blocks of flats behind
the water-front and rained down upon the town.

*See Appendix 5.

Standing guard over the RAF Headquarters in Canea were two LACs from 33 Squadron, Chris Pendergast and his friend, Albert Moore. As the crumping of the bursting bombs came nearer, both airmen dived for cover. At the same time there was a terrifying sound of rushing air, a tremendous explosion and, for Albert Moore, oblivion.

At Maleme landing-ground I had joined Ken Eaton in the Lewis-pit and throughout the morning had witnessed a procession of strafing Messerschmitts falling out of the skies, raking Bofors guns, hitting the riddled wrecks now littering the perimeter, time and time again diving upon the solitary Hurricane below us. Bullets clanged among the petrol drums bordering the road like hammer blows and ripped into sand-bags around the gun-pit but, because of the depth of its protecting pen, the CO's aircraft seemed to be bearing a charmed life. So did Eaton, squinting along the sights, swivelling his machine-gun this way and that, mingling his tracers with their crackling cannon shells.

In the middle of bedlam, a replacement Hurricane arrived. Above the hullaballoo we could hear the Merlin engine's thoroughbred drone as the aircraft skirted the hills. The pilot must have seen that the 'drome was under attack but nevertheless prepared to land. He was probably out of fuel. We followed his passage breathlessly. One-o-nines crowded above and behind him. Then ... wheels down ... full flap ... he swung out to sea on his final approach. He was coming in down-wind. Agonizing seconds passed.

'He's going to make it!' Ken yelled in my ear.

Then the aircraft was falling like a plummet. It hit the sea with a mighty splash. The waters closed over and were calm once more. Eaton was swearing coarsely at the 109s as they screamed past in triumph.

Now Heinkels were flying in from the east. They were too high for the Lewis but Eaton still hammered at the fighters. We did not see the bombs dropping.

A deafening metallic explosion suddenly darkened everything. A bomb had hit the sand-bags and exploded in the pen below. The gun-pit caved in upon us and I was conscious of a searing pain across my back. I thought that I had been hit. Ken was underneath me and I struggled to shift the weight of the sand-bags pinning me down. Then I could hear McKenna's voice. He and the gang, swarming out of their trench, ran to the pit and pulled it apart. They lifted the hot machine-gun muzzle from my bare back and the pain went. Eaton was eased out, eyes, nose, and ears choked with earth. He was white as a sheet. He sat down groggily on some sand-bags retching. Then Corporal Willy Cann put a shoulder under his arm and led him away to his tent. The rest of the erks picked up their rifles and returned to their trench.

Down below, the Hurricane blazed and crackled away in the pen with exploding ammunition in the wings showering sparks into the air like a Roman candle. There was nothing we could do about it. Another casualty was the Lewis-gun. I was setting about rebuilding the gun-pit when a fresh formation of Heinkels drifted in over the hills. Once bitten, twice shy, this time I watched the bomb-doors open and saw the falling bombs flash silver in the afternoon sun.

There was a slit trench across the road. I made a dive for it, although against my better judgement — I always had a claustrophobic aversion to trenches, tin hats, or anything which hampered movement. Two elderly Cretans, who had been running down the road, piled in beside me. At the same moment there was an ear-splitting explosion and once again everything went dark. I had been buried twice in the space of 15 minutes! I choked at the fine soil and thrust my head upwards in a panic. The earth was like flour. Struggling free at last I looked around. Fighters were shooting up the far end of the landing-ground, strafing the vineyard where Salmon and his gang hung out and over the 30 Squadron Crash Centre.

The Cretan civilians had vanished ... At first, the erks who had raced down the slope again did not believe me when I told them they were there. A severed human ear lying in the crater finally convinced them. Then, digging frantically, they recovered both men. An urgent call was sent to the Crash Centre and 30 Squadron airmen, driver LAC Betts and orderly LAC Darch, answered it immediately. Still under fire, they tumbled into their ambulance, drove down the short track, bounced over the Maleme-Canea road and down the slope to the landing-ground, arriving in a great cloud of dust.

With Betts zig-zagging wildly, they made a left-handed sweep past the burnt-out Fairey Fulmar towards Eaton's gun position disregarding the fighters overhead. Betts clung to the wheel as he swung the ambulance violently from side to side. The fighters roared low overhead and then turned for home. The ambulance slewed to a halt by the aircraft pens. We loaded the two Cretans on board but one died shortly afterwards.*

I found Ken Eaton in his tent. The past few days had taken a lot out of him. His eyes were bloodshot; his clothes still caked in white dust; his face was smudged with dirt and cordite; he looked years older than himself. I thought that it would be a good idea if the two of us had a break. I persuaded him to come with me to search the neighbourhood for a decent meal. We crossed the long Iron Bridge which bore the road over the dry and stony bed of the Tavronitis river and were lucky to find the first of a huddle of houses on the far bank to be a tavern. Here, among a crowd of friendly Cretans, our smiling host and his good wife prepared for us a chicken dinner, assisted by their dark-eyed little children, Kosta and Antigoni.

We had hardly sat down when suddenly, above the babble of villagers' voices in the crowded bar, came the crash of bombs. From the aerodrome a formation of Heinkels flew low over the Iron Bridge strafing the village as they hurtled past. Cannon shells shattered the tavern shutters sending glasses and bottles rolling and bouncing through the air as everyone dived for the floor amid broken glass, spilt wine and food. The Heinkels, roaring overhead, pulled up over the hills and came in for the second shoot-up.

Antigoni, the innkeeper's child, had rushed out into the road during the uproar. Now she stood terrified, gaping at the on-coming aircraft. Eaton yelled

*A report and recommendation were sent back to base. The award of the Military Medal for Bravery in the Field was approved for both men but one was cancelled on the eve of being Gazetted. See 'After Crete', and also Appendix 4.

at me, raced out of the doorway, scooped up the girl, and threw her down behind a low wall across the road, covering her body with his own.

Inside the tavern there was instant uproar. Then two Cretans ran outside — right into the path of the on-coming bombers. Tracers bracketed them. They stood in the middle of the street shouting and waving their arms. Tiles scattered from adjacent housetops. Cannon shells and machine-gun fire stabbed the dusk in yellow streaks. Miraculously unscathed, the two men now ran gesticulating up to Ken. Roughly they pulled him to his feet and shouted at the top of their voices, *'Eisai patrimenos? Eisai patrimenos?'* — meaning, 'Are you married?'

Eaton had committed a major breach of etiquette. He had been alone in the company of an unmarried girl — aged seven. He should have requested a chaperon . . .

The next day commenced with the usual bombing attack. LAC Dixie Dean, returning from the landing-ground towards the tented camp, was unaware of the proximity of the approaching bombers until, suddenly, the ground around him was straddled with exploding bombs. He recalled being hurled through the air but remembered nothing more until he found himself in the New Zealand 7th General Hospital near Canea with shrapnel in his left thigh, three fractured ribs and a great pain every time he tried to breathe.

In the next bed was Vic Wyatt, an Australian, wounded in the chest but, nevertheless, self-appointed assistant to the needs of the young airman. This strangely suited pair were to forge a lifetime friendship.

Unbeknown to Dixie Dean, 33 Squadron airman Albert Moore lay grievously wounded nearby with no less than *sixty* pieces of shrapnel embedded in his body. He had survived although the bomb outside the RAF Headquarters at Canea must have exploded almost on top of him. The RAMC had rushed him to an emergency tent in the New Zealand 7th General Hospital.

Maleme had become non-operational at last. Reluctantly forced to admit that it was suicide to continue under the conditions prevailing, Squadron Leader Howell had sent our last remaining Hurricane back to Egypt. Instead of choosing one of his own pilots he sent Sergeant Bennett, the last of the 80 Squadron pilots, as a deliberate gesture from 33 to 80 Squadron. It was a salute to a figher squadron, the longest serving in the Balkan War, whose pilots had fought so valiantly alongside 33 Squadron and won their whole-hearted admiration. Flight Sergeant Salmon and a bunch of airmen had gone too, flown out from Suda Bay by Sunderland. With foolish optimism a gang of us commenced building a new aircraft pen at the eastern end of the aerodrome. But not for long.

At the first sound of approaching aircraft we dived behind our newly-made wall and, being marooned out on the airfield, felt decidedly uncomfortable. Twenty yards away Marine gunners stood coolly around their even less protected Bofors surrounded by shell clips and ammo boxes.

Out of the bright morning sun the fighters poured down upon Maleme in

a ragged gun-blazing horde — about 40 Me109s. With a sound as though the
sky was being ripped across like calico, they flattened out, flashing across
the sandy ground. Behind the unfinished pen the erks watched, fascinated
— and then rubbed their eyes in disbelief for dozens of bombs following the
Messerschmitts were whizzing across the width of the aerodrome. Released
too late they flew on either side of the airmen, little bombs with their ringed
markings clearly visible. Then, still appearing to maintain a height of a few
feet from the ground, they disappeared towards the sea.

Unfortunately the Messerschmitts were more lethal. Cascading empty shell
cases behind them they climbed out to sea, turned and dropped out of the
sky one after the other, diving headlong for the Bofors guns. On the site nearby
the team of squaddies, bared to the waist, were feeding in clip after clip. Candescent shells curved skywards like strings of pearls. But still the Messerschmitts in line astern flew straight down the gun-sights raking the men with
their deadly fire. Two Marines fell over a heap of ammunition boxes. The
gun stopped for a moment — then restarted as another soldier took over the
loading. The air above the site was ablaze with incendiaries but the Germans
flew on through the hail of fire. They swooped away from the target at the
last moment, almost scraping the aerodrome with their bellies. I recalled a
conversation of the previous day with one of these gunners.

'If you keep on firing straight at the flakers,' he had said, 'they'll always
give in first.'

But this time the Luftwaffe were out to destroy the guns. The gunners knew
it too and were fighting for their lives. More and more Messerschmitts joined
in the attack. One by one the guns ceased firing until only a solitary Bofors
blazed defiantly at the yellow-nosed killers. There were many casualties among
the gun-crews that morning.

By the old aircraft pen someone had replaced the wooden gun with a Vickers
'K' and stocked up the pit with ammunition. Jubilantly, I took possession and
throughout the afternoon was able to get in some choice shooting. Nearby,
Ginger Stone was also pleased with life. He had been having a run of bad
luck with his Brownings. They had packed up on him during every raid but
now they were working perfectly. Most of the other airmen from both squadrons were with the CO back in camp, practising an invasion 'dummy run'.
Plans were already made for the erks to spend the night on the hillside as
a precaution.

By late afternoon the aerodrome wore the desolate appearance of an out-
of-season seaside resort. Wisps of black smoke drifted from the littered beach,
across the sandy strip, and over the road which curved eastwards towards Pirgos
like a deserted promenade. The Bofors concert party had closed down and
Ginger and I were the last of the side-shows. Only the Germans still arrived
by the score like vulgar sightseers to poke about in the litter dumps of wrecked
aircraft.

Without Bofors to worry them the Messerschmitts cruised to and fro across
the airfield. There was a German pilot banking and looking down at us and
Stone and I followed him as he flew slowly past. Three rings ... then two

... then half a ring on the gun sights when suddenly the fighter pulled up, heading for the sea and belching smoke. A chunk of metal cowling clattered on the aerodrome. Ginger and I were shouting to each other excitedly but our jubilation was short-lived.

Sailing over Kavkazia Hill came 18 Heinkels. Formating on the leader they dropped their bombs in a long stick and we watched them most of the way. Then the earth erupted suddenly among the New Zealanders up the slope ... then down the rising ground towards us. A sudden series of explosions straddled our two gun-pits; the world blacked out in a dozen showers of dust and clods of earth. Something smacked into the front gun-sight of my 'K' and knocked it loose so that it swivelled round. Instinctively reaching to screw it back again the hot muzzle seared my fingers.

Ginger Stone, covered in white dust like a miller, was standing by my pit scratching his head and muttering: 'Well, flake me!' as he surveyed the pattern of craters all around him. The last bomb had fallen just in front of his Brownings.

Sometime later Squadron Leader Howell came down the camp road and walked over to us.

'Any luck?'

'Yes sir, I think we pranged a 109. There's a piece of it out there on the 'drome somewhere,' said Stone.

It was getting dark. The CO paced out the nearest craters and congratulated us upon our escape. Then with a final word of encouragement he retraced his steps and we watched him until his form lost its shape in the half light beneath the olives. Upon his shoulders had fallen an impossible task. He had fought the Germans to our last Hurricane without sparing himself. Now, having turned down the chance of flying our remaining aircraft back to Egypt — where the squadron was reforming and where he was also needed — he had the responsibility of the Maleme airmen in his charge on an island threatened with imminent invasion. I sensed that he was a very tired man. Behind his ready smile lay a great weariness. But fate held worse things in store for him, for within a few hours his martyrdom was to begin ...

I left Ginger Stone at his tent. As I walked away he called after me:

'See you down the 'drome first thing tomorrow?'

Whether or not he made his lonely way back to his Brownings that fateful Tuesday morning I shall never know.

8
20th May 1941: Morning

'Any foothold, or success against the troops in any particular position must be immediately *counter-attacked.*'

Major-General B. C. Freyberg VC,
Commander-in-Chief, Crete.

Fifth New Zealand Brigade had been given the task of defending Maleme aerodrome and the five miles of coast from Maleme to Platanias village. Plantanias was held by 28th Maori Battalion and 21st and 23rd Battalions held a ridge of hills one mile from Maleme, and 22nd Battalion the aerodrome.

Lieutenant-Colonel Andrew, VC, had positioned 22nd Battalion's five companies at readiness in a circle around his headquarters, which were situated on the northern slopes of Kavkazia Hill. On the morning of 20th May, as a precaution, the airmen had moved within these defences before first light.

Most of 30 Squadron waited with the New Zealanders 'A' Company in a gulley which led past headquarters towards the summit. More to the west, 33 Squadron were stationed in another gulley or else in trenches with the New Zealanders. Here 'D' Company held a line from the RAF tented camp southwards and covering the open ground by the Tavronitis.

Guarding the aerodrome perimeter was 'C' Company with a platoon facing the river-bed north of the iron bridge, another between the beach and the far side of aerodrome, and the third platoon covering the road. Holding the eastern approaches, Headquarters Company centred on Pirgos village just down the road, and 'B' Company lay on the eastern slopes of Kavkazia Hill and across the Maleme–Vlakheronitissa track.

The only additional force was a platoon from 21st Battalion who were returning from a patrol and accidentally became caught up in the battle. They posted themselves in what was to become a most important position, on the Tavronitis river bank south of 'D' Company.

Defending Maleme that morning were 620 New Zealanders, 85 Marines, 55 Fleet Air Arm and 229 officers and airmen from 30 and 33 Squadrons.

Messerschmitts, the sunlight flashing on their wings, approached rapidly from the sea. They swept low over the airfield strafing the Bofors and the empty aircraft pens. Then they turned their attention to the hillside defences. For 20 minutes or so they flew up and down the New Zealand lines firing their cannon at the rising ground around the hill.

The erks sheltered in the slit trenches with the soldiers. During the previous afternoon, groups of airmen had received instructions from a New Zealand sergeant. One section, including Tug Wilson, was directed to defend an area from a large tree to the Iron Bridge. When Wilson enquired as to what he should do if a parachutist landed behind him he was informed by the Kiwi that he would have been wrong to have noticed.

'That's outside your area,' explained the sergeant. 'It's the job of somebody else to take care of him ...'

Now, at about 7.30am, in the silence that followed the departure of the fighters, the sergeant was going from trench to trench telling everybody to 'stand down'. There would be no invasion that day ... 'If Jerry was coming, he'd have been here by now!' they were told.

So the 33 Squadron airmen left their trenches and made their way back to the RAF camp. By my side Burwell from 11 Squadron had slept through the strafing but I could only think how hungry I was. When the last fighter droned away in the distance, Ken Eaton, McKenna and Jones also set off past me down the hill for some breakfast.

Elsewhere the erks had the same idea and we would hear them as they picked their way down the slope chatting and laughing. A similar exodus from the hill was taking place among the 30 Squadron airmen, who like us, had mistaken the German attack for the usual morning strafe.

I gave Burwell a shake but he preferred to finish his sleep and I left him there to run and catch up with the others; he was not seen again. At my tent Eaton and the others went ahead while I made a quick search for a pipe which I had lost. It was shortly after finding it that I became aware of the growing noise outside.

From the tent doorway I looked up and saw a vast armada of aeroplanes approaching. The throbbing of their engines grew to a crescendo. Then bombs started falling and the air reverberated with sound. Above flew Ju88s, Heinkels and Dorniers, wave after wave. Bombs fell in sticks around the base of the hill, among the New Zealanders, and through the RAF camp. For half an hour or more the bombs rained down. The explosions tore out the soft

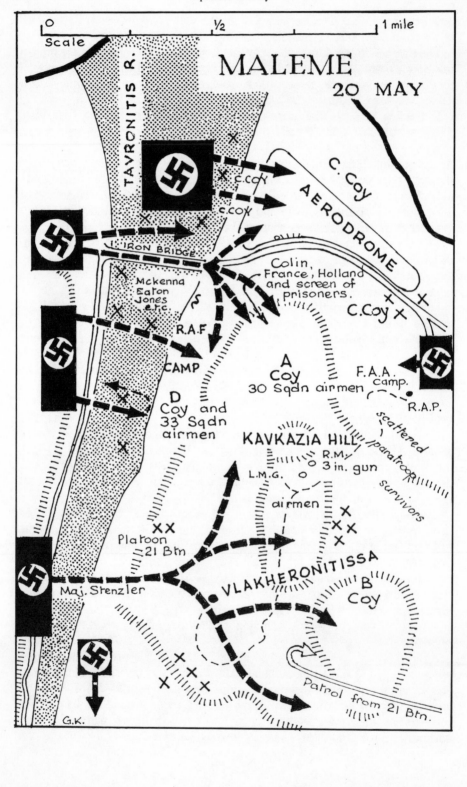

0   Scale   ½   1 mile

MALEME
20 MAY

TAVRONITIS R.

AERODROME

C. Coy

C. Coy

IRON BRIDGE

Colin, France, Holland and screen of prisoners.

C.Coy

Mckenna Eaton Jones etc.

R.A.F

CAMP

A Coy 30 Sqdn airmen

F.A.A. camp.

R.A.P.

D Coy and 33 Sqdn airmen

scattered paratroop survivors

KAVKAZIA HILL

R.M. 3 in. gun

L.M.G.

airmen

Platoon 21 Btn

VLAKHERONITISSA

B Coy

Maj. Stenzler

Patrol from 21 Btn.

G.K.

soil, lifting it skywards until it hung in the air like a blanket, blotting out the sun.

Fresh aircraft thundered in large formations out of the afternoon sky. On all sides I could hear the screaming of the bombs and the occasional metallic clang of shrapnel as fragments of bomb-casing flew in every direction. I had grabbed my rifle and dived into a one-man hole a few yards away. There was a violent eruption ahead of me and, through the haze, I thought I saw the bomb lift a man off the ground but I could not be sure. The next bombs burst behind me among 'D' Company lines and I started to breathe again — but not for long.

Above me, I heard the sound of rushing air. A glider swooped low through the curtain of dust, silent and sinister, and disappeared westwards. Almost at once there was a crackling and a cracking through the olive trees — a second glider was careering straight towards me. I had no time to avoid it. It skidded into the tent, slewed half-round, showering me with loose soil and stopping in a cloud of dust with one wing dug into the bank behind me. Another glider piled in close by.

I ducked under the wing feeling pretty scared. Before I could reach the bank leading to the high ground the door of the nearest glider opened. Out jumped a dazed-looking German and I fired and shot him at almost point-blank range. He fell backwards on to a second glider-trooper now standing behind him. I had time to eject and re-load. The second man was holding his head with his hands. I fired again and he spun around and collapsed, his body blocking the doorway. I sent a third bullet into the darkness of the doorway.

This could not go on forever. I moved backwards to the bank ejecting the empty case as I went. The next round jammed. Sweating and swearing I wrestled with the bolt but it refused to budge. The rest of the Germans were piling out by now while out of the corner of my eye, I could see more of them racing through the trees from the second glider. It was the longest second of my life! A low-flying Dornier, a 'Flying Pencil', droned by at treetop height, its gunner spraying the hillside; there appeared to be endless yards of it and I found time to wonder if it would ever pass by.

Then I was clambering up the bank, clawing at the loose earth, running towards 'D' Company trenches, with bursts of rapid fire following me. Bullets sliced through the trees and flicked into the ground. I reached the trenches but found them deserted. The place should have been crowded with soldiers and airmen but there was not a soul in sight!

One of 'D' Company's eight Tommy-guns lay beneath a tree loaded with a drum. A spare clip lay by it. Without pausing to consider the incredulity of my find or my extreme good fortune, more suitably armed I made my way cautiously back down the slope to the top of the bank. The two bodies lay where I had left them but the glider seemed deserted. I raked it through from nose to tail just in case.

Returning up the hill, I eventually found six New Zealanders in a trench. They were still sheltering with their 'heads down' and blissfully unaware that gliders were landing. However, they soon cottoned on and went looking for their comrades to share the good news.

In another trench I found two RAF corporals, Stevenson and Price, who had been in Chiefy Salmon's gang. Together with a few of the New Zealanders we made our way to the summit of Kavkazia Hill. The summit sloped to the south and then dropped sharply into a valley separating it from a village on the next hill named Vlakheronitissa. We arrived out of breath leaving the shelter of the trees behind us. Three sand-bagged emplacements stood ahead, two of which housed Lewis machine-guns. Here also the place was deserted. All hell was being let loose. Bullets were flying in all directions. Most of the firing was coming from the area around the Tavronitis river where we could see more gliders piled up.

We made a dive for the nearest gunpit, jumping over two Marines lying on their faces in the entrance. We took them for dead but as soon as Stevenson grabbed the gun one of them leapt to his feet and grappled with him like a man demented. The combined shock of the bombing and the gliders, together with the sheer incredulity of the situation had been too much for his mind to take in. He and his companion had already decided that it was all up. They even thought that they stood a better chance of being made prisoner if they did not offend the Germans by shooting at them; a good example of how the minds of two, otherwise reliable, soldiers can be demolished by sheer panic. We quietened the poor blighters down and, after a while, they regained their composure.

Now airmen and New Zealanders were arriving on the hilltop in ones and twos. They spread out finding what cover they could. A bloody-faced sergeant from 30 Squadron took the second machine-gun.

It came as a shock to us as to every Allied defender in Crete that morning that the enemy were not, in fact, soldiers but German *airmen* with a uniform under their jump-suits not unlike the colour of the Royal Air Force, Home Service issue! In an attempt to avoid future confusion all sorts of identification devices were hastily thought up. Some airmen tied handkerchiefs around their arm, others ripped off the lower part of their RAF trousers to make improvised shorts.

The handkerchief idea did not work well as they slipped off too easily and one late arrival from 30 Squadron who had known nothing of these arrangements was nearly killed. The other airmen, trigger-happy, fired upon him and made him keep his distance until he had identified himself. Fortunately for him, further interrogation was cut short by the arrival of about 30 Me110s strafing the hill with cannon and machine-gun fire. The place was alight. Cannon shells smacked into the emplacements, spewing out the sand from the flimsy bags. Stevenson on the Lewis fired off a complete pan with his fingers tight on the trigger.

The whole German airworks were cruising past the hill. Never before had there been such a vast concentration of aircraft as over the square mile of Maleme! Sometimes Me109s flew on a level or below our height. They rarely fired now but hung over the Maleme area giving moral support to

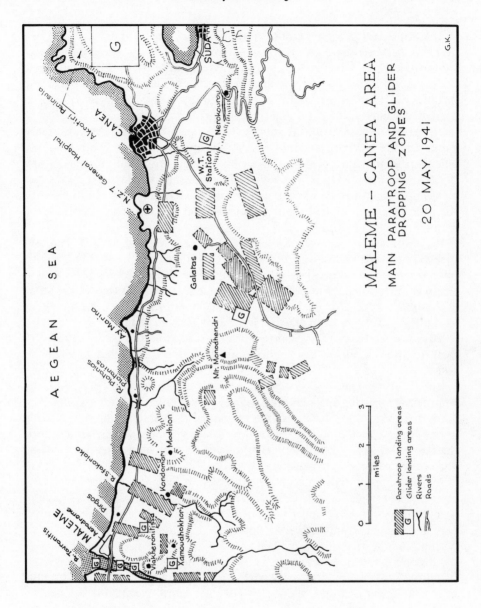

MALEME – CANEA AREA

MAIN PARATROOP AND GLIDER
DROPPING ZONES

20 MAY 1941

Paratroop landing areas
Glider landing areas
Rivers
Roads

the glider troops.

The skies cleared for a moment. Then the paratroopers arrived. Flying low over the sparkling sea came an armada of Junkers 52 troop-carriers. In impeccable vic formation they made a left-handed circuit of the area dropping their human cargo as they went. Green, brown and occasionally white parachute mushrooms hung in the air from the Tavronitis round to Pirgos village, in a broad circle.

They floated away from the Junkers like soapsud bubbles. And still more came. On the hill the airmen of 30 and 33 Squadrons joined with the army defenders in firing at every German within range. They fell on all sides and it was sometimes difficult to know which target to pick. The dead were probably hit several times over as they fell among the living. The few who reached the ground alive grabbed their parachutes and instantly vanished into the shrubbery.

In the middle of all this, a Kiwi entered our gun-pit and, incredibly, commenced counting and noting all the used cartridge cases — as if back home on a firing range. When he saw my Tommy-gun he asked for it back as it really belonged to the New Zealanders. Limited in range it was of little value at the time and, in any case, I had used up most of the drum on the glider in the RAF camp. I exchanged it for a Lee Enfield rifle.

Then a fresh load of paratroopers straddled the south of the hill and every man was potting at Germans who loomed suddenly large out of nowhere, feet first.

Both Lewises were red hot and down on our left the 3-inch guns of the Marines were firing through open sights. The Junkers were being knocked all over the sky. One aircraft was out of control and careering towards a string of parachutes; another was on fire and we could see men leaping out to escape the flames while, by Maleme beach, a troop-carrier hit the sea with a wing and, in slow motion, cartwheeled into the water with a mighty splash.

An isolated parachutist, caught by a thermal, drifed away over the sea, receding from us towards a watery death, pulled down by the weight of his equipment. The loss of life must have been fantastic. Those who did survive, however, quickly vanished from sight.

Approaching from the mountains a new formation discharged a mass of paratroopers above the ridge to the east of Maleme where the two reserve battalions of New Zealanders lay concealed. For a while there was the sound of distant firing and then silence. We did not know at the time but we had witnessed the almost complete destruction of Student's III Battalion, Sturm Regiment.

Meanwhile this ill-fated battalion's remaining company, the 9th, was approaching from the south, droning slowly towards us along the intervening valley. Seated in one of the Junkers was Jg Walter Goltz, an ex-apprentice locksmith for the German railways at Brandenborg. Next to him were his friends, Kurt Hammermann, Heinz Jeremais and Karl Ehrenhofer. All four were 18-year-olds who had been together from parachute school days at Wittstock/Dosse until they joined the Sturm Regiment at Halberstatt.

At 4am that day they had washed and breakfasted on coffee and Schinken-wurst sausage. Weapons were then tried out before they shouldered their parachutes and marched for a mile to the aerodrome at Megara, near Athens. Now, as Walter sat in the vibrating darkened aircraft he tried to overcome his apprehension by thinking of his childhood sweetheart, Lisalotte. They planned to marry one day . . .

The door opened, breaking his reverie, and the Junkers filled with sudden sunlight. At the same moment bullets peppered the fuselage and the wing was hit with shellfire. The aircraft banked steeply, out of control. Walter, fourth in line, tried hard to stand and maintain his balance with others shouting and pushing him frantically from behind . . . The Junkers was plunging earthwards . . . Hammermann, Jeremias and Ehrenhofer, the first three to jump, were already dead, hit by a hail of bullets from New Zealanders and 30 Squadron airmen in 'A' Company trenches on the eastern slopes of the hill.

Walter felt the wind tear away his goggles as he hurled himself from the doomed aircraft. A bullet sliced through the baggy part of his trouser leg. Other bullets grazed ankle, knee and thigh . . . After what seemed an eternity, he landed in some bushes by an old stone hut. All was still and he was alone.

From the hill we watched the stricken Junkers, trailing smoke and losing height as it arched across the eastern end of the airfield and splashed into the sea.

Another 9th Company, III Battalion, German preparing to jump at the same time was Dr Friedrich Merk. A tough, 30-year-old, devotee of Student since secret training began in the 1930s, he was still smarting from a heated argument prior to take-off! It was bad enough that medical staff and doctors were made to wear conspicuous white parachutes, making them a special target for the enemy, but it was the last straw when the senior officer at Megara tried to insist that he and all his men should jump wearing *gas masks* as well!

He crashed into some bushes, landing on his rubber knee pads, and quickly grabbed the tell-tale white parachute, dragging it under cover. Taking stock of his position, to his dismay he found himself in the middle of a Royal Marine anti-aircraft site although, fortunately for him, the sky was too full of parachutes and the defenders too busy blazing away at them to notice him. He pulled the bushes around himself and kept very still.

Further out in the 'No Man's Land' of the valley, two brothers from Essen had landed, one of them badly wounded. His brother did what little he could and then went off upon a frantic search for medical assistance oblivious to duty or to war.

The German plan was simple enough: to take Kavkazia Hill, to silence the Bofors guns around the landing-ground, and to capture the Iron Bridge intact. Without the Iron Bridge, reinforcements dropped in undefended areas further west could not be fed quickly to the assembly point in the RAF camp. Without control of the aerodrome perimeter troop-carriers could not be flown in. Without holding Kavkazia Hill the whole operation would fail.

The assault upon Kavkazia Hill from the south was undertaken by glider troops under Major Koch, who landed on the south-east and south-west slopes. Reinforced by paratroopers they secured a footing on the hill while many of the defenders still had their heads down in trenches and were unaware of gliders or paratroops.

Pilot Officer Crowther, left in charge of the 30 Squadron contingent, quickly realised the gravity of the situation. He soon gathered together a group of airmen and some two dozen leaderless New Zealanders.

The Germans suffered heavy casualties under withering fire from 'B' Company on their flank which, combined with fire from Crowther's airmen and Kiwis, drove them from the hill. Major Koch was severely wounded and the remnants of his scattered troops were forced to detour and dig in as best they could. Six of Koch's gliders straddled 'D' Company defences and took heavy casualties. A further three gliders landed in the RAF Camp, two of which I encountered.

Glider-troops under Lieutenant Plessen had more success. Landing in the river mouth with 16 gliders, Plessen stormed the east bank of the Tavronitis. Here the New Zealanders were overrun and the first two Bofors guns captured although Plessen was killed in the fighting.

But the greatest success came to the gliders of Major Braun. His men were able to seize the Iron Bridge and drive a wedge between 'D' Company and 'C' Company. This vital region north of the RAF camp was bitterly contested and casualties were heavy among the Germans, who lost their officer as well as some complete crews who had the misfortune to land within 'D' Company lines. The survivors, however, created havoc in the RAF camp.

From the hillside, Squadron Leader Howell saw the gliders coming in and set off down the slope to look for airmen still in the camp. He was accompanied by Flight Lieutenant Woodward, Pilot Officer Dunscombe, and Commander Beale, CO of 805 Fleet Air Arm.

Even at this stage it was apparent that some airmen were cut off by the enemy but nevertheless three parties of erks were collected together. Two groups under Woodward and Dunscombe gathered from the eastern end of the camp near the airfield made their way independently to the south of the hill.

Squadron Leader Howell took his party of airmen up the eastern slopes of the hill and positioned them behind a stone wall along with some New Zealanders. They prepared to withstand any attacks from the Tavronitis. Howell left them there and descended the hill once again with Commander Beale. They were looking for airmen still cut off and they also intended to destroy the squadron documents. Two isolated airmen with rifles defending a slit trench joined them and the four proceeded towards the Orderly Room.

There was a good deal of small arms fire on all sides as the Germans fanned through the camp and Commander Beale, who was leading, collapsed suddenly, hit in the stomach. Squadron Leader Howell bent over him when another burst of firing at close quarters shattered both his arms. One of the airmen was at the same time hit in the ribs.

Commander Beale and the airmen, seeing the blood gushing from the CO, forgot their own painful wounds, made a rough torniquet around one of his arms, and attempted to move him across the bullet-swept open ground to the shelter of the gulley. With five paces to go Howell fainted and fell to the ground. His companions lifted him and somehow carried him to some cover by a wrecked tent.

Beale, although in agony himself, set off to organize a rescue party. After he had gone, Squadron Leader Howell, regaining consciousness, persuaded the two airmen who had loyally stood by him to make their escape but both men were subsequently captured.

The Commander was more successful. A rescue party of airmen made their way to the edge of the camp and reached the CO who was by this time unconscious again, but when they saw him lying motionless in a pool of blood and covered with flies they mistook him for dead and left him there.*

Meanwhile, in the lull after the early morning strafing, telephonist Colin France had snatched some breakfast before reporting for duty but had hardly set off towards the aerodrome when the first wave of bombers approached. Behind the dining tent, half way up the slope was the first aid post, a natural cave protected by a stone wall. With bombs falling on every quarter Colin and some other airmen scrambled up the hillside and reached safety inside.

For a long while the noise outside was deafening as waves of Junkers 88s, Dorniers 17s and Heinkel 111s saturated the area with high explosives. The very air seemed to vibrate with the roar of aircraft engines and bursting bombs interspersed with the calico-ripping sound of machine-gun fire.

Soon casualties began to arrive. One 30 Squadron airman was wounded and shocked completely dumb. They were tended by the 30 Squadron Medical Officer, Flying Officer Cullen, although himself weak with dysentery. He was assisted by his Medical Orderly, Norman Darch.

Suddenly another airman staggered through the entrance. His clothes were tattered and earth-stained and there was blood running in rivulets down his bare right side where he had been injured. He blurted out that a bomb had landed in his trench, killing three airmen and badly wounding three others.

Some time later, he casually announced, almost as an afterthought, that gliders had been landing, there were Germans in the RAF camp and he had seen parachutists . . . Dead silence followed this shattering revelation and then everyone was talking at once. It was agreed that the best course was to join the New Zealanders further up the hill.

Flying Officer Cullen set out with Norman Darch hoping to reach the New Zealand Medical Officer, Captain Longmore, at his Regimental Aid Post on the eastern slope of the hill. He was followed by Colin France, another airman and a corporal. Unfortunately, in the excitement, the corporal accidentally shot himself in the leg with his revolver and they had to return to the cave.

*He was destined to remain on that spot for a long while before the Germans found him. His fight to recovery and his adventures which followed make his book *Escape to Live* one of the best stories to come out of the war.

Commander Beale was made prisoner when the first aid post to which he had been taken was overrun by the enemy.

Aircraft still droned overhead. Colin, positioned on a ledge further up the hill, could now hear small-arms fire and an occasional shout coming from the camp. He peered through the bushes with his loaded rifle at the ready.

Suddenly, some distance below, there was an airman moving up the hill followed by another man in blue with a red swastika flag draped around his shoulders. With a shock the young telephonist realised that both men in blue were Germans! He took careful aim and fired; the second German jerked and fell suddenly. But, by now, there were other Germans on the hill above him. Once again he returned to the cave but had hardly arrived there out of breath, when a hand-grenade exploded outside. A guttural voice shouted, 'Come out with your hands up!' Outside the cave entrance were six paratroopers, armed to the teeth.

With helmets discarded and hands held high the small group of airmen were forced down the slope to the RAF camp. They passed the body of a fair-haired German clutching a red flag and Colin realised with a shock that he had ended this young man's life. He glanced at his captors uneasily as if they knew that he had been the culprit. He prayed there would be no reprisals.

At the same time, within the camp and caught in the German mesh were a party of 30 Squadron airmen, including LAC 'Dutch' Holland, a tall storekeeper. They had taken refuge in a stone hut, firing at the Germans until their ammunition ran out. Germans had not been long in coming. Glider troops kicked open the door and advanced upon them with level machine-pistols. In the brief silence Holland edged his way to the front with fists clenched and raised but waiting for the shot which must surely come. Instead, one of the intruders barked: *'Spricht jemand Deutsch?'*

Holland, greatly relieved, answered that he spoke German. They asked him where they could find water and the storeman led the party, Germans and airmen, through the trees to the irrigation ditch which ran around the foot of the hill.

Distrustingly, their captors insisted that the airmen drank some water first of all. The erks felt that they could do with a drink at that moment. Then, finding the water not poisoned, the Germans motioned their prisoners to be seated and quenched their thirst with collapsible beakers. The airmen remained under guard for an hour or more. When their officer left the Germans became more friendly and passed around chocolate and cigarettes. Here, by the canal, the prisoners were to remain for some time while the battle raged elsewhere.

There were still airmen holding out in parts of the camp but their single-shot rifles were no match for the automatic weapons and hand grenades now turned upon them. Some men who had been on their way to the dining tent had only their mug and eating irons with which to defend themselves. One by one most of the isolated defenders were killed or captured.

The party of prisoners, including Colin France and his group and with late arrivals, soon swelled to some 30 or more men.

Flying Officer Tom Cullen, accompanied by Norman Darch, had headed eastwards and came across a small group of wounded. The Medical Officer stayed to assist but sent the loyal Darch forward to find the New Zealand lines. Unfortunately, the 30 Squadron Medical Officer and his group of wounded were soon surrounded by paratroops and captured.

Norman Darch reached the New Zealanders but was twice wounded in the back on the way. He, too, was eventually taken prisoner.*

Near the dining tent Paddy Rennie all but ran full tilt into a party of glider troopers who were by now sifting through the RAF camp on every side. He threw himself to the ground behind a bush. Waiting a tense moment he lifted his head cautiously and squinted through the foliage. In front of him was open ground — about six yards — and then some shrubs. Now and again he could catch a glimpse of blue-green uniforms behind the leaves. The sun sent shafts of light into the clearing. The thick green grass and the leaves of the nearby olives glittered in the morning sunshine. Behind the Germans rose Kavkazia Hill and safety. Just a few more yards, just a minute sooner, and he would have been safe.

Time passed slowly. He dared not move. There was still sounds of fighting among the tents. Overhead, aircraft cruised by, rarely firing, afraid of hitting their own men. Then there was a shout and a shot close at hand. Two New Zealanders burst through the bushes behind him and dived down by his side. Bursts of Schmeisser fire followed them, the slugs snipping through the trees overhead. A German parted the bushes across the clearing and stood for a moment, gun at the ready. The firing ceased abruptly and, evidently satisfied, the glider trooper returned to his colleagues.

Paddy lay wondering why the enemy across the clearing did not move off towards the battle which he could hear raging near the end of the road. As if in answer, one of the Kiwis nudged him and whispered:

'Look, digger. They've set up a machine-gun!'

Sure enough, facing them and resting upon a hastily prepared earthwork, projected a Spandau's deadly snout.

The New Zealanders knew what they had to do. From a knapsack over one shoulder the first Kiwi had produced some hand grenades. He handed one to Rennie.

'I'll run out first,' he said softly. 'You two jokers follow up and finish off what's left of 'em, OK?'

Two heads nodded.

Grasping the unfamiliar object, Paddy was really scared now. As he lay pressed to the ground his heart thumped so loudly, that he felt sure that the Germans must hear it above the noise of the battle. Lying in one position for so long he felt unable to make any rapid movement when called upon to do so.

Now the Kiwi was crouching. He had straightened the release split-pin and brought the grenade close to his face, ready to bite the ring with his teeth

*Tom Cullen and the wounded remained where they were for some time. Later on, when it was safe to do so, they were moved across the Tavronitis to a house in the village. The Germans provided some medical supplies and instruments and the 30 Squadron Medical Officer coped with the wounded as best he could.

... then he was on his feet and running.

Up sprang the second New Zealander. Rennie was still on one knee when the Spandau opened up. Bullets spat across the clearing. He could not stop himself now ... he was out in the open, driven by a reflex which he tried too late to arrest. Both Kiwis were dead several times before they slumped to the ground. Neither had used their grenades. Down fell Paddy also. He lay still. The machine-gun spattered hot lead into the bush which had been their shelter. Bullets whistled past a few inches above the three bodies. Then, evidently satisfied that there was nothing left alive, the Germans ceased fire.

To the Irishman lying there it was the end of life. In his numbed brain he could think of nothing except lie still. Even his heart did not seem to thump any more. Sprawled out in full view of the enemy he feigned death and waited to die.

A long time afterwards he was conscious of voices ... guttural German voices close at hand ... Glider-troops were casually examining the other bodies. He dared not look, but he could sense them as they stood over him. He held his breath. A boot prodded him not too gently in the ribs. Then the voices sounded distant. The Germans had retired to their hide-out.

At that moment he became conscious of the grenade still held in his clenched hand. All the time that went before his mind had been blank, but with the realisation of what he possessed hope returned. For a while he lay biding his time. About him the war went on. Aircraft still droned constantly overhead, somewhere to the right trench mortars came into action. But his private war concerned only five men and a machine-gun...

He had changed his position slowly — moving an inch at a time until his left hand gripped the ring of the release pin. He acted suddenly with no time to reconsider. Rolling on his face, he prodded himself to his knees by this elbows and at the same time tugged the grenade from the pin, hurled it, and fell flat upon his face again.

There was a loud explosion a few yards away, and he was on his feet running. He did not pause to examine the havoc but raced towards the hill. From behind came no sound. No one tried to stop him. He was free. He raced up the hill — towards what?

The RAF camp was now in German hands — but not entirely. In a trench by the Tavronitis bank a handful of determined erks still held out. McKenna, Eaton, Dixon and Jones, taking shelter here at the commencement of the bombing, had been joined later by Banks and Chiefy Firman. The flight sergeant, blown up by a bomb, was suffering from shock, and lay in the trench bottom taking no part in the action.

The remainder, overlooking the river-bed and the Iron Bridge, probably saw more of the glider landings than anyone, and were soon firing into the Germans as they scurried for shelter. Then two gliders crashed through the olives behind them,* but they swung around and engaged the attackers from that quarter also.

*Probably the same gliders I had encountered.

For a while they held out with considerable success and inflicted several casualties among the Germans around the tents, but, as the New Zealanders relinquished their hold upon the bridge area, more and more of the enemy filtered through the camp. By the time the badly mauled remnants of 'D' Company's right flank had fallen back to prepared positions behind the irrigation ditch, McKenna's party had been left in an impossible position. Before them were the Germans crossing the bridge in strength; behind, glider troops held the RAF camp.

Nevertheless, while guarding their rear, the erks maintained a steady and accurate fire upon the reinforcements as they ran across the bridge. They were targets too good to miss. Three Germans they dropped in a row; then their comrades gave up the attempt, preferring to cross under cover of the bridge pylons and run the gauntlet of the more distant fire from 'D' Company lines.

Meanwhile, on Kavkazia Hill it was time to take stock of our position, and three of us slipped away through the bushes to reconnoitre the southern slopes. The little German Jew, Hess, was leading. He and Taffy Williams, a wireless mechanic who was the third member, were magnificent. We searched the area from a grassy mound half-way down the hill. Plenty of dead bodies sprawled about the valley, but at first we saw no live Germans.

To our left, where the Vlakheronitissa track fell away to the valley, an occasional flare shot skywards and once a multi-coloured cluster went up together. On the hill east of the track were 'B' Company, and they were probably having a fine game destroying German containers which had fallen so providentially in their midst.

Lying due south of us, Vlakheronitissa, a handful of white-walled houses like grazing sheep on the hill-side, appeared deserted, but to our right, near the glider-infested Tavronitis, we could just make out 21 Battalion's gallant platoon, who were heavily engaged and battling it out in isolation. Two gliders lay across their positions.

On the open ground before us a drama was being enacted as a Kiwi dragged an injured man towards 'B' Company lines. With one arm hanging limp over his comrade's shoulder, the wounded soldier stumbled slowly forwards.

Suddenly Vlakheronitissa came to life. Sporadic firing echoed from among the houses. We pinpointed some firing which came from a bend in the track below, but whether or not it was directed towards the couple of New Zealanders we could not tell. Hess and Williams were quickly in position, sniping at the enemy and I followed suit. We gave the group by the track several rounds, but all the time anxiously watching the progress of the two soldiers. They staggered on slowly towards the cover of some trees. Then we saw another Kiwi from 'B' Company running out to meet them. Throwing the wounded man's across his shoulder, the new arrival quickly pulled the pair to safety.

Unbeknown to us at the time, over the next ridge near Xamoudhokhori village the officers and airmen of 252 AMES (Radar and W/T) under the command of Flight Lieutenant Babcock and twenty-one New Zealanders under Lieutenant Wadey manned a perimeter wire with five Lewis machine guns protecting the transmitter and receiver vans within their 'technical site'.

They had found plenty of targets among the descending paratroops and the gliders released overhead as they swept silently towards the southern slopes of Kavkazia Hill. In the nearby village all the Germans were dead but at a price. Many Cretan civilians who had resisted them also lay dead or severely wounded in the main street.

We returned to the summit, reporting our observations to two artillery officers in one of the sand-bagged enclosures. They had planned to use the hilltop as an observation post, but had soon been out of touch with their guns. Now they had assumed control of the heterogeneous troops still arriving in penny numbers. The senior officer, Captain Williams, was relieved to learn of the New Zealanders on our right wing, and we settled down to guard the gap to the south between them and 'B' Company.

I went back to Stevenson and Price in the Lewis-pit. From here we could watch the long line of mortars on the far bank of the river which was sending a barrage over our heads — most of the shells panting past and landing somewhere in 'A' Company lines.

Although as the morning progressed, a few isolated paratroops moved up the hill towards us they were soon dispatched. Most of the time, to conserve ammunition, only Alfie Price, the armourer, who was a crack shot with a rifle, continued firing at any worthwhile target which presented itself. But there was quite a degree of excitement. On one occasion a German suddenly appeared among the shrubbery a few feet away and opened up with his Schmeisser. Everyone shouted a warning at once.

Stevenson swivelled the Lewis and his sudden burst splashed across the man like water from a garden hose. He fell to his knees and pitched forward, his face buried in the mountain thyme and his hands reaching out stiff before him. We took his gun and drank the coffee in his water bottle.

Hess was worried about his paybook. His chances of survival would be slight if he were captured and his nationality discovered. After a conference with Stevenson and Price, we made a bonfire of it.

Stragglers still arrived from the RAF camp, dishevelled and out of breath. The majority bore some mark of battle. Bullet-sliced tin hats were common, and one erk had the paybook in his breast pocket cut in two by a bullet. There seemed to be far more near-misses than casualties. Many brought incredible tales of their individual escapes. One opportunist, fighting a running battle through the tents, had deviated to the stone hut and collected the 'shoot' school money on the way. His shirt bulged with the handfuls of worthless currency. But the most remarkable story came from a young 30 Squadron airman who had run full tilt into the arms of a glider trooper. The German disarmed him before he had recovered from the shock, presented him with a packet of cigarettes and three lemons, gave him a swig of coffee, and told him to 'beat it!'

Sturgess, the armourer, and a 30 Squadron officer named Black appeared together, Sturgess weak with dysentery, Black with a sprained ankle. An inseparable couple, they were to sit by the stone wall discussing classical music all day. Jock Fraser had found himself with a group of 30 Squadron airmen.

Pilot Officer Crowther organized them into a defensive line around the north-eastern summit of the hill overlooking the RAF camp. In a lull in the firing, two airmen on his right raised their heads a bit too high. A machine-gun opened up and both men were killed, hit in the chest. Fraser managed to drag both airmen away from the edge and called Crowther who helped him to carry them to an open space near the AA gun and covered them with groundsheets.

I came across Jock some time later and he insisted upon lending me his Italian .44 revolver and some .45 ammunition for it.

Presently Flight Lieutenant Woodward arrived. He sat himself down on the grass and watched the proceedings with a slightly bored expression upon his face. Hess took me German-hunting down the southern slopes again. He was certainly a great lad for this sort of thing. He had led German patrols across 'No Man's Land' during the First World War, so he told me. Now he was killing Germans . . .

We were retracing our footsteps when Hess made a quick gesture to take cover. I soon saw why. Between us and the summit lay a paratrooper. In his hands he held a sub-machine-gun. He was resting on one forearm with his back turned towards us, and he had not seen us.

I lined him up in my rifle sights, loath to pull the trigger at such a sitting target. He was a dead duck. As I hesitated Hess ran up to him, shouted in German, and prodded him in the back with his rifle. The Schmeisser clattered from the German's grasp. Hess kicked him flat. The paratrooper, letting out a shriek of agony rolled over, clutching his leg with both hands. We could now see that it was soaked in blood.

We took away his gun and examined his leg while Hess questioned him in German. He produced a flick-knife with a swastika-marked handle for us to hack at his clothing. His bared leg was a sickening pulp of red, bullet-shattered flesh and bone. The poor devil must have caught a burst from a Lewis. He was in great pain; agony contorted his sweating face. I felt pity for him. No longer a matchstick man to knock down, a mere clay-pipe target at a fairground, the enemy became a human being for the first time.

I heard myself saying: 'All right, old chap,' as we eased him under a shady bush.

He found us a field dressing, and we did what little we could to staunch the flow of blood. I marvelled at Hess, chatting to him and bandaging him up as tenderly as if he were caring for a brother. It didn't make sense.

I left the two Germans to their gossiping and returned to the hilltop for some water, dodging an inquisitive Messerschmitt on the way. Nothing much could be done for the man. We had no medical supplies or orderlies to administer them. Our own wounded lay about the summit unattended. What water we possessed came from the radiator of a derelict truck, and was rationed out for our wounded only. However, on the pretext that it was needed for a wounded Kiwi, I acquired a small quantity of the rust-coloured liquid and returned to Hess.

By the time I had reached them, Heinrich, the paratrooper, and Hess had become soul-mates. A wad of family photographs were going the rounds:

brother Willi in the Marine U-Bot Waffe, Uncle Karl in the Wehrmacht, Mum, Dad, and girlfriend. The German seemed eager to turn out his pockets for us, and when he produced a large document which Hess assured me was his Record of Service — a most unlikely thing to carry into battle, I would have thought — I glanced at his date of attestation and could not resist telling him to 'Join up and get some service in', all of which Hess dutifully translated. As I was rewarded with a bewildered expression on the German's face, I could only presume that no such phrases existed among the German troops.

Finally, Heinrich instructed us on how to use his weapon and then we left him.

That morning, six miles away in the New Zealand 7th General Hospital near Canea, Dixie Dean, 33 Squadron flight rigger, had finished his early break-fast and Vic Wyatt, the Australian in the next bed, just about to shave when they heard a series of deafening crashes.

'Hell! We're being bombed!' the Aussie shouted in disbelief as earth and shrapnel from nearby explosions splattered their tent. Anticipating a quick exit, both men grabbed their clothes and dived under their beds where the mattresses gave them some slight protection.

German bombers, ignoring the many large Red Crosses displayed, were pattern-bombing the hospital, straddling the tents with high explosives! For a long time the bombs rained down, destroying tents and killing and wound-ing bed-patients and orderlies. Shrapnel ripped lethal patterns in the canvas and there was black smoke, cordite and dust.

Suddenly there were parachutists bursting through the tent doorway, machine pistols menacing and wildly yelling 'Hande hoch! Hande hoch!' Outside was more yelling and shooting.

Lieutenant-Colonel Plimmer, CO 6th Field Ambulance, one arm in a sling, left his slit trench with raised arm. Captain Lovell, also unarmed, was by his side. Both were fired upon at close range and Lieutenant-Colonel Plim-mer was killed.

Dixie Dean felt a gun muzzle prod him and, forgetting the pain in his ribs, was out from under the bed like a shot. Regardless of protests from the New Zealand orderlies, in no time bed patients were forced to their feet with hands held high. Some asked permission to dress or, at least, put their boots on but the request was refused and both sick men and orderlies were roughly prodded through the doorway.

Outside, Dixie and Vic Wyatt looked around in disbelief. The New Zealand 7th General Hospital was a mess; tents destroyed, smoke, fire, and a row of 20 patients laid out for burial, killed by the bombing.

It was later discovered that some of the nursing staff managed to hide and a few of the less brutal paratroopers allowed other orderlies to remain with the worst bed cases like Albert Moore who could not be moved. The remainder, staff and pyjama-clad bed patients, totalling some 300 men, were herded over to the 6th Field Ambulance where they waited uneasily.

There was consternation among the Germans when a New Zealand personnel carrier drove past. Occasional bursts of firing could be heard although from which side was not certain. The Germans then decided to move behind a screen of bed patients and orderlies in the direction of their comrades whom they erroneously believed were in the possession of Galatas village a short distance away.

To this end, some immediately disappeared through the olive trees leaving behind a dozen or so paratroopers who had now been joined by the angry Luftwaffe pilot shot down at Maleme the previous Thursday. His hand was bandaged but he was waving a Schmeisser enthusiastically.

Forward moved the prisoners, some supported by orderlies, many hobbling along the stony ground in bare feet. Dixie Dean, who could hardly breathe, lay heavily against the loyal Australian as they staggered along. The party was ordered to turn right at the Maleme-Canea road junction and then to move over some rough terrain, those with bare feet the best way they could. Now and again rifle shots would ring out and several patients were hit. Then there was a sudden burst of firing and one of the paratroopers and three New Zealand Ambulance staff dropped dead. A further New Zealander was wounded. The patients repeatedly yelled out that they were British but it made no difference.

By now they had climbed a small hill. The Germans took up positions behind a stone wall while the prisoners dived for the ground finding what cover they could. Vic Wyatt and Dixie Dean peered down from the brow of the hill towards a small valley. To their consternation New Zealand soldiers were approaching in full view of their guards. Some of the Germans swung around, made gestures for silence and pointed their guns in a threatening manner. And all the while the New Zealanders, a patrol from 19th Battalion, were walking into the trap.

Then one of them was heard to comment loudly, 'There's none of the bastards over here!', and the party moved away. However, shortly afterwards, the patrol was seen to be returning and once more the Germans signalled for absolute silence. Then, seeing a sudden movement, one of the New Zealanders opened fire. Before the paratroopers could stop him the Luftwaffe pilot, unable to contain himself, fired back with a Schmeisser burst and the game was up.

The ensuing battle lasted over an hour. Soon realising that there were many unarmed prisoners as well as Germans to contend with, the New Zealanders skilfully outflanked the enemy, picking them off one by one until all but two had been killed. Dixie Dean was taken with the other patients and orderlies to the safety of the battalion headquarters.

9
20th May 1941:
Afternoon

By midday, General Meindl, wounded while trying to cross the Tavronitis under the Iron Bridge and directing operations from a stretcher in the village, was really worried. He had made far less progress than had been anticipated, not having succeeded in capturing either the aerodrome or the hill which overlooked it. Apart from his small initial successes, the position was rapidly becoming one of stalemate, with his troops unable to shift the stubborn New Zealand defenders, and the Kiwis, without reinforcements, too few in number to win back the small German gains.

The failure of the gliders of Major Koch to take Kavkazia Hill at the onset had been followed by a far greater catastrophe. His III Battalion of paratroopers had all fallen short of their intended drop zone. Instead of landing virtually unopposed as indicated by German Intelligence, they had all fallen two miles from the aerodrome, fair and square upon the New Zealand support battalions.

The German commander, all his officers and more than two-thirds of his men had been killed. The remaining troops were scattered over a wide area and, apart from their nuisance value, could not affect the immediate battle.

Meindl therefore decided upon an all-out attack upon Kavkazia Hill, calling for support from dive-bombers and trench mortars to blast the summit and demoralise the defenders. Two companies of his IV Battalion were sent, under Major Stenzler, down the river bank to cross south of the New Zealand defences and attack the high ground with an outflanking movement from the south. He ordered the remainder of his available troops to enlarge their hold on the bridge area, and engage the northern defences of Kavkazia Hill.

Hopelessly isolated, McKenna's party still held on grimly to their trench on the edge of the river-bed near the Iron Bridge. They had been receiving plenty of attention from the Germans in the camp. They had accounted for at least 15 of them, but not without suffering casualties themselves. Nobby Banks had been killed and little 17-year-old Tubby Dixon also, shot through the head. He had lived for another hour, but had died without regaining consciousness. The four survivors could not hope to fend off the next attack, being by now without rifle ammunition. Their total armament now consisted of an Italian .22 Biretti of Eaton's and Chiefy Firman's revolver.

Something had to be done. There was always the possibility of there being a few rounds of ammunition left behind in the nearby tents, and Ken Eaton decided to leave the trench and make a search. He handed McKenna the Biretti and clambered out. Cautiously he crept towards the nearest tent . . . the others watched in silence with bated breath. Then he had reached the doorway and disappeared inside. Too late they saw the Germans over to the left. Suddenly opening fire, the enemy raked the tent through and through.

McKenna and Jones watched the doorway for a few more moments — but Ken Eaton had made his last unselfish gesture.

Eaton was dead and nothing had been achieved. Then, shortly afterwards, Jones spotted a full bandolier hanging from an olive tree by the tent. Undeterred by Eaton's fate, he too climbed over the trench edge. Immediately seen by the watchful enemy behind the trees he ran the gauntlet of their fire, reached up for the ammunition, and calmy disengaged the canvas strap from the branch. With bullets humming all around him he unhooked the bandolier and raced back towards the shelter of the trench, regaining it unscathed.

While it lasted, this fresh supply was a godsend. Keeping a weather eye open for attacks from behind them, the two airmen returned to sniping at the bridge, where the enemy were once more attempting to reinforce the camp. When their ammunition ran out again they decided to leave their position and make a bolt for the hill. This time luck was with them all the way. Encumbered by the still-shocked flight sergeant, they were successful in reaching the New Zealand lines after some exciting moments creeping around parties of Germans among the olives.

Meanwhile, within the RAF camp they had left behind them, the Germans were preparing to attack the hill from that direction and, being desperate, were about to resort to desperate measures.

Collecting all available men en route, a German officer hurried through the trees to the clearing where the RAF prisoners were being guarded. He lined them up before him, stomped up and down and treated them to an uncontrolled tirade of abuse. Being in German his words were lost to all but three of the bewildered men, Dutch Holland and two German Palestinians in a panic in case their Jewish origin was discovered. Then he pulled a few of them out of the line, including the two terrified Palestinians, shouted at them afresh and dealt them several brutal blows. He concluded his Nazi psychopathic display with an order to the German guards to turn the prisoners round with their hands raised.

The Nazi moved out of earshot and Holland had an opportunity to ask one of the friendlier guards if they were going to be shot.

'*Werden wir ershossen?*'

'Not today, anyway,' mumbled the German turning his head away.

Colin France, fully expecting to be shot in the back said his prayers. Every airman there expected the worst and it was almost a relief when the Nazi officer returned and shouted, 'March!' instead of 'Fire'.

The prisoners were then marched towards the aerodrome and halted where the trees ended. The landing-ground, littered with corpses, fairly hummed with the vicious cross-fire coming in all directions. To their right the ground sloped up towards the New Zealand defences halfway up the hill. The airmen were separated into groups of nine or ten and told to move up the slope and shout out, 'Don't shoot!' when they neared the defenders.

Crouching behind the airmen, the Germans prodded them forward with their Schmeissers. They walked into the wicked fire from the soldiers up the hill. Men were falling to the ground, their blue uniforms causing them to be mistaken for the enemy.

To the right of Colin France, Ginger Hutchinson crumpled up suddenly and fell with a New Zealand bullet in his stomach. Ignoring the hail of fire and the Germans behind them, Colin and another airman crouched down to help their comrade. There was no sign of blood but a considerable bulge in his trousers where, it appeared, his intestines were oozing through a bullet wound to the right of his navel but lower down. They attempted to bandage him with a field dressing but the Germans prodded them forward again. Ginger Hutchinson was helped to his feet and staggered forward with one hand holding his stomach.

Then they could hear New Zealand voices telling them to duck. They threw themselves upon the ground. There was a burst of firing, then silence. They were free!

At the same time, there was a confusion within the two other groups of airmen. The advance up the hill came to a halt. More airmen fell mortally wounded, and the German captors were rapidly losing their screen.

Dutch Holland was told to walk up the hill to the New Zealanders with the ludicrous suggestion that unless the aerodrome was surrendered all hostages would be shot! With raised hands the 30 Squadron storekeeper climbed upwards, slowly at first, then faster as the defence trenches loomed nearer.

Before his message could be delivered, however, the defenders had sized up the situation. Firing ceased and the New Zealanders were standing up in anger, shouting at the crouching enemy. From the summit of Kavkazia Hill we could hear the cries of 'Shame!'

But by now Pilot Officer Crowther of 30 Squadron, leading a party of airmen, had forced his way down the hillside to catch the Germans with flanking fire. At the same time New Zealanders and a few airmen led by Corporal Harrison pushed down the enemy's other flank. Confusion reigned. The prisoners, realising that it was now or never, bolted for the hill, leaving the Germans bereft of cover. The bunch of paratroopers were hit from three directions. In a moment nothing but an untidy row of dead Germans remained. Over half of the prisoners had also been killed, but some 14 reached safety.

Ginger Hutchinson's wound was tightly bandaged and he was placed in the open back of the army truck on the summit. The remainder were given rifles and manned the defences alongside the New Zealanders. The attack on Kavkazia Hill from the north had turned into a massacre. The assault from two other directions was soon to come.

Without warning, mortars found the summit's range, the first three shells exploding among the sand-bagged emplacements. The sudden attack had sent the defenders scurrying from the post. They evacuated the area and retired to the shelter of the stone wall which fell away down the south-eastern slope along the Maleme-Vlakheronitissa track.

Hess and I saw the shells falling as we were returning from the valley. Between explosions, another more disturbing sound could be heard: rapid automatic fire crackling through the trees like burning timber from the direction of 'A' Company. It appeared that a battle royal was being fought out down there. Because of the wooded slopes which obscured our vision, and lacking knowledge of the strength or disposition of the New Zealanders between us and the aerodrome, we had no means of gauging the outcome. For all we knew, Germans might overrun the hill at any moment. It was a time to stand firm, and now the emplacements were unmanned.

Wisps of cordite-smelling vapour hung above the scene, and supporting Spandau fire swept the hilltop. We dived flat upon the ground, watching with fascination the stream of bullets moving slowly along the stone wall, loosening the soil and ricocheting off the rocks. Then we bolted for the first gun-pit. The Lewis had vanished. We must find it quickly. The Spandau stopped for a moment, and we ran for the wall, vaulted over, and fell among a crouching line of New Zealanders, Fleet Air Arm, Marines and airmen.

The machine-gun was retrieved along with several pans of ammunition. The mounting was permanently lost. Most of the men were willing to return with us, and we divided forces; one party of airmen to guard the southern slopes and about a dozen New Zealanders to take the northern end. We carried the Lewis to the latter position, keeping well to the east of the summit to avoid the vicious bursts of machine-gun fire which still made movement hazardous. The spare ammunition was carried by a Kiwi called Smiler, a small, lean, bright-eyed soldier, whose brown, weather beaten face gave the impression of an animated walnut. We jammed the gun against a tree root while the others sprawled on the ground beside us in a semi-circle. Rifles at the ready, they peered down through the trees in the direction of the anticipated assault.

Behind us, in the shadow of the army truck with the drained radiator, lay two wounded Kiwis. One croaked hoarsely for water. Handing over the Lewis to Smiler, I crept back to him and helped him to drink some of the precious liquid. The other soldier was dead or unconscious. I found a third casualty in the open back of the truck. He was a young airman and he had a broad bandage around his stomach. I suddenly realised that he was Ginger Hutchinson, an LAC from 'A' Flight. I had not seen his rescuers lay him there previously. He whimpered softly for water, although three water bottles stood by his side.

Preoccupied with Ginger Hutchinson, I had not noticed the dive-bombers gathering overhead. The boy, he was not older than 18, was holding my arm and whispering:

'Is it because this bandage is so tight that it hurts so much?'

Then the first load of bombs came screaming down. Fingernails dug into my arm. His face was a mask of terror. The great noise drowned my words.

The Junkers dive-bombers hurled themselves down upon us out of the clear blue sky, bomb following bomb in rapid succession. The Stuka sirens harmonised with the nightmare screaming of the bombs into an obscene death psalm. A dark, cordite-stinking tunnel imprisoned us, cutting us off from the world outside. Then there was a loud explosion and a terrifying gust of wind and I was hurled to the ground and pelted with stones and thrown one way and blasted back again. I was hanging on to the edge of the world by my fingertips. The ground opened beneath me and my mouth filled with grit. As my senses reeled, my arm was being tugged, and it was Smiler dragging me away.

'Run for it!' he bawled.

Then we plunged through the exploding, erupting, choking darkness, stumbling over bodies, and they faded from view engulfed in a new wave of smoke, dust and noise. Smiler was staggering under the weight of the Lewis as well as the ammunition pans. When we reached daylight again, a New Zealander cannoned into us.

'What shall I do with this, digger?' he croaked.

He was staring stupefied at his smashed shoulder, where the blood had saturated the front of his shirt and was running down his arm and dripping off the tips of his fingers.

The Stukas departed and the defences on the north side of the post were re-established; airmen and New Zealanders filled the gaps. By a miracle the army truck, more likely than not the aiming point for the Stuka attack, escaped the bombs. Ginger Hutchinson was transferred to the New Zealand Regimental Aid Post at the western foot of the hill.

Fortunately for us, the determined resistance of the New Zealanders in their trenches holding the 'D' Company positions, assisted by Marines and airmen, combined with 'A' Company New Zealanders, had blunted the German attack. The enemy retired once more to the RAF camp.

Colin France and other 'human screen' airmen had been given Canadian Ross rifles and 12 rounds per man. This .300 rimless weapon, handed to us by the Navy, was guaranteed to jam after the third or fourth round. It had nearly cost me my life when faced with glider troopers earlier that morning.

With two New Zealanders from 'A' Company, Colin found a spot over-

Above *Germans descending upon the plain of Thessaly.*

Below *11 Squadron at Menidi.*

Left *'Paddy' Duff, 11 Squadron, Menidi, 'wrenched a Lewis machine-gun from its mounting and, like a man berserk, advanced down the centre of the aerodrome firing from the waist at the on-coming fighter-bombers . . .'*

Below *Menidi: 'Already a cloud of smoke hung like a black pillar in the morning air . . .'*

Below right *Menidi: end of the 'Flying Pig'. '. . . a gaunt skeleton of twisted struts and bays.'* (J. Dowd)

Right *Menidi: a blazing Greek Junkers on the tarmac.* (J. Dowd)

Above left *More chaos when a 'Chev' breaks down during the next retreat.*

Left *11 Squadron airmen retreating from Greece.* (J. Dowd)

Below left *The SS* Dumana *in Cretan waters.* (J. Dowd)

Above *11 Squadron airmen passing HMNZS* Ajax *in Suda Bay.* (J. Dowd)

Right *Squadron Leader E. A. Howell OBE, DFC, 33 Squadron CO, Maleme.* (E. A. Howell)

Above left *LAC Jack Diamond, wounded and finally rescued by Commandos.* (Jack Diamond)

Above *LAC Colin France: captured twice and escaped twice.* (Colin France)

Left *LAC 'Dixie' Dean. Wounded and used as a human shield by the Germans at the New Zealand 7th General Hospital.* (Dixie Dean)

Above right *Maleme: the author's diary entry.*

Right *Aussie Vic Wyatt.* (Dixie Dean)

Far right *A New Zealand soldier, Crete.* (The New Zealand Ministry of Defence, Wellington, NZ)

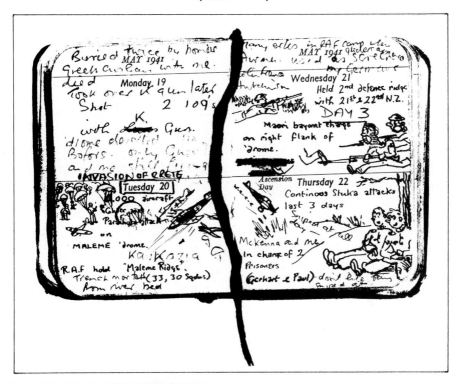

Above *An Me109 shot down by ground fire at Maleme, crashed on the beach near Platanias. First on the scene, Cretan ladies hacked off the pilot's finger to obtain his ring. The pilot later played a key role in the attack on the New Zealand 7th General Hospital.*

Below *The last Hurricane out of Maleme. The last Gladiator flown out was never seen again.* (Edward Howell)

looking the aerodrome with instructions to look out for German snipers who were taking pot-shots at the defenders. They fired at various objects which could have been snipers and presumably were successful as no more sniping was reported. The Ross rifle had fired 12 rounds and was now useless as no other rimless ammunition was available.

The assault from the south-west under Major Stenzler fared little better. Having given the resolute platoon from 21 Battalion — which was still holding that flank in isolation — a wide berth, the groups of Germans fanned out towards the hill. Two companies of paratroops struck out east, aiming to drive a wedge between 'A' and 'B' Companies on our left, while another party, attacking north, established themselves in small numbers between us and 'D' Company.

'B' Company stood their ground and throughout the afternoon no headway was made. The second party, although making no serious attack upon 'D' Company's rear, succeeded, for the moment, in cutting off communications between that flank and battalion headquarters.

The third group, attacking the southern end of the hill, met with heavy fire from a handful of airmen and New Zealanders shooting from well-concealed positions. Accurate fire from rifles and one or two captured Schmeissers sent the Germans scurrying for cover. However, one reckless paratrooper reached the summit alive and started throwing concussion grenades before he was killed. We raided his pockets for tobacco and food, and I took his pipe. Some time later, when no one was looking, I slipped it back into his pocket.

Meanwhile, by noon, Walter Goltz, survivor from the 9th Company, III Battallion, had found seven of his comrades. All were wounded, one seriously. There were no signs of the other 132 paratroops from his company.

Behind the stone building, near to where he had landed, one of them had found a short ladder which became a makeshift stretcher for the badly wounded man. Further down the slope they came upon a narrow irrigation canal which ran parallel to the coast and around the foot of Kavkazia Hill to the RAF camp. It offered cover of sorts and the paratroopers, with their badly wounded colleague between them, sunk quietly into the water, moving stealthily through the New Zealand positions. They had been instructed, if isolated, to link up with the main Sturm Regiment forces who, according to their briefing, should be holding Tavronitis. Hours later they reached the RAF camp undetected.

Further up the hill, Dr Friedrich Merk still remained among the bushes motionless while Marines wandered about their defensive positions all around him. Like many a paratrooper that day, he cursed the inefficiency of the Luftwaffe High Command in sending him to battle under a hot Cretan sun, wearing clothing designed for the attack on Narvic, near the Arctic Circle!

Running with perspiration due to his stifling clothes, his 'Standard Arctic Rations' had soon melted, the chocolate with the bacon and spiced sausage, and slopped about at his slightest movement.*

*After the battle a Nazi reporter asking a paratrooper what was his worst experience, received the reply: 'Going without food for a week!'

However, during the Stuka attack on Kavkazia — which had been all too close for comfort — he had managed to reach his water bottle and take a quick swig of the lukewarm coffee which he had brought with him from the officers' mess at Megara.

Smiler, Hess and I left the summit and set up the Lewis on a grassy ledge facing the Tavronitis. From here we could fire down, over the heads of 'D' Company defenders, upon the mortars and machine-guns on the far bank. The light was slowly failing, but the Germans thought it worth their while to shoot at us from this long range, and we had a few lively duels with them. We had the advantage of height, and, as they were using tracer, they were easy to pin-point.

Water was still our main concern. There wasn't a man on the hill who would not have given six months' pay for a decent long drink. It was natural, therefore, that a petrol can standing in the open farther down the slope should arouse our interest. For a long while we convinced ourselves that it was brimful with cold clear water. Eventually, Smiler, unable to resist the temptation, threw caution to the winds and crept down after it. So intent were we on watching his progress that we barely noticed the approaching aircraft. Just as his hand touched the can, there was a scream overhead as a score of Me110s dived upon the hilltop. From his exposed position he was forced to watch the cannon shells as they ploughed past him up the slope in long furrows, destroying everything in their path, flashing across the summit like a cat-o'-nine-tails.

Above us, men fell over each other running for cover to the emplacements. A canvas awning over two wounded men caught fire. A soldier, running to the rescue, fell to the ground. The fire spread. Some soldiers' kit was alight. For a full half-hour the fighter-bombers roared around and around the hill. Every time that Smiler attempted to join us, diving aircraft sent him to the ground again. It was almost dark when they left. Our relief at their departure changed to bitter disappointment when we discovered the Kiwi had risked his life for a can of dirty, soapy, washing water.

The firing died down; apart from a few sporadic bursts in the distance, all was uncannily quiet. Behind us the hill crackled and smouldered. Men were moving about above us, silhouetted by the flames. Where we were seemed as good a place as any to spend the night. We settled down to watch and to listen while the shadows changed and darkened on the distant hills until exhaustion overtook us and we fell asleep. The Germans had achieved no significant gains. Tomorrow we would counter-attack, and then Hitler's invincible air-army was going to get the biggest drubbing of all time.

General Student, directing operations from his headquarters in Athens, must have felt likewise. He had now committed most of his airborne troops on a score of targets along the length of Crete. Not one of the three landing-grounds was in his hands and, besides Maleme, only at one point, near Galatas, were his troops established in force. Even that position would change rapidly if a landing-ground was not soon made available to enable reinforcements to be flown in.

Lack of alternate aerodromes, the very reason which had made the island difficult for the RAF to defend, now denied him the opportunity to build up reinforcements. In one day's fighting at Maleme he had already lost 2,500 killed and 500 wounded, all elite troops. With General Meindl among the wounded, the remainder's chances of survival could not be rated high. On the morrow these same tired men could hardly be expected to withstand the inevitable counter-attack.

Only one last gamble remained. All his hopes had now to be pinned on the success of the seaborne landings. His survivors at Maleme, supported by reinforcements landed on the beaches and by his few remaining paratroops, might just hold the aerodrome long enough for the infantry to be flown in. A slender hope indeed.

But unfortunately, Lieutenant-Colonel Andrew of 22nd Battalion did not know this. Contact with his brigade commander had become increasingly difficult, communications failing completely by late afternoon. The brigadier could not have failed to appreciate the crucial importance of the airfield, but perhaps did not fully realise the desperate position Colonel Andrew *thought* he was in. He therefore saw no immediate reason to send forward his support battalions.

In the late afternoon a counter-attack mounted by Colonel Andrew without outside assistance or co-operation with his other companies, failed to dislodge the enemy. His only reserve of men — one platoon and five men from a Bofors crew who begged to be allowed to take part — had followed the two infantry tanks down the road towards the Tavronitis. The results were disastrous. The leading tank reached the river-bed on its own, turned north under the Iron Bridge, and became embedded in the soft ground, where it was captured. The second tank went into action with its turret jammed, and, when the crew found that they had been issued with the wrong-sized shells for the breech block it was withdrawn. The infantry still bravely pressed home their attack, but were cut to pieces out in the open.

Throughout the day, Andrew inexplicably found it difficult to maintain contact with his own companies. All telephonic communication had been disrupted ever since the early morning bombardment. Faced with an ultra-modern invasion, he was reduced to keeping contact with runners. Unfortunately he never once went forward to see for himself and thought that German infiltrators were often killing his messengers before they could get through. As a result of this he assumed, quite incorrectly, that 'D', 'C', and probably Headquarters Companies, from whom he had received no word, had been overrun. If the Germans had already knocked out three of his companies, he did not rate the chances of his two remaining companies as very good. He did not know either that the German paratroop reserves were relatively small. Brigadier Hargest had received optimistic reports from the two support battalions, and was under the impression that all was going well; when Andrew asked for permission to withdraw, Hargest must have assumed it was only a local withdrawal to sort out his perimeter. This basic misunderstanding could never have occurred if the batteries of Andrew's only antiquated wireless set had not failed at the crucial moment.

Andrew thought his situation hopeless, and although some reinforcements were already on the way, he decided to salvage 'A' and 'B' Companies, and gave the order to withdraw. This fateful decision played no small part in the final loss of Crete.

While we slept on in blissful ignorance, the columns of men started to file off the high ground behind us. The 30 Squadron airmen set off in two parties, accompanied by the artillery officers. Colin France had already left the hill. Out of ammunition for his Ross rifle, he had volunteered as a stretcher bearer and was already lost in the 'No Man's Land' between the hill and the support battalions on the next ridge. He was with a party, 20-strong. Some of the wounded lay on stretchers, others on planks. Leading them was Captain Longmore, the Medical Officer, and 30 Squadron's Intelligence Officer. In the darkness they stumbled their hesitant way until it was decided to rest where they were until daylight.

Meanwhile the two groups of 30 Squadron airmen had been more succ-cessful. After a most hazardous journey through country alive with small pockets of Germans, both groups were to gain the safety of 23rd Battalion lines.

The platoon from 21st Battalion, under cover of darkness, vacated their untenable position along the Tavronitis and reached the main body of men in time to retire with them. Led by a sergeant, they had brought with them three wounded. They had lost their officer and another man in the fighting.

By midnight the withdrawal had been completed, and two hours later a covering force which had belatedly arrived from 23rd Battalion to reinforce Colonel Andrew had also pulled out.

As the New Zealanders moved out, the Germans moved in. Creeping up the undefended slopes, they sent out probes along the ridge . . .

10
Kavkazia, 'No Man's Land' and Stukas

First to realise what had taken place was 'D' Company's commander, Captain Campbell. He had picked up the rumour from a stray Marine while in search of water for his men. After further investigation had convinced him that the withdrawal had been a complete one, he decided upon immediate evacuation. He knew that his badly mauled company would not be strong enough to withstand the morning assault unaided.

He therefore divided his New Zealanders, along with some 60 RAF and Marines, into three parties. The depleted platoon from his right flank he sent southwards with the badly wounded. They were successful in evading the cordon of Germans, and two days later reached the south coast over the White Mountains.

The remainder set off over the hill moving eastwards in two groups. Lieutenant Craig took his platoon and wounded to the south and then turned east but here the enemy were astride his route in force. He turned back and tried a more northerly path but, as daylight came, he realised that they were surrounded. Ordering one section to slip away, because of the wounded they carried, he had no choice but to surrender.*

Captain Campbell's party, consisting of 26 New Zealanders and the RAF and Marines, were more successful. They were able to pick their way through

*See 'After Crete', page 198.

the paratroops and, by first light, hide up in a concealed spot in front of 21st Battalion defences.

By good fortune the retiring soldiers passed close to our position, and a Marine came across to arouse us from our sleep. I shouldered the Lewis, the soldier lifted the ammunition pans, and we quietly joined the moving column.

The journey was a gruesome one. A stink of blood and ersatz coffee pervaded the air, overpowering even the aroma of the shrubs that everywhere perfume the Cretan scene. Crumpled German corpses littered the countryside, lying in the strange individual attitudes where sudden death had overtaken them. We stumbled over them in the darkness, treading on stomachs, gargling hollow moans from lifeless lips. A few bodies hung from trees, twisted in their harnesses; unpleasant, yielding, fleshy obstacles to blunder against in the darkness.

Jock Fraser was startled when he found himself alone among a large group of these, hanging lifeless on every side. Then he discovered a young parachutist on the ground. He was alive with dreadful stomach wounds. The boy was begging for water. Feeling guilty because he was unable to assist, in his best schoolboy German, Jock told him, *'Wir haben kein wasser.'* He gathered up his parachute and made it into a pillow for his head. In the darkness, Jock thought that he saw a look of gratitude in his eyes.

Some yards further on a New Zealander appeared from nowhere and told him that the youngster would not last the night out. He had watching the whole episode and Jock sensed that the Kiwi was probably the man who had shot the German in the first place.

But other paratroops were fit and far from dead. Passing close to a party of sleeping Germans, Campbell's CSM rather recklessly tossed a grenade among them 'for good luck'.

In the early hours of 21st May, Dr Friedrich Merk from Wilhelmsfeld, 9th Company survivor, had been aware of movement and muffled voices for a while and then, silence. After waiting a little longer he crept cautiously out of the bushes to stretch his cramped limbs. By the half-light the gunsite appeared to be deserted. Nearby he discovered two British soldiers in a shelter, both badly injured. As he started to examine their wounds and do what he could for them the irony of the situation struck him; all those years of pre-war training and his first patients — enemy soldiers!

For Captain Longmore and his small group of stretcher cases and orderlies, including Colin France from 33 Squadron, marooned in 'No Man's Land' without coats or blankets, the night was bitterly cold. At about 4 am cries for help were heard. After searching among the bushes they came across the two parachute brothers from Essen, survivors from the ill-fated III Battalion. One was badly wounded in the chest and hand. While the Medical Officer attended his injuries the other brother was profuse in his gratitude.

At dawn, when the first Messerschmitts appeared overhead, the German told Captain Longmore to make a circle of stretchers and asked the orderlies to remove their headgear. He produced a red, white and black swastika flag which he spread on the ground. He also made a white cross of sorts from other strips of material. The significance of these preparations were soon apparent when the first flight of fighters flew low overhead, waggling their wings in acknowledgement.

The 30 Squadron Intelligence Officer set off for the New Zealanders on the next ridge but had no luck. There were bullets flying in all directions but whether from Kiwis or Germans or both he could not establish. He returned to Longmore with the clear conviction that, for the moment, the wounded could not be brought across the exposed fire-swept ridge.

The party sheltered on the edge of an olive grove, only a stone's throw from safety . . .

Daylight found us lying under the trees in a valley west of 21st Battalion. Here we were joined by the survivors of Headquarters and 'C' Companies who had also obtained late information of the evacuation. 'C' Company and the Germans had been sharing the western corner of the aerodrome for most of the day. Carrying their wounded they had tiptoed away, crossing the landing-ground in stockinged feet with their boots tied around their necks.

With the dazzling dawn came the first distant droning of aircraft. The sound grew suddenly louder and a flight of Messerschmitt 110s skimmed the tree-tops and everyone went under cover, still as death. Me109s followed on their heels, strafing anything and everything. Somewhere behind the next ridge a large mortar boomed an occasional missile on to the aerodrome.

During a lull we tried to make contact with 21st Battalion, who promptly fired upon us. Eventually, recognition having been established, we moved up to join them.

The new line was established with 21st Battalion on some high land at right angles to the sea and known as Vineyard Ridge, and with 23rd Battalion to the north. Survivors from Kavkazia Hill still continued to arrive throughout the morning, among them several RAF and FAA personnel. They were immediately sent into the trenches according to where they entered the defences. Roughly speaking, 30 Squadron airmen remained with 23rd Battalion, while 33 Squadron survivors spread out along Vineyard Ridge. A cheery-faced Marine corporal, who had staggered all the way from Kavkazia Hill with my ammunition pans, found a trench for us to set up the Lewis.

Meanwhile the defenders of 252 AMES Radar 'technical site' at Xamoud-hokhori had become more isolated as each hour passed. During the night a Maori patrol reached them down the Pirgos track. They were looking for Colonel Andrew and said that they were to relieve troops in the aerodrome area but later the airmen saw them turn back they way they had come. Soon the little enclave of airmen and New Zealanders heard disquieting sounds of men from the hill moving eastwards away from the battle area . . .

Their position was heavily strafed by Me109s in the morning and they were further dismayed to discover that not only had Stenzler's Germans returned to the top of the hill to their south but, to the north, another swastika flag was displayed. They could see enemy troops in the intervening valley. News also reached them from stragglers that the aerodrome area was in German hands and many RAF had been made prisoner.

The news of 22nd Battalion's evacuation came to General Student like a death-sentence reprieve. After spending the night in near despair, he now seized his opportunities with both hands. Colonel Ramcke, a tough 52-year-old veteran, was ordered to Maleme to take over from the wounded Meindl until reinforcements could be flown in. Ramcke's men were to be stiffened by the dropping of the last paratroop reserves. The Motor Sailing Flotilla, now at Melos, was directed to the Spatha Peninsula between Maleme and Kastelli, regardless of air reports of British warships in Cretan waters. Junkers 52s, with desperately needed ammunition and urgently requested anti-tank guns, were sent to attempt a landing on Maleme aerodrome.

The first of these ammunition Junkers landed, discharged its cargo under heavy fire, and managed to fly off. A second plane also got down in one piece, but was raked with machine-gun fire and finally blew up after a direct hit from one of 23rd Battalion's mortars. No further attempts were made to land. The Germans would wait for the paratroop reinforcements to clear the way.

At 8.30 am, preceded by packs of fighters and figher bombers, the Junkers transports approached the coast by the Tavronitis. It was like the previous day on a smaller scale but this time the Germans would be falling in a safe area with few guns to endanger their descent.

Nevertheless, they viewed the next few seconds with apprehension as they awaited the signal to jump. Reports were already circulating back in Greece of many paratroopers being drowned on the previous day. Released too soon and dropped over the sea, the weight of their equipment had given them no chance for survival.

Three friends, Heinz Osterman, Gerhard Hänel and Franz Ullrich prepared to jump in the second wave of aircraft. For Gerhard Hänel there was another worry besides the chance of being dropped into the sea. He had crashed an army vehicle back in Greece and, despite a still sprained ankle, he was flying to Crete in the hope that retribution for the accident would not follow him . . .

Then he was swinging over the coastline and making a hard landing among the boulders of the Tavronitis riverbed. His friends landing nearby joined him and they made for the village. The Iron Bridge was still under fire from New Zealand snipers who had not retreated with the main body. The small group of Germans had to cross the Tavronitis underneath the bridge, running from pier to pier.

On the aerodrome the Germans were quick to consolidate their unexpected good fortune despite constant shelling from British guns. Walter Goltz, III Battalion survivor, after a night in Tavronitis village met up with an old friend among the new arrivals. Together they organised Army and RAF prisoners to trundle the wedge of 50-gallon petrol drums off the aerodrome. Originally they had been placed there to be ignited by incendiary bullets from Ken Eaton's machine-gun should the Germans attempt a landing. No such landings occurred and, anyway, the gun-pit and Lewis had been previously destroyed by a bomb, but, as a diversion, during invasion morning 'C' Company New Zealanders had attempted unsuccessfully to set the drums alight with hand-grenades.

Germans worked on the Bofors guns and soon had one into action. Others dug fresh trenches. Their greatest worry was always a tank-supported counter-attack from the New Zealanders.

Walter Goltz and his friend were ordered to tow a 'Pak' gun to the eastern end of the landing-ground to guard the road to Pirgos.*

Others also manned the airfield trenches against the expected Panzer attack while the main force made preparations for an advance against the New Zealand defences to coincide with the second parachute drop later that day.

From a hill on 21st Battalion's left flank we looked out over a tree-studded valley towards our old positions south of the aerodrome, and awaited the German attack. But the enemy, hardly believing their good fortune, took their time in clearing the area, and throughout the morning our chief discomfort came from the air.

A frail looking Henschel, the eyes of the Luftwaffe, meandered continually up and down the ridge looking for targets worthy of attention. Then up would come the inevitable dive-bombers. Within minutes the chosen area would be plastered with high-explosives, the torn and bleeding men dragged out of the line like bundles of red-stained rag. Two mortars in the valley behind us continued firing defiantly with one eye upon the circling planes. The mortar crews escaped the attentions of the ferreting spotter aircraft by quickly covering up with branches after each shell.

We began to dread the Stukas. At the slightest movement the ugly, bent-winged Junkers circled the spot with their oil-stained bellies turned towards us. One by one, in leisurely fashion, they peeled off, screaming down in a vertical dive, air-brakes extended, sirens wailing, to release their bombs with deadly accuracy and then pull out on automatic control with the crew blacked out, rejoining the defensive circle as the next Stuka sped on its way towards us.

There was a Kiwi ducking along from trench to trench, handing out bully beef and biscuit sandwiches, one for each of us. We ate hungrily. For many this was the first food for 30 hours. We remained very thirsty, and nothing could be done about it.

Firing came from the direction of Pirgos, on the coast, where some New Zealanders, aided by the Cretans, were still holding out. But, although we fully expected the enemy to attack during the morning, our only visitors came from quite another quarter when a donkey loaded with laundry bundles, suddenly broke through the bushes to be followed by an old Cretan couple. They had come from a nearby village in order that 'the *Inglisi* soldiers should fight in clean clothes.' We watched the strange trio move along Vineyard Ridge on their mission, impervious to the attentions of the ever-present aircraft.

The Marine and I discussed our withdrawal, which puzzled us as it had

*The 260-pound Schwere Panzerbuchse. A lightweight version of the heavy anti-tank rifle, the 2.8 cm Pzb 41, had been developed for airborne troops. It was fitted with small aircraft-type wheels and had no shield.

most of the men. Why had we given up such a commanding entrenched position without a fight on, what we all thought, was the eve of victory? We concluded that, somehow, it was all part of a plan to launch a strong counter-attack
that day.

'Even Jerry can't go on losing men at this rate,' argued my companion. 'If
we push him now, he's had it, chum. He's got no reserves — unless there's
another bunch of silly flakers in Greece waiting to commit suicide like they
did yesterday. Wait and see, chum, Jerry's right up the flaking creek without
a paddle!'

It was only as the day progressed and no signs of an advance became apparent
that we began to have doubts.

But we were only two men in a trench. What we did not know was that
between us and Canea there were determined pockets of paratroop survivors
who were playing havoc with our lines of communication to the extent that
New Zealand Intelligence were still unaware of the implications of our withdrawal. The only way to obtain a true appreciation of the situation was for
staff officers themselves to come forward. As these had to run the gauntlet
of sniping Germans, it was not, therefore, surprising that no clear picture
presented itself and that no immediate counter-attack was mounted.

Coupled with this uncertainty at brigade headquarters was the fear of invasion by sea. This hazard was always in the background, and the battalions
of fresh troops whose presence at Maleme would have made victory certain
were retained to guard sectors of the coastline.

In fairness, it should be said that this was the first mass parachute assault
ever attempted. There was no precedent. The logical point had not occurred
that, whereas a sea invasion *might* lose us the island, German control of an
airstrip made the loss of Crete a certainty.

During the afternoon there was a prolonged Stuka attack upon the New
Zealand positions. At the same time the second half of Student's reserve of
paratroops were dropped between Pirgos and Platanias.

The Germans, under a Captain Gerike, held in readiness to the east of the
aerodrome, advanced against the New Zealand defences, into the 'No Man's
Land' between Kavkazia and the next ridge.

It was upon 23rd Battalion, stiffened by Marines and airmen, that the full
brunt of the assault was felt. With fanatical bravery the fresh enemy forces
hurled themselves at the New Zealanders, rushing the slopes and firing at
almost point-blank range. They fell by the score to the steady fire from rifle
and machine-gun. Soon the dead lay about in heaps, the remainder, depleted
in numbers, fell back.

As they retired towards the aerodrome they came across Captain Longmore's
group of stretcher cases and orderlies. Colin France barely had time to jam
the Luger he was carrying into the fork of an olive tree before he was captured. The party was escorted back to Maleme village and Colin France was
immediately put to work retrieving wounded paratroops.

But for the Germans worse was still to come. The second half of the paratroop
reserve, dropped between Pirgos and Platanias, could hardly have chosen a

more unhealthy spot. The area, given as 'safe' by German Intelligence, was well within 5th Brigade's perimeter, and Platanias bristled with the Maoris of 28th Battalion, only too eager to get to grips with the enemy. The invaders found the New Zealanders ready for them. Germans were killed or scattered to the four winds before they could form up. But for those falling within 28th Maori Battalion lines one could almost feel pity. Leaping out of their trenches like unleashed hounds, the Maori boys fell upon the enemy with fixed bayonets in a terrible skirmish, wiping out every invader.

At the technical site near Xamoudhokhori, the airmen and New Zealanders had been defending their perimeter with rifles, Lewis and Bren guns throughout the morning. The commanding officer of 252 AMES, Flight Lieutenant Babcock, still maintained W/T communication with Canea and it was from HQ RAF that they received instructions to join the nearest army unit. Preparations were therefore put in hand to destroy equipment, cypher books and the two vans.

At 2.30 pm Lieutenant Wadey, the New Zealand officer, had set out to find Colonel Andrew for instructions. It had been agreed that the Colonel should be asked either to sanction a withdrawal or, better still, as their fortified technical site was in such an excellent position, to send reinforcements to assist the airmen in holding it. He was also to report that they still had a first class W/T link with Canea.

James Britton recalls the outcome in his book *Record and Recall: A Cretan Memoir* (Lightfoot Publishing):

> He returned about an hour later with the news that 'matters were so bad they could hardly be worse.' The road to Canea was in German hands and the valley below us was said to have German troops established a little to the south of it. The Colonel would agree neither to our withdrawal nor to the supply of additional troops. We were to stay where we were and hold out as long as we could. We were promised that a patrol would be sent into the village after nightfall.
>
> At a conference of the three officers it was decided to blow up all apparatus during the first bombing raid on the unit — and so avoid publishing the fact.

However the decision had barely been made when they became aware of an ominous vamping drone in the northern sky. A large formation of Ju87B Stukas with Messerschmitt escorts had already singled out 252 AMES for attack.

For 45 minutes the bombs rained down upon the defenders. On all sides the ground erupted in sudden explosions of earth and shrapnel. Large calibre bombs swung out from under the oily bellies of the attacking dive-bombers and burst on and around the technical vehicle area. Two of the Lewis gun pits were destroyed. Then Messerschmitt fighters dived down upon the stricken site with cannon and machine-gun fire. The airmen blasted back at the attackers as best they could but several were killed or wounded. Flight Lieutenant Babcock was hit in the shoulder by a bullet. Immediately below the transmitter van, Wadey, the New Zealand officer, standing right next to Pilot Officer James Britton, was seriously wounded by shrapnel.

Carrying their wounded, under a cover of dust clouds from the bombing, the surviving airmen tried to reach the New Zealanders on Vineyard Ridge. Britton and a sergeant returned to the site to ensure that both vans had been destroyed and that no live personnel remained.

After more adventures, some eventually reached the comparative safety of the Ridge while others escaped over the White Mountain. James Britton and 33 other ranks (including six wounded) returned to Egypt. The CO and 13 other ranks were missing.

The almost complete destruction of Student's second wave of reserve paratroops by the Maoris, following so soon after his losses during the unsuccessful assault upon 23rd Battalion, brought him no nearer to conquering Crete. Now he was really worried that the inevitable New Zealand counter-attack would be launched before the arrival of his seaborne reinforcements. He therefore decided upon desperate alternative action.

In the late afternoon the sky to the north darkened as a large fleet of transport planes approached low over the sea. The 100th Mountain Regiment were flying in regardless of the cost! Lumbering across the landing-ground, the Junkers came under heavy fire from our northern positions, but, before they had stopped rolling, the Germans were leaping from them and racing for cover. More and more transports piled up behind them until the aerodrome was overflowing with aircraft and could take no more. The Junkers upon it were being smashed by mortar fire. Then, with reckless disregard for the machines, the German pilots threw them down along the beach and down the slope above the aircraft pens. Crash-landed Junkers littered the coast from Maleme to Platanias. The dozens of burning and shot-up wrecks had transformed the place into an aircraft junkyard. Under the rising plumes of smoke the slaughter of Germans went on, the Mountain troops going down under a barrage of hot lead as they dived from the crashed aircraft.

As the reinforcements arrived on the aerodrome they were helped by their colleagues to reach the shelter of the trenches and sandbagged emplacements.

Major Schaette, a fanatical Nazi, had been briefed to protect the landing-ground from attacks from Kavkazia and the west where Student thought, quite incorrectly, there were strong reserves of New Zealanders. With a force of Mountain troops he set off westwards with some sense of urgency to capture the Spatha Peninsula, where the Small Ship Flotilla was expected, and nearby Kastelli. He was to achieve the first objective easily. He did not find the expected 'strong New Zealand reserve forces' but, at Kastelli, the stubborn resistance of three New Zealand officers leading a handful of gendarmes and local militia was to delay him a further three days! Afterwards he was to exact a dreadful revenge upon the people of Kastelli.*

Meanwhile, at Maleme, I Battalion, 100th Mountain Regiment, under Colonel Utz, had set out to reinforce the still-active Major Stenzler to the south.

It soon became apparent that Stenzler constituted a most serious threat. He was deploying his paratroops, now reinforced by a large part of 85th Moun-

*See Chapter Twelve.

tain Regiment under Utz, around the southern flank of Vineyard Ridge with
the obvious intention of cutting us off from Canea.

Six miles to our east lay 3rd Parachute Regiment, which had dropped the
previous day and already threatened Galatas and the Canea road from the
south. No concerted efforts had been made to remove this threat. The defenders
in the vicinity were still keeping one eye cocked for the threatened sea invasion. Unless we counter-attacked soon we would be hopelessly surrounded.

'Follow me, you chaps, and don't make too much noise.' As the light was
falling, Flight Lieutenant Woodward, our only surviving officer, gathered his
airmen from the trenches in the hope of leading them to Canea. Hard friend-
ships had been made during the day between the erks and their New Zealand
hosts — the affinity of those who had shared a common danger — and there
was some handshaking as they left.

'Best of luck, you "Rare As Fairy" jokers!' some of the Kiwis called out
after them.

Chiefy Firman would not come. He was sitting in a trench with the back
of his tunic split open by a bullet and refusing to budge. There was no time
to argue and we left him there. We did not see him again.

Saying my adieux to my Marine friend and handing over the Lewis to him,
I shouldered a rifle and walked down the eastern slope of the hill to join up
with the others under the trees. They had discovered a muddy puddle when
I arrived, and were taking it in turns to lie on their faces and drink. Dead
leaves were a nuisance but everyone was too thirsty to care. As 'Goon' Gummer, a Servicing Section Fitter, remarked: 'Nothing too big will go down if
you clench your teeth . . .' To all of us it tasted like nectar.

We gathered around while the imperturbable Woodward explained our position. Parties of Germans lay between us and Canea, cut off from their units,
operating in bands ranging in size from half a dozen to larger groups. We
hoped to pass through them undetected.

Soon the airmen were moving cautiously to the north of Kondomari in single file along a path as twisting as an olive bole, each man carrying items
of German equipment as well as his rifle and a blanket or two filched on
the way from discarded dumps of kit.

Half a mile farther east, another RAF party joined us out of the shadows
including Jeffers, Paddy Smith, McKenna, Jock Fraser, Sturgess, Tug Wilson and Black, the 30 Squadron officer. The combined parties moved on quietly
through the trees.

We had only travelled for ten minutes or so when, without warning, a
machine-gun opened up ahead, shattering the eerie stillness of the night. Someone called out *'Kiora Katoa'*, the Maori password we had been instructed
to memorise, but was answered by a whole rattling barrage of small-arms
fire. Germans lay astride our route in the darkness ahead.

Flickering pin-points of light flashed and danced around the trees to our
right. The bullets, fortunately aimed too high, were singing overhead and slicing
off the leaves in the trees behind.

The door to Canea had been closed. It would have been foolhardy to proceed in the darkness. There were a few moments of indecision. Then Woodward ordered us to turn about, and we were scrambling for cover. The airmen dispersed and wandered back in ones and twos to Vineyard Ridge again. Failing to find the Marine with my Lewis, McKenna, Paddy Smith and I huddled up under a tree and went to sleep.

Still lying by the wrecked tent in the RAF camp Squadron Leader Howell was motionless. Always acutely conscious of a tormenting thirst, he was too weak to move even a finger. For two long days the Cretan sun had beaten mercilessly down from a blazing sky, the heat agitated the swarms of flies which constantly settled all over him. The nights seemed bitterly cold and, whenever he drifted into unconsciousness, the pain from his wounds and the dreadful craving for water soon aroused him again and renewed his deep desire for relief through death.

But this was not to be for there were yet many incredible adventures in store for this son of a Scottish parson. Already the big black shiny flies had come to the rescue, laying their eggs in his large open wounds. By now he was crawling with maggots. They fed upon the decaying flesh and prevented the inevitable gangrene from taking hold.

By now it had dawned upon Hitler that Crete was not going to be the walkover that the advocates of air conquest had led him to believe. The initial German loss of life — the very flower of his hand-picked troops — had appalled him. He had been equally astounded by the stubborn resistance of the illequipped defenders. The promised victory now seemed a long way off.

But, although the setbacks and failures of the day had also depressed Student, by nightfall he was more confident in facing the morrow. Not only were the seaborne reinforcements on their way but at Galatas, as at Heraklion and Rethymnon, paratroops appeared to be successful in pinning down the defenders and preventing them from strengthening Maleme. Although the aerodrome was still under machine-gun and mortar fire, every hour brought him in another 20 troop-laden transports. Confident that no New Zealand counter-attack would now be launched, he decided to remove their threat to the landing-ground by a drive through to Canea the following day. To ensure success, all reinforcements of men and materials were now switched to the Maleme sector.

His plan contained two erroneous suppositions. Even while he issued his instructions, the Royal Navy, despite the loss of two cruisers and four destroyers, were moving in for the kill. They found the first flotilla of caiques and transports in the open sea and blasted them to Kingdom Come. Within a short time hundreds of Germans were drowning or clinging desperately to driftwood in the hopes of reaching the islands. The second flotilla was intercepted and destroyed later in the day.

The gun flashes out to sea could be seen by the defenders all along the coast. They were seen by Brigade HQ where the irony of the victory must have been apparent. In tying down so many Allied troops to the coast defences the two German flotillas had more than justified their existence.

And Student was wrong to assume that there would now be no New Zealand counter-attack for already the decision had been made the previous day. The 28th Maori Battalion and 20th Battalion of 4th New Zealand Brigade were to regain the aerodrome; 23rd Battalion was to straighten their line and recapture the mortar and machine-gun positions and also to hold themselves in readiness for mopping-up operations; 21st Battalion was to move against Stenzler on the flank and regain Xamoudhokhori. Unfortunately this involved moving 20th Battalion from the outskirts of Canea up to the Maori start line at Platanias. 4th Brigade, already understrength, had been further depleted when part of 18 Battalion had been given the task of escorting the King of Greece to Egypt. All movement had become increasingly difficult and by midnight the new troops were not in position. The valuable hours of darkness slipped away as zero hour came and passed. By the time half of 20th Battalion had arrived, Lieutenant-Colonel Dittmer and his Maoris could wait no longer. The advance commenced in the hopes that the remaining troops could catch up as and when they arrived.

11
Counter-Attack and Ambush

Forward, between the road and the sea, raced 20th Battalion's two companies, into the fire of the German strongpoints with the Maori boys on their left. Their objectives: the aerodrome and Kavkazia Hill. Along the road in support trundled three tanks. With little else but their rifles and bayonets the New Zealanders cleared out the heavily armed German pockets of resistance as they advanced. By dawn they had covered 2,000 yards and were parallel with our positions along Vineyard Ridge, two companies of Maoris passing through 23rd Battalion's northern defences.

But with daylight came the Luftwaffe. Staffels of fighters and fighter-bombers buzzed angrily overhead. Their devastating cannon and machine-gun fire ripped down the ranks of advancing New Zealanders while stubborn German troops on the ground blasted them with freshly-landed artillery, mortars, and Spandaus. Every tree concealed a machine-gun. Bofors guns added to the carnage, sending strings of candescent shells snapping and cracking down the road into 20th Battalion's 'D' Company at point blank range.

The advance continued against a wall of hot lead. All three tanks were now left behind, disabled. There was house to house fighting in strongly-held Pirgos. Single-handedly Lieutenant Upham wiped out a machine-gun post and killed eight Germans and, when two further machine-guns raked his platoon with their fire from the shelter of a house, Upham rolled a grenade inside, killed or wounded eight more of the enemy while no less than 12 more surrendered.

All the while the New Zealanders were being met with heavy bursts of small-arms fire, machine-guns and, at near point-blank range, the cracking shells from two Bofors guns. Then the 20th Battalion men were running through a bamboo thicket and across open ground into the concentrated machine-gun fire. Casualties mounted. Covered by three of his men, Lieutenant Upham dived for a gulley, reached a Bofors, and killed the gunners with grenades.*

Daylight and they had reached the aerodrome, holding on to their exposed positions with great courage. They fired the transport planes littering the perimeter with their only anti-tank rifle. Into the maelstrom tri-motored Junkers were still landing and taking off with fresh troops pouring out and rushing straight into the slaughter . . .

Over on 20th Battalion's left, the Maoris had chanted their thigh-slapping *hakas* and charged the enemy with equal ferocity. With them raced a company from 23rd Battalion and the remnants of 22nd Battalion's 'C' Company, who had held the aerodrome perimeter so gallantly throughout invasion day. The Germans left their machine-guns, turned their backs and fled; the Maoris, yelling and shouting terrifying 'Ahh's', followed, striking them down with red-dened bayonets to the eastern boundary of Kavkazia Hill. Now resistance was stronger. Running on like demons through a hail of lead the Maoris did not slacken their pace. The sight of the carnage that they dealt among the enemy nerved them to fight more fiercely on. The wounded staggered onwards with their comrades, impaling the Germans scrambling out of their path. When machine-guns pinned down some of them, Colonel Dittmer, the battalion commander himself, charged past his men taunting them with:

'Call yourselves bloody soldiers!'

Farther along the ridge, the airmen with 23rd Battalion, who made a local withdrawal against strong German pressure the previous evening, stood by their new positions alongside the New Zealanders. Rifle in hand they prepared to thwart any attack along the thinly-held flanks while two platoons advanced cautiously from the centre of the line. Caught between sniping fire on either side and unable to consolidate positions gained on the previous night the Germans retreated before the New Zealanders' determined advance. Then 23rd Battalion were able to re-establish themselves in their old mortar and machine-gun area once more. From these positions the defenders, who had been given a mopping-up role, awaited developments.

Meanwhile, on the southern flank, 21st Battalion had also attacked from the south of Vineyard Ridge. Stevenson, Gummer, Price and Hess were among the foremost of the airmen who followed the New Zealanders into battle moving quickly against Xamoudhokhori.

Germans, barricaded behind doors and windows in the village, sent a vicious fusillade across the intervening valley. Spent bullets whined and ricocheted about the ears of the advancing men. Moving from cover to cover the airmen joined in the attack, firing into the end houses. The noise of the battle, the continuous crash of rifles, the Spandau and Schmeisser bursts echoing across

*For this and other courageous actions throughout the campaign, Lieutenant C. H. Upham was awarded the Victoria Cross. He was later given a bar to this decoration.

the valley filled the mind with a strange exhilaration which forced out fear.

There was a Kiwi writhing in agony on the ground. Farther on, an airman no one recognised lay huddled in a ditch. Now the end houses were silent. A German, retreating down the street, straightened suddenly as if he had run into an invisible wire. He pitched forward full-length in the dust.

With fixed bayonets the advance continued. There was close fighting among the houses with the enemy holding out stubbornly to the right. Their automatic fire raked the area sending the attackers under cover with their dead and wounded lying in the street. The Kiwis dragged a machine-gun up the clock tower which commanded a good field of fire to the west of the village. The soldiers moved into the attack again. Xamoudhokhori was captured within three bloody hours of the start of the action.

Now the advanced continued along both sides of the Vlakheronitissa track against heavy machine-gun fire. To the left the company commander was killed. With every yard the volume of fire increased. A young ex-school teacher, leading a patrol farther south in an attempt to outflank the enemy, ran into deadly fire and he too lost his life.

Progress had been slightly better along the right of the road and several pockets of resistance had been wiped out. The enemy were driven to the outskirts of Vlakheronitissa itself. But by now the New Zealanders had to run the gauntlet of the line of Spandaus and mortars along Kavkazia Hill, firing into their flank. With a larger proportion of the battalion killed or wounded it was becoming hourly more difficult to hold on to the recent hard-won gains. The Germans were too thick on the ground. The Battalion's 'D' Company, a raggle-taggle assortment of RAF and Marines, and our old friends from the Tavronitis — 'D' Company of 22nd Battalion — were now the only reserves left.

Advancing over the newly won ground north of the Vlakheronitissa track, this force fought their way through the enemy-held territory ahead of them. The Germans fell back to strengthen the village on the hill and then turned to meet the resolute attackers with a barrage of small-arms fire. Unable to drive the enemy from their strongly-held positions in the houses, the New Zealanders raced past them, down the village street, and down to the Tavronitis. Once again the 26 survivors of 'D' Company, having sustained further casualties, occupied their old positions above the river bed.

But the supreme gallantry of the New Zealanders was of no avail. The line of Spandaus firing from the high ground around Kavkazia Hill could not be reached. All that could be done had been done.

It was the Germans who were now counter-attacking. Wasting no time they had quickly regrouped their vastly numerically superior forces. Now there was a great danger of a decisive break-through and the extended New Zealand columns were hurriedly recalled to Vineyard Ridge to block the gaps in the line. Machine-gun and artillery fire pursued them while Stukas hovered like vultures overhead.

Among the dead bodies left sprawling in Xamoudhokhori street lay Hess, the little German Jew.

A party of soldiers and airmen, still holding their hard-won positions near the village, ceased fire when a German officer walked towards them waving a white flag. A prisoner walked beside him. The German told the New Zealanders that they were surrounded and called upon them to surrender. If they refused, he said, they would be blasted by the Stukas. The soldiers replied with a curt, unprintable, two-worded expression with a sexual connotation and the officer quickly retired. Later on the party regained 21st Battalion lines without too much difficulty.

The roles of the combatants had now changed. Determined to pursue the original plan of a breakthrough towards Canea, the Germans were attacking all along the front. RAF and New Zealand prisoners, driven at pistol point on to the aerodrome, were made to clear a path through the smashed and burning troop-carriers enabling still more reinforcements to be flown in. Supported by artillery batteries, countless Spandaus, and trench mortars, the Germans forced their way into the New Zealand defences. Once more savage, brutal, hand-to-hand fighting was the order of things. Lacking machine-guns, and in some cases even rifle ammunition, the attacks were warded off with bayonet and rifle butt. The contest could not have been more uneven.

All that was best from the Nazi armoury poured in against the battleweary defenders. New Zealand casualties mounted in direct proportion to the rate at which fresh German infantry were ferried from Greece. Only their indomitable spirit saved the front from collapse.

And still into the gap between 21st and 23rd Battalions the hordes of Germans poured, with the Maoris pulling quickly into position behind the ridge. The enemy troops lining the skyline hurled grenades down the eastern slope. As the roar of the exploding bombs subsided the Maori boys tore up the hillside with a blood-curdling yell which echoed round the valleys. They fell upon the startled Germans with fixed bayonets and chased them back the way the had come.

McKenna and I had been called out of the line to guard two German parachutists back at Battalion HQ. We found them in a clearing near the battalion commander's tent. They were a good-looking pair with true 'Nordic' blue eyes and flaxen hair. Paul and Gerhart were their names. They both spoke several languages, including Classical Greek and, no doubt, were typical of the sort of men recruited for the Paratroop Regiments at that time. Soon they were giving us the usual bumph about the Germans being cousins to the British with whom they had no wish to fight. Then, with typical arrogance, Paul added:

'When Germany wins the war, I, personally will be very glad.'

When McKenna exploded, the prisoner postulated: 'But how can you doubt that Germany will win? After all, who has won all the battles so far?'

There were a few enemy snipers about, infiltrating from the south and firing from the cover of trees to our rear. Our parachutists did not take kindly to them and crouched together with their backs against a thick olive trunk. Here the four of us remained while, with monotonous regularity, tri-motored Junkers flew in to land over our heads, sweeping down in vics of three. To the south, a continuous stream of wounded were being carried to a Regimental Aid Post behind us. One of the casualties was a German major and our prisoners asked to see him. To make a change of scenery we agreed.

We followed a track out of the tree-studded valley and past a large bush festooned with contraceptives, fluttering in the breeze. A trail of them led from the pocket of a parachutist lying dead among the foliage. For some reason, I felt glad that he was dead ...

We found the major inside the white-walled RAP on the hilltop. McKenna took the two prisoners inside and I left them to their heel-clicking and saluting. Outside, in a crude shelter lay the overflow of wounded. Here British and German lay side by side with little enmity left between them. Geordie Tweddle was among the medical orderlies. As he bent over his blood-soaked charges administering water to them, he told me how he had volunteered as a stretcher bearer and had been out all morning bringing in the wounded under fire. I shared my German tobacco with him and told him of Flight Lieutenant Woodward's move to evacuate the RAF at the next opportunity. He gave me a tired grin.

'I'm mair use here,' he said.

True to his calling, he remained there with the MO until they were made prisoners of war when the post was overrun.

A Schmeisser opening fire from near at hand, sent us diving flat upon the ground. Bullets traced a zigzag pattern along the RAP wall. New Zealanders from over the brow of the hill ran crouching through the bushes with their rifles — heading towards the sound. For a little while sporadic shooting echoed across the valley, hunters and hunted hidden among the swaying greenery. Then the firing ceased. The soldiers returned to the hilltop. No prisoners had been taken.

Almost immediately one of the Kiwis fell, hit by another sharpshooter. This time the firing seemed to come from the RAP itself but, although the angry soldiers searched the area, no sniper could be found.

McKenna and I, glad to leave the place, took our prisoners back towards the trees. At every step we expected a shot in the back and we walked close to the two Germans all the way. For some while afterwards the German at the RAP continued to take his occasional toll of passing soldiers before his luck deserted him. He was discovered hidden under a large red cross flag on the RAP roof. A single rifle shot tumbled him down from the tiles.

Stevenson and Gummer, sweating and smoke-smudged, with empty bandoliers over their shoulders, came back to us in the clearing. They brought news of more German infiltrations behind us from the south and even as they spoke firing broke out close at hand. Coming from two directions twin streams of bullets zipped past us. A runner outside the battalion commander's tent jerked his head backward suddenly, a hand clapped to his face. Blood spurted from his cheek, slashed from eye to chin. His officer dragged him to cover. Our prisoners won the race to a nearby ditch. Along with several others we remained spectators to a minor war now raging in the valley. The indefatigable Kiwis stalked the intruders and then there was stillness.

That night McKenna and I took turns in guarding the prisoners. Desperate for sleep ourselves, we spent a miserable night listening to the contented snores and grunts of our charges. Then, by first light on the following day, they were taken from us.

That same night the Germans back in Tavronitis village were again having to count the cost of their reckless Cretan adventure as casualties from the day's fighting started to arrive, soon to overflow the main street.

Squadron Leader Howell (who, that day, had been discovered) recalls the dreadful scene in his book, *Escape to Live.*

> Every lurch of the stretcher was agony. I passed out again into merciful obli-
> vion. Then I was lying among a crowd of other wounded and dying men in
> the village street. There was someone close to me on either side. One was silent,
> he was dead. The other was one of my own airmen. I was delirious . . . Soon
> I was carried into a little shop on the village street. Here, Flying Officer Tom
> Cullen was doing the work of ten men. He had dysentery when the blitz came
> and crawled out of bed to attend to the wounded . . . Now he was attending
> to all the wounded as they were brought in. He had been on his feet for three
> days and nights. And his only helpers were untrained men. My fitter sergeant
> from 33 Squadron was helping in the 'operating theatre'. The Intelligence officer
> from 30 Squadron was his anaesthetist. I was put on a table, only half-conscious.
> A piece of torn parachute fabric was laid across my face and ether poured on
> it until I passed right out. Cullen then operated on my shoulder and cleaned
> up and bandaged both wounds . . .
>
> Later I was carried into another little house on the side of the street. . . There
> was a constant stream of wounded through the little door. Soon they were every-
> where inside. There was no room to walk between the bodies on the floor.
>
> Night came and darkness added horror to the scene. Men were groaning and
> crying out. Men were dying. Men were bleeding and being sick over each other.
> The sounds and the smells were indescribable.

Along the wall of a larger building on the left hand side of the street more stretchers were piling up. For the paratroops this was their first encounter with the dreaded Maoris and, from time to time, several of the wounded could be heard muttering the word 'Maori' in awe.

Dr Friedrich Merk, working inside, had hurried to the village and had been fighting to save lives for many hours into the night. It was an experience he was never to forget.

The counter-attack failure followed by such swift reaction on the part of the enemy had left us in an unhealthy position once more. Chances of extricating ourselves diminished hourly as fresh troops of 100th and 85th Mountain Regiments continued their enveloping movement around our southern flank. Once joined to 3rd Parachute Regiment's two battalions near Galatas they could cut the road behind us in strength and isolate the brigade.

When the battle had commenced it had been a matter of inferior versus superior weapons. Now, with the steady build up of troops landing at the rate of 500 an hour, the Germans faced us with something approaching 10,000 men — most of them fresh. Of the 1,591 New Zealanders in the three battalions once guarding Maleme, only 530 remained to hold the line with the Maoris. RAF casualties had been in the same proportion. Two-thirds of the defenders were killed, wounded, or missing. There remained no choice but to withdraw at once to the old Maori positions at Platanias, leaving a Maori rearguard to cover the retreat.

By 6.30 the next morning we set off in single file, moving south east. The rough mountain track traced its winding way through terraced vineyards and abundant shrubbery into which we dived each time aircraft flew over. A Staffel of Stukas came at us from the east; foul, black and ugly, with their vultures'-feet undercarriages reaching out as if to try to snatch us up as they approached. We froze. They passed over and seconds later we heard them blasting into the luckless columns from 23rd Battalion who were taking another route north of Kondomari. Then more Stukas appeared and we froze again but they also passed low overhead without altering course. Almost hovering in the cloudless sky above us, a solitary Henschel 'Spotter' kept its vigil.

An uneasy feeling of urgency and expectancy pervaded the grim-faced line of soldiers. There were more things than aircraft to occupy their minds. Stentzler's Germans were travelling fast on a line parallel to us. They peered anxiously at the rising ground to the right which dominated the path. We could sense the enemy watching us all the way.

Up paths, down paths, through fields, and across shallow streams the single file of men meandered with each soldier keeping an eye on the man in front. Once he had been swallowed up by the bushes ahead, those who followed were lost in the labyrinthine landscape. Only the guide knew the way. And all the while we wondered whether the Germans were occupying the higher ground ahead of us, awaiting our arrival.

Sturgess was delirious with dysentery. His constant companion, Black, his own ankle still swollen, now tried to support him in turn. Later on, the 30 Squadron officer hobbled, one-footed down the column to us, greatly distressed because during an aircraft alert his colleague, Sturgess, had disappeared. McKenna cut a stout stick for Black and he rejoined the line while the four of us searched the length of the column. We waited until the last man had passed us but Sturgess had vanished without trace. Eventually we had to give up the search and joined the tail of the file.*

The going was becoming even more difficult. By the sound of things we were walking into a battle. The chatter of machine-guns from the north grew even louder and the Germans had several of our Bofors guns in action, shelling the retiring columns. They seemed much too close for comfort.

We spread out along a shallow stream, a small tributary of the river Platanias. Tug Wilson could not resist falling on his knees and, with his tin hat, scooping up some of the crystal-clear water and drinking deeply. Further upstream and round a corner of the hill he found the body of a paratrooper

---

*He had collapsed into some bushes where he was found by two New Zealanders and carried to the Field Hospital. From there he was successfully evacuated to Egypt.

suspended upside down from overhanging branches. His legs were entwined in his parachute cords and his head submerged in the water ...

Still following the tributary, we left the shelter of the hills, traversing a small flat meadow where the stream met its parent river at right-angles. Rifles above their heads, the leading men were sinking up to their waists in the water, fording the river against the strong current. We moved forward to follow them.

Suddenly, the German machine-gunners opened fire. A hail of bullets from the hills slanted across the clearing among the men now dashing for scanty cover, and into the soldiers and airmen in the river. They kicked into the black earth, following the line of crouching men, and crawled along the water's edge. And almost immediately other Spandaus opened fire from the hills around us.

We unslung our rifles. McKenna and Stevenson were standing in the line of fire, then, ducking low, searching the hills in vain for a target. A soldier got to his feet. I saw the big man standing there in the clearing, swaying, and then he collapsed. Four bullets thudded into Jack Diamond from 'A' Flight, as he lay face downwards in the mud by the water's edge — fortunately finding no more vital region than the fleshy part of his buttocks. A corpse in the river turned over and started to drift away. Men were trying to crawl stealthily backwards the way they had come. The Germans, sitting tight behind their guns, still sprayed the clearing.

McKenna started running towards the water and we followed him with the bullets sizzling and splashing all around. A man lay groaning behind us in the open.

I heard McKenna: 'To hell with it! Get across! It's our only chance!'

We raced after him, plunging into the cold water and struggling to keep our balance. Up the bank and we dived full length behind a row of tall bamboos — affording cover but no protection. The bullets crackled and snapped through them. Up on our feet again and moving forward. Suddenly, without warning, McKenna was running crouched up — back to the water's edge. Taken completely by surprise we lay still, watching him as he grubbed about in the mud with the bullets thudding into the ground beside him. Then he was racing back to us. In one hand he held a bunch of onions which he waved at us in triumph.

'Saw them as we climbed out of the river,' he explained and started sharing them out. We had almost forgotten how hungry we were ...

We were not out of the wood yet. Bullets still searched the area as we came to the next obstacle — an irrigation ditch, deep and muddy. Too wide to jump, it had to be forded. But once the water had risen to our shoulders we could find no way of lifting ourselves on to the far bank. Those who had gone before us had churned the clay into a slippery paste.

While we floundered, helplessly, the bushes ahead moved and parted and then a hulking Maori stood surveying us and grinning from ear to ear. He reached down for our rifles and dragged us out dripping, one by one. The Maori, who had a bullet wound in his leg, said:

'You jokers should be all right now. This is Maori territory.'

He made it sound as if we were entering an impenetrable fortress. When I showed concern for his leg he only grinned again.

'I'm jest waiting here to catch the bastard who done it,' was his only comment.*

---

*He was standing in the American Bar, Cairo, when next I saw him and I had the opportunity to buy him a drink.

12
The Road to Canea and Traivoros

We joined the rest of the survivors farther up the hill and set off for the Maori HQ. Then, so near and yet so far from our destination, the men in the column began to lose touch in the dense undergrowth and much time was wasted in finding each other. Soon the four of us, who had kept together, were laughing aloud as heads bobbed warily up and down in the greenery — each time a fresh head popped up all the others popped down again in case the additional head belonged to a German. But we should have known that Germans did not live long within Maori boundaries. The remainder of the journey to their HQ was completely uneventful.

The headquarters was hidden in a copse south of Platanias village. Here we caught up with Willy Cann and a few others we had thought to be missing. The Maori boys gave us a free hand with a pile of bread stacked on the grass and we ate it under the trees with a slice of bully and the onions which McKenna had salvaged. It was a meal fit for a king! For a little while we rested in this peaceful olive grove and chatted with our happy-faced hosts. I thought that it would be hard to find another race possessing such fierceness and contempt for pain yet combining these qualities with the impish love of practical joking and good humour which is the inheritance of the Maori.

But meanwhile the battle sounds grew in fury. Germans were pressing hard on three sides, the main assault coming from the coast where the weight of numbers and superior equipment of Ramcke's fresh troops were overwhelming the New Zealand rear guard. To the south, 100th Mountain Regiment had already passed our new positions and were curving round behind us to cut the road at Ay Marina on the coast. Also, thrusting north and barely half a mile from the Mountain troops, 3rd Parachute Regiment had taken Stalos in their drive to close the door behind us. Every hour that passed brought the balance down still farther on the side of the enemy. The 21st and 23rd Battalions were already in positions east of Platanias. All other troops were being sent farther back to strengthen the Canea area.

The dozen or so of us thanked our kind hosts for their hospitality and struck out for the coast road. Diamond, with four bullets in his buttocks, came too. He had declined the Maori offer to get him to Canea by hospital truck.

Climbing the track towards Platanias village, the sudden sharp crash of nearby German artillery sent the erks diving for cover among the bushes. For a while they lay listening to the shells screaming overhead and watching the ground farther up the hill erupting all around, thrusting up geyser-like fountains of earth and rock. Mortars joined in and then two vicious Bofors which the enemy had towed to Platanias bridge with captured RAF trucks. Then the Bofors shells started raking the bank they had just left, by the Maori HQ. Strings of burning explosives crackled through the bushes and among the trees. Caught between the two fires the airmen bolted uphill for the village rather than remain in their unhealthy position.

Debris-littered Platanias stood on the hilltop resentfully silent, like a ghost town. The village seemed to be weeping quietly to itself; its battered whitewashed houses eyeing us suspiciously as we crept down the main street. Only the desultory fluttering of a sheet of paper pinned to a demolished porchway disturbed the sepulchral stillness. It advertised in English that tea, lemonade, and cakes had been sold in the house sometime in the past. A young New Zealander sprawled dead beneath with the flies clustering on his blood-soaked tunic and swarming over a large pool of blood in which he lay.

The harsh vamping of Stuka sirens broke upon the silent scene. Then, gathering overhead the dive-bombers flew around and around, waggling their bent wings, sniffing the air for fresh prey. We left the village as the pointless demolition started all over again.

With the dust and smoke hanging over the stricken cluster of houses on the hilltop behind us, and over the still smouldering buildings lining the seashore, we joined the Canea road. On the beach a Messerschmitt 109 lay new and artificial-looking with its nose in a clump of feathery reeds. With the airmen's in-bred curiosity my companions forgot the war for a while and left the road to clamber all over it. Not until their 'technical' examination had been completed did they move on again.

A few minutes later they were all lying full length in a shallow ditch, holding their breath while three hedge-hopping Me109s flew down the road towards them. We soon discovered that fighters were maintaining a standing patrol between Canea and Maleme, passing low overhead at intervals of 15 minutes. It was a nerve-racking business. Sometimes there was no opportunity to find cover and the men could only sprawl by the road edge and keep very still.

There was a 30 Squadron Palestinian beginning to crack up under the strain.

Then he lost his head completely; darting across the path of the fighters he scurried towards a small stone cottage on the other side of the road. A Messerschmitt flicked a wing — taking a good look. It was time to move quickly. Before the Germans could come back again the party had all bolted into the cottage behind the Palestinian.

A few moments later cannon shells were exploding outside, scattering tiles from the roof like playing cards, their bullets thudded into the walls like hail stones. In one darkened corner sat an old woman, softly sobbing and crooning to herself. The erks felt suddenly ashamed for having invaded her house and left her their few blankets.

Ay Marina lay half a mile farther east; a friendly line of limestone cottages leading down from the hill where the sturdy womenfolk stood, holding out water pitchers to the weary airmen from their doorways. Their words of encouragement were still ringing in our ears when we came to the bomb-cratered 7th General Hospital another three miles down the road.

For eight hours that day the Luftwaffe had been raining high explosives and incendiaries upon Canea and, when we arrived, a large area was already engulfed in flames. A new relay of Stukas flew in just as we reached the debris-heaped outskirts of the doomed town and civilians hustled us into a large cellar. Smiling Cretans jumped to their feet, insisting that we took their seats and we were too weary to protest.

Half an hour later, as we again walked the rubble-strewn streets we were beset by other civilians, hostile this time, who, mistaking me for a German under escort — although I was carrying a rifle — tried to drag me from the centre of my friends and lynch me. Fortunately a red-cap on a motorcycle arrived in the nick of time. He glanced at the various items of German equipment I was carrying and then he as well was not satisfied with my appearance. He took me, protesting, to police headquarters where it took some time to convince my interrogators that I was harmless. When they released me, I soon found the rest of the erks in a bomb-scarred college sharing heavenly bliss with their feet under a cold tap. Here were more of 33 Squadron men including Taffy Williams whom I was pleased to meet again.

Unfortunately, one of our party had not made the journey. Jack Diamond, with the pain from his four wounds increasing hourly, could not keep up with us on the road to Canea. Rather than make a fuss he had given us the slip and returned to the Maori camp where he joined a small group of wounded; two Australians, four New Zealanders and a British Army captain. The captain, self-appointed leader of the party, convinced them that, although there were Germans between them and Canea, he knew the terrain and could land them on a cross-country detour to Suda, by-passing Canea. As it turned out, he would have done better to have followed the road as we had done.

The little party hobbled painfully into the wild Cretan terrain. Overhead, a Fieseler Storch spotter plane hovered briefly and then moved north over the New Zealand positions. The inevitable Stuka attacks which followed were not aimed in their direction.

Within a short distance from the town of Suda, they were about to con-

gratulate the captain when they saw ahead of them, as large as life, a group
of Germans making little attempt to conceal themselves. They made a dive
for the bushes amid the mountain sage, then, slowly crawling backwards, moved
further inland. They had not travelled far, when to their dismay, they again
found more Germans. A third attempt was little better. Painfully, they retraced
their steps and moved towards the coast only to encounter yet another pocket
of Germans.

Nothing more could be done. Lying concealed, heart in mouth, they awaited
the night and then, as quietly as their injured limbs could manage, successfully crept between two of the groups. True to their reputation, the Germans
appeared to prefer day rather than night action.

New Zealand Medical Orderlies found them when they reached Suda. They
were taken to a Greek Orthodox Church, used as a temporary hospital. At
last their wounds were dressed and they had their first long sleep in days.

At about this time, back in Egypt, AB Parsons, a Royal Marine, was loading
his equpiment aboard the mine-laying destroyer, HMS *Abdiel*. Previously,
he had been allocated as a member of a Bofors gun crew at Maleme but,
due to a stomach upset, he had stayed in Egypt and missed the German invasion. Now, with 200 Marine reserves they were boarding the fastest destroyer
in the Mediterranean to join their comrades in a wild dash along the long
northern coast of Crete, usually avoided at all costs because of the inevitable
prolonged Stuka attacks. However, destroyers *Jaguar* and *Defender* had survived the journey on the previous day.

Back in Canea the 33 Squadron survivors clambered aboard a couple of
Chevs that evening and left the shattered, smouldering capital, still under constant air attack. We journeyed to Traivoros, some miles east of Suda, arriving at midnight.

Sprawled out on the springy turf we slept the sleep of the dead, lying within
a few paces from where the trucks had dropped us. Some even lay in the road,
too exhausted to walk another step. It was the first real sleep most of us had
had in five days and nights.

We awoke later with the sun streaming through the trees. Untidy gaggles
of Messerschmitts and Junkers already roamed the countryside, darting this
way and that way among the sleeping villages below like hounds searching
out the scent, but the cluster of white buildings up the bank, the dusty track
holding Suda Bay in its noose, and the far-away tinkle of goat bells, belonged
to a world at peace.

In the distance the guns around Suda boomed and, now and again, bent-
wing Stukas gathered over some peaceful hamlet and blasted it out of existence — but they did not bother us. Once, two truckloads of Cretan Gendarmerie drove past with the moustachioed policemen, smart as guardsmen,
clutching their carbines and proudly singing a patriotic song which could be
heard faintly like an echo long after they had gone.

Then in the afternoon, a Blenheim dived low over the Bay with three gun-
blazing Messerschmitts on its tail. It was the first British aircraft we had seen

that week and we felt enraged frustration that we could do nothing to save it. The bomber did not stand a chance and crashed into the water.

Flight Lieutenant Woodward and another 33 Squadron officer named Mitchell, whom we had picked up, held a roll call. We numbered 41. Sixty-one men had been lost ...

Woodward, still a tower of strength and still looking immaculate, decided to alleviate the 'boredom' now we were out of the fighting line for the first time by organising a swimming party. It was quite a success. Soon we were following him through the ancient and knotted olives and down over a sequence of grassy terraces to the water's edge. A Greek destroyer lay at anchor nearby. For most of us, who had lived in the same clothes night and day for a month and who had not washed for a week, the pleasure of cleansing our filthy bodies was made none the less enjoyable by the driftwood and oil floating on the surface, stemming from the graveyard of shipping at the other end of the Bay.

Meanwhile, while we rested a while and wondered about our immediate future, the build up of enemy troops continued at Maleme and the Germans had taken Galatas. Their fresh, well-fed, hand-picked battalions now advanced supported by a mass of heavy equipment and the ever-present dive-bombers. The wheels of the Nazi war machine were now well-oiled. No longer did they anticipate much resistance from the diminishing numbers of red eyed, unshaven, hungry New Zealanders opposing them with very little else but their great indomitable spirit.

Their astonishment was therefore beyond description when, on the evening of 25th May another counter-attack was launched. Preceded by a mixed medley of blood-curdling college *hakas* the veterans of 18th and 23rd Battalion charged through the cross-fire of countless machine-guns back up the hill into Galatas. When the enemy left their guns and fled in terror westwards they were followed by the yelling pack of Kiwis in what has since been described as the fiercest action of World War Two.

But there was never a chance of recapturing Maleme. All the fighting troops could do was to hold on long enough to gain a little time.

During our second afternoon at Traivoros, a New Zealand officer, caked white with dust, roared in on a motorcycle. He told Woodward that we must prepare to evacuate over the White Mountains to the south coast port of Sfakia, on the opposite side of the island. The Kiwi, who looked all in, said that he was returning to his section which was now fighting a rearguard action west of Suda. Canea had fallen. There wasn't much time left ...

Now, it seemed that all the gallantry displayed in the New Zealanders' dogged resistance, fighting action after action by day and marching by night, could not alter that inevitable result. The enemy appeared to grow two heads in place of each one lopped off, like the hundred-headed Hydra of mythology. Without the RAF over Maleme to burn out the monster's heart — to act as the red-hot iron of Herakles — the extermination of the Nazis had now become a mathematical impossibility.

On 26th May the decision to evacuate had been confirmed and the main body of troops were moving off southwards to Stilos on the way to the coast.

The depleted battalions of our old friends of 5th Brigade, together with two battalions of Australians, grimly awaited the enemy onslaught along a line west of Suda. It had been seven days since they had last washed, slept, or had a square meal; for seven days they had been constantly engaged with the enemy.

Colonel Jais, commanding the Battle Group of 141st Mountain Regiment, with orders to cut the Suda road expected to brush aside such light opposition. Instead the Germans ran the gauntlet of the whole line of defenders who, seeing them break and run, leapt from their trenches and charged them: I Battalion of 141st Regiment lost over 300 men killed.

For Jack Diamond the time spent in the Greek church at Suda were full of confusion. His wounds were becoming more painful and he could no longer walk. At one time, in his delirium, it seemed that Germans had entered the building, posted guards and told patients and orderlies that they were now prisoners of war. Then later, they had gone.

A long time elapsed and then outside was a lot of noise and shouting and a Commando burst into the church.

'All who can walk,' he said, 'make for the harbour. A ship is waiting to take you off!'

The temporary hospital emptied rapidly as walking wounded assisted by orderlies made for the docks. Soon the 'A' Flight airman was on his own. He tried to crawl towards the door but the pain was excruciating. Then there was a broom against the wall. Somehow he dragged himself to his feet and hooked it under his arm like a crutch. With every step agony, he eventually hobbled into the street outside. Then the shaft of the broom snapped and the airman fell to the ground with a force which all but winded him. With the determination of one who knew there was no second chance, he commenced crawling again, ever nearer to rescue.

Fortunately, four more Commandos appeared at that moment. They picked him up and carried him to the dock where HMS *Abdiel* lay preparing to sail. In no time he was strapped to a sea stretcher and hoisted aboard. Soon the destroyer was underway.

Junkers 88s caught them at first light and, for 60 miles, a running battle ensued with bombs bursting near-misses on all sides, thumping ack-ack, pom-poms, and soldiers joining in with rifle fire. However, the Germans did not have this unfair contest all their own way and at least one of them was seen to crash into the water. And then the skies cleared.

After his mad dash along the northern coast of Crete, Royal Marine Parsons had disembarked at Suda with the other 200 reserves. Two days later destroyers landed a further 750 Marines. One of the many sad results of the Cretan campaign is that these superb men who had received long training to be employed in offensive and harassing operations against the enemy were, due to the circumstances of the battle, forced into a defensive role. After a spirited rearguard action they had been told to lay down their arms and surrender. Marine Parsons had raced towards his own capture . . .

The resistance of the Australians and New Zealanders was so great that, at first, the Germans had no idea that men were moving southwards. Believing that they had now trapped the defenders around Suda, the bulk of the enemy forces proceeded to push along the coast to relieve Rethymnon and Heraklion.

Not only the stubbornness of the British forces troubled the Germans. The ill-equipped Greek army units in Crete were fighting magnificently along-side their allies. But the Cretans were the biggest headache. Before the first glider had landed, the villagers had drawn their long knives, seized their ancient arms, and prepared to set upon the invaders. A proud race of warlike people whom four thousand years of invaders could not tame, they ruthlessly butch-ered the isolated groups of Germans. A hundred years of Corsair blood in their veins steeled them to give no mercy and to expect none in return. Deprived of their young men who had been trapped with the Cretan Division of Alba-nia, old men, women, and even children, armed with nothing better than kitchen knives on sticks, charged down on the enemy machine-guns with demoniacal fury. On 26th May 5th Mountain Division war diary reported:

> Armed bands are fighting fiercely in the mountains using great cunning, are cruelly mutilating dead and wounded. This inhuman method of making war is making our advance infinitely more difficult.

Here the Germans obviously drew a distinction between the actions of a proud people defending their homes and their own humane practices such as the bombing of defenceless villages.

During our last afternoon at Traivoros a Dornier flew over the village drop-ping leaflets. They threatened reprisals upon anyone committing such crimes 'against international law'.

High above us the tiny specks of light which were a thousand sheets of paper twinkled in the evening sun. Children from Traivoros raced about the village street laughing and shouting as they jumped for the elusive sheets, printed alternatively in Greek and English. As we stood there listening to the shrieks of villagers' laughter, we could not have visualised the ruthless treatment which the conquering Germans had in store for Crete. What they had accused the Cretans of doing in the heat of the battle, these 'enforcers of international law' were to repeat a thousandfold when they had occupied the island. Vil-lages were to be obliterated and old people and children alike were to face torture and the firing squad.

At the time we had no way of knowing that the first of many major German atrocities had already occurred at Kastelli, a few miles west of Maleme. Here, on 20th May, 78 well-armed paratroops fought with the 'Ist Greek Regiment', a hastily recruited rag-tag of locals. The Cretans of Kastelli had few modern weapons and those without modern rifles fell upon the invaders with flint-locks and knives. Soon all but 17 Germans had been killed.

Three days later Major Schaette, who had landed with the Mountain Divi-sion, probed westwards and came across their unburied corpses. Because some had died of knife wounds he came to the erroneous conclusion that they had been captured and then tortured to death.

To the population and the military forces on Crete

It has been brought to the notice of the German Supreme Command that German soldiers who fell into the hands of the enemy on the island of Crete have been illtreated and even mutilated in a most infamous and inhuman manner.

As a punishment and reprisal therefore it is announced as follows:

1) Whosoever commits such crimes against international laws on German prisoners of war will be punished in the manner of his own cruel action, no matter be he or she a man or a woman.

2) Localities near which such crimes have been perpetrated will be burned down. The population will be held responsible.

3) Beyond those measures further and sharper reprisals will be held in store.

The German Supreme Command

Right *19-year-old Gunner E. Telling manning Suda Bay defences with a Naval Pom-pom.* (Telling)

Below *Paratroops in Greece emplane for Crete.*

Bottom *Paratroops over Suda Bay.*

Left *Paratroops over Crete.* (Imperial War Museum)

Below left *Gliders over the Tavronitis. The RAF camp is left of the road.* (National Soaring Museum, Multi-Media Collection)

Bottom left *A crashed glider beside the Iron Bridge.*

Right *Ju52s attempt to land at Maleme.*

Below *A Ju88 bomber lands past Ju52s at Maleme.* (Imperial War Museum)

Bottom *Maleme: German paratroops bring one of our Bofors guns into action.*

Above *Maleme airfield on or after 22nd May. The exposed aircraft pen we were building on the morning of 19th May is on the right of the 'drome. South of the white road, from right to left, is the Crash Centre, Servicing Section, backing onto vineyards, and, where the road bends, the Flights and aircraft pens. Further south, the irrigation ditch, which helped to conceal Walter Goltz and other paratroops, winds through the vineyard and along the base of the hill.* (Imperial War Museum)

Below *Maleme: this enlargement of the bottom left-hand corner of the photograph allows the drama of 18th and 19th May to be easily traced.* (Author)

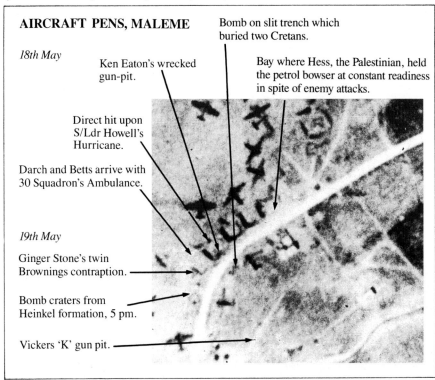

AIRCRAFT PENS, MALEME

18th May

Ken Eaton's wrecked gun-pit.

Bomb on slit trench which buried two Cretans.

Bay where Hess, the Palestinian, held the petrol bowser at constant readiness in spite of enemy attacks.

Direct hit upon S/Ldr Howell's Hurricane.

Darch and Betts arrive with 30 Squadron's Ambulance.

19th May

Ginger Stone's twin Brownings contraption.

Bomb craters from Heinkel formation, 5 pm.

Vickers 'K' gun pit.

Above *Survivors from Crete arrive at Alexandria.*

Right *The author with Australian survivors from Crete, on top of the Great Pyramid at Gizeh.* (Author)

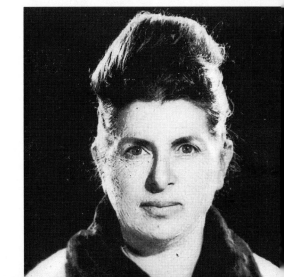

Right *Maria Fiotakis. 'She gave me food and, very much against my will, forced upon me some money. Before I left she kissed me on both cheeks, she had been crying too.'* — Colin France, who tells his story in an appendix to this book. (Colin France)

Adonis Bridsolakis, who also fed Colin France when he was at Therisso. (Colin France)

Colin France escaping from Crete on the Greek submarine Triton. (Colin France)

The story of 33 and 11 Squadron's last encounter is told in an appendix. Here an 11 Squadron Blenheim receives a direct hit at LG125. (Author)

Right *LG125. 33 Squadron's Hurricanes burn.* (Author)

Below *A 33 Squadron Hurricane in unusual livery.* (Author)

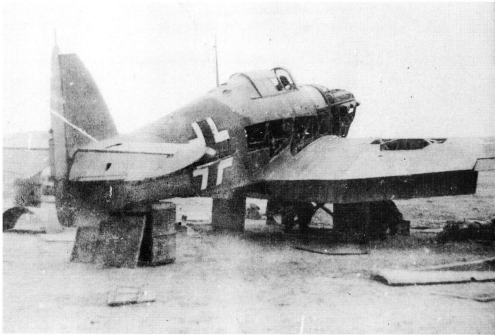

Above *After Crete: the author and a Ju87B Stuka.* (Author)

Left *33 Squadron's famous 'prop' with the Squadron operational record of wartime 'kills'.* (33 Squadron, RAF Odiham)

Two New Zealand officers tried to convince him otherwise and their statement was backed up by the released 17 German prisoners who all said that they had been well-treated. However, Major Schaette was blind to their words. When his men had rounded up 200 Cretan civilians, young boys and old men included, he had them murdered in groups by firing squad. In the First World War the Germans were described as 'cringing in defeat, arrogant in victory.' In the Second World War it seemed that for a few nothing had changed.

Flight Lieutenant Woodward was flying out and that evening he said his farewells with a firm handshake for all of us. The remainder crammed into two trucks and set out upon the long journey to Sfakia. For hours the vehicles climbed the twisting rocky track which, as we neared the mountain peaks, lost itself among the boulders. In the darkness the drivers groped their precarious way upwards and southwards. It was cold. Then, by three in the morning we were over the top of the last hill. Far below, the ribbon of track twisted around a series of hair-pinned terraces for 3,000 feet. The trucks descended cautiously in bottom gear, hugging the inside of each sharp bend, until the huge boulders which had impeded our travel, blocked the way completely and we could ride no farther. One lorry, wedged between rocks, we covered with blankets, the other was pushed over a precipice. A long way farther down could be discerned a dark area, hidden in shadow. We were told to reach it on foot.

Singly we groped our way crabwise down the slippery scree. Nothing but pitch black darkness could be seen below. If there was a way down, the path was buried in obscurity. We arrived at the bottom exhausted, many of us minus the soles of our shoes. The airmen lay among the rocks and went to sleep.

13
11 Squadron: Port Detachment

While exhausted but resolute bands of Kiwis and Aussies fought the advancing German juggernaut at Suda, the gallant defenders at Rethymnon and Herkalion still held out in isolation yet confident of an early victory. German forces dropped upon them in the afternoon of Invasion Day had failed disastrously to gain either objective and soon had been sent, with heavy loss of life, scurrying for distant shelter.

There were a dozen airmen at Rethymnon and about 200 at Heraklion who took up arms with the defenders and fought as infantry throughout the action. With the Australians, Greeks and Cretan Gendarmerie, at Rethymnon and the Australians, Black Watch, Leicesters, Yorks and Lancs, and Greeks at Heraklion, they held the two airfields against all comers and, at Rethymnon, were soon taking the offensive against the invaders.

For the Germans, everything had gone wrong. Due to confusion and dust on the Greek airfields and the unexpected heavy losses in aircraft at Maleme, air support had to be drastically curtailed. Consequently, the uncoordinated parachute descents had developed into chaos. Two battalions of paratroops, dropping at Rethymnon, fell at different times and over three unconnected areas. While the first wave did succeed in gaining a temporary foothold on the eastern edge of the airfield, the second force sustained heavy casualties both in the air and on the ground and were chased out of Rethymnon town by the moustachioed Cretan Gendarmerie. The third group, landing upon Australian positions south of the road, were completely destroyed and their commanding officer captured along with all their heavy weapons.

At Heraklion, also, the invaders had died in the hundreds. Such confusion had reigned among them that late arrivals were still making for the heavily defended airfield, confident that it had been already captured. Except for small parties of snipers, the German survivors finally fell back to the high ground to the east. Others, falling around the town itself, made no headway in the bitter street fighting which raged throughout the night.

By the following day the defenders were doing even better and were able to replenish their armament with light guns, dropped upon their lines in error out of the sky. As the Italian artillery they were using sent up a high percentage of 'dud' shells, these weapons made a welcome change.

At Rethymnon on 23rd May, with the Germans now bottled up and the Australian and Greeks resorting to a series of attacks to dislodge them from their few remaining strong points, the enemy tried to 'work a fast one', sending a delegation under a white flag to demand immediate surrender on the grounds of a German victory in all other sectors. That was the day after the Maori counter-attack at Maleme when the fate of Crete still hung in the balance, with Canea virtually cleared of the enemy and all sectors holding their positions. In fact, on paper, things did look bright for the defenders that day and hopes were further raised by the dispatching of 12 Hurricanes from Egypt to Heraklion. The first one arrived around midday but, of the others, five were shot down or forced back by naval gunfire, and the other six found themselves in the middle of a heavy air attack over Heraklion town. By the time they had landed, four had been damaged and the Flight was easy meat for a force of strafing Messerschmitts the next morning. Nevertheless, the RAF in Egypt were able to hit back with suicide raids upon Maleme with Marylands and Blenheims by day and Wellingtons by night while, at Sidi Barrani in the Western Desert, 274 Squadron, offspring of 33 and 80, sent long-range Hurricanes on their desperate journey towards Crete with little or no combat time left to them when and if they arrived. Aircraft followed aircraft in this expensive gamble and few returned. It called for great courage from the pilots who still awaited their turn. All the same, from isolated tales picked up after the event, several of these fighters gave a good account of themselves before they were destroyed.

Meanwhile, in the Suda area, the 30 odd-airmen working in and around the town met with various adventures of which the following account of what befell the 'Port Detachment' is perhaps typical.

This party of 13 men under a sergeant had been selected to remain behind when 11 Squadron evacuated early in May. They comprised eight aircrafthands, three motor transport drivers, and two storekeepers and were based in a two-storied school building on a hill above Suda Bay and near Nerokourou village. Their billet in the top floor commanded a splendid view of the Bay, the Akrotiri peninsula across the Bay, and Canea to the north. On the ground floor were collected flying clothing, aircraft parts, and kindred stores while down the road, hidden among the olives, lay a petrol and oil dump. The unit's function was to collect, hold, and distribute stores as they arrived on the island but, because the Luftwaffe had soon practically established a blockade, there was little to do all day except watch the continuous destruction of shipping in the bay and then retire to the local tavern in the evening to drink and hear the BBC News announcing their usual: 'Enemy aircraft have again attacked targets in Crete but have caused no serious damage...'

Food had been a problem until they were fortunate enough to engage a local war widow to cook for them. They quickly discovered what a gem of a person they had acquired. Her name was Maria and she had recently lost her husband on the Albanian Front; but she was a naturally cheerful woman and soon livened up the place with her singing and happy chatter to her small son, Michael. Such contentment could not last. On 19th May the detachment was ordered to Maleme.

The invasion came as they were preparing to leave the village the following morning. One place being as good as another in a widespread parachutist assault, the erks prudently doubled back up the hill towards the tavern which as Stan Wingrove, one of their number, put it 'offered thick local-quarried rock walls for protection, wine for courage, and, incidentally, the best view.'

It was from here that they watched the mass formations of fighters, bombers, and then gliders and their tugs, arriving over their targets. To the left paratroops fell around Pirgos and the 7th General Hospital, but for the moment the gliders were the biggest worry. Sent to destroy what was considered one of the two most dangerous gun sites in the Canea area, the German Altmann detachment of 15 gliders headed for the Akrotiri peninsula but, forced by the mountains to approach from the Suda area, they fell foul of the concentrated AA fire around the bay. The force soon lost its cohesion and for a while the air above the harbour was filled with damaged and broken Dornier and Junkers tugs ploughing through a red and black rash of exploding ack-ack with the hastily cast off gliders scattered far from their allotted landing points. The surviving Germans soon discovered that the gun site they had been sent to capture was a dummy one and, although some of the force held out for a few days, they were all captured by the Northumberland Hussars, having lost 48 killed and 36 wounded.

The second gun site attacked by gliders lay half a mile down the road from Nerokourou. Two-thirds of the attackers landed on or near the site and soon were engaged by the gunners in a bitter struggle which only ended after all the defenders bar seven had been killed. The Germans then turned their attention towards an adjacent wireless station but were driven off by a sharp counter-attack.

Back at the schoolhouse and still undecided what to do, the airmen found themselves the centre of a crowd of excited Cretans begging for guns to go and kill Germans. The drivers, who had revolvers, gave them their rifles. Then they made off down the road towards an army unit holed up in a monastery. Here they spent some part of the day with the soldiers, preparing to withstand the anticipated assault from the direction of the wireless station. An army officer stood on a trench parapet viewing the battle through field glasses and giving a running commentary.

But the Army showed little interest in the RAF men. Resentment against them was still strong and the soldiers had their work cut out trying to feed and accommodate the numerous spare squaddies who continued to turn up throughout the day. Therefore, during the afternoon, as there seemed to be no immediate German drive towards the monastery, the erks made their way cautiously back up the road, keeping under cover all the way.

Reaching their school building without mishap, they were greeted with some sad news. Nerokourou village had been bombed and Maria, their cheerful cook, had been killed. The airmen turned out their pockets and sent all their money to the now orphaned Michael.

For a further two days they stayed put and had a panoramic view of the battle all around; troop-carriers by the score plying between Greece and Maleme, shelling and mortar fire, and the ever-present fighters and bombers patrolling the village tracks, making all movement an extremely dangerous and haphazard affair. One night they rolled out of bed to see the waters to the north erupt into a succession of coloured flashes and violent explosions as the Royal Navy waded into the German sea-borne flotilla . . .

Then came a message to take their trucks to pick up some petrol from Suda jetty that afternoon. By the time they arrived gangs of soldiers were already working feverishly to unload the fuel from a Greek caique. The cans were being dumped in sacks on the wharf. But the first formation of dive-bombers appeared as soon as the airmen commenced loading their vehicles. In the general scramble to place as much distance as possible between himself and the petrol, Stan Wingrove leapt for a slit trench among the AA guns, falling on top of another airman as the first Stuka went into its dive.

In an instant the peaceful jetty became a raging inferno against an ear-splitting background of ack-ack guns, whining shrapnel, rattling machine-guns, and earth-rocking bomb explosions. A bright and fearsome wall of flame roared skywards, engulfing the Greek schooner which was receiving hit after hit. Blazing petrol on the jetty shot suddenly in every direction from the exploding pile of cans, rocketing high into the air in streaks of red and yellow fire. Looking for fresh targets, the Stukas now flew down the path of the guns, screaming down within the ring of bursting shells as if they intended to fly into the trenches themselves.

The other airman, crouching with Wingrove, face streaming with perspiration, reached inside his shirt, fingered a rosary, and started to pray.

'I usually wanted to pray at times like this,' Stan Wingrove said afterwards. 'And there was something else I usually wanted to do. But nothing could make me leave the shelter of the trench to do it.'

Eventually the noise died down except for the crackling of burning wreckage about the jetty and the survivors of the attack crept out of their trenches and groped their way through the wall of choking black smoke. The ship had vanished and one of the RAF trucks was a charred wreck. Fortunately the two other vehicles escaped with minor damage.

By the following day the little detachment had found their way to Traivoros where they were cheered to witness the shooting down of a four-engined Focke-

Wulf Condor by a Hurricane over the Bay. But they were less cheered when they contemplated their new assignment. The Royal Marine Commandos needed petrol at Suda which would have to be fetched from the RAF dump west of the Nerokourou road. The 'Detachment' had fallen in for the job. They could be given no guarantee that the Germans were not already in possession of the dump.

They set out in two truck-loads, travelling rough along hillside tracks to avoid the strafing Messerschmitts who still patrolled the main roads. Even so, every few minutes Cassidy, the leading driver, bounced his vehicle quickly under cover of the olives as hostile aircraft hurtled low overhead. They were held up for an hour near Suda while a large enemy formation blasted a nearby wood. Then, as they pulled the trucks past the now cratered and leafless area they came upon a crowd of Aussies carrying out their dead and wounded in long lines.

Much later, as they neared their objective, they were caught by low-flying Messerschmitts and, in the confusion, the second truck was lost. Then Cassidy's truck broke down and refused to restart. The seven airmen, Jim Weddell, Bill Taylor, Joe Wilkinson, 'Bruiser' Northway, Peacock, Wingrove and Cassidy were scratching their heads and wondering what to do next when they became suddenly aware of nearby sounds of small-arms fire, machine-guns and mortar bombs, coming from the olives on the other side of the petrol dump. Germans were fanning out through the trees ahead; 85th Mountain Regiment was curling around the south of the Allied line and towards Suda.

Still intent upon rescuing the petrol, the party of erks struck out for the Suda road intending to persuade some army transport to help them as the other truck had still not appeared. There was not much time left. Already the enemy were holding part of the wood.

But when they reached the road all ideas of obtaining transport vanished. Marching troops, falling back on Suda, packed the road; Marines, Australians, and Kiwis, dragging their unwilling feet through the dust. The airmen fell in with some British troops and Cassidy met a 'towny' from Liverpool with a wounded leg whom they were able to assist.

There was nothing left for the airmen to do on the island now that their transport had gone and, when the seven fell in with some erks from 230 (Sunderland Flying Boat) Squadron on the other side of Suda who told them that a Sunderland was expected to land in the Bay that night to pick them up, they decided to leave with them.

That evening about 50 airmen boarded an assault craft and sailed out into the Bay. All night they drifted around waiting and listening — but the only aircraft around were German. In the shivering dawn they remained unmolested spectators of the grim battle raging along the shore near Suda and, when they thought that the town had fallen, they prudently steered for a point along the coast farther east.

From here they climbed ashore and rejoined the main stream of retreating army — all except Cassidy who had disappeared. They followed the soldiers blindly with no knowledge of what was happening or where they were heading for. They were never to forget the next nightmare 48 hours.

14
Retreat to Sfakia

When I awoke I found myself at the bottom of a rugged wilderness of such awe-inspiring dimensions that I had difficulty in remembering where I was, so much having taken place in the past eight days. My head filled with rapturous wonder as my eyes took in the scene.

We were lying between huge boulders on the floor of a stony ravine cutting deeply into the flank of a range of mountains as wild, desolate and unearthly-looking as the mountains of the moon. Tall pine trees touched fingertips as if dancing a stately Greek *hassariko* before, what seemed at first inspection, a sheer drop of several hundreds of feet capped by a terrace wall, barely visible. We had found our way down that cliff in the darkness!

Serrated mountains, 7,000 feet high, arose above the cliff looking grey and forbidding in the early morning. Everything was rougher and more spectacular than the northern slopes of the island. The ravine clawed its ragged way past us, down among rocky headlands, to the boulder-strewn seashore.

A distant sound broke into the silent scene. Aircraft were about. We scanned the southern skies anxiously. Then we could see two black specks moving quickly across the sea towards us.

'Look, they're Blenheims!' someone shouted and we gave a cheery wave to the bomber boys as the familiar silhouettes became plainer.

But Sandy Powell, a sergeant whom we had picked up near Canea, was yelling: 'Get under cover. Don't you know Ju88s when you see them!'

As we dived for shelter the Junkers sailed overhead passing straight up the ravine and over our truck on the ledge above . . . They droned away into the distance without altering course and we heaved a sigh of relief. We wanted this to be a nice quiet and peaceful evacuation when it came; none of Dunkirk's dive-bombed beaches for us if we could help it. So as not to tempt fate a second time, we quickly made up a party to take care of the remaining truck. After the exhausting climb back up to the terraced track there was little destructive pleasure in sending the faithful old Chev on its last bouncing, splintering, glass-tinkling journey.

Back at the cliff foot again we explored the ground farther down towards the sea. We followed the ravine until its broad bed shrank momentarily to a narrow fissure between two massive limestone shoulders. Through this gateway it opened out again suddenly into a glorious mossy wonderland in every shade of green where grew maidenhair fern in profusion with blue vetch and yellow alyssum. Here we made our home, sheltered by deep recesses in the rock face from the prying eyes of the occasional patrols of German aircraft.

Water was still the chief problem and a party of erks set off with a large container between them to climb to Komitadhes village perched on a distant jut of limestone. Eventually reaching the houses they met a Cretan woman who, seeing their blue tunics, ran down the street shouting in warning:

'Germanos! Germanos!'

The container was at last filled and peace restored to the aggressive villagers. Painfully the airmen hauled the water back to the ravine over the rough terrain. One of them had lost the sole of his shoe on the way.

The state of our footwear was serious. The down-at-heel boots and shoes with which we arrived on Crete had not survived the gruelling test of the mountains. Paper-thin soles reinforced by paratroop rubber overshoes which had lasted us to Traivoros had been soon ripped to pieces in that long hectic climb down the cliff on the previous night, and already many men were hobbling among the sharp rocks with their feet torn and bleeding.

But our hardships were slight in comparison with the bulk of the retreating army who were at that moment approaching on foot over the White Mountains. Few forced marches in history since the days of Xenophon can compare with the retreat from Suda to Sfakia.

The battle had turned into an endurance test in which self-discipline became the essential quality for survival. Faced with ridge after ridge of heartbreaking cliffs the little army, beside itself with indescribable weariness resulting from lack of food and sleep, harassed by enemy aircraft, climbed onwards towards the sea, turning to fight their pursuers, time and time again, the fighting units holding back the Germans to allow the rest to pass through them. Those who fell by the roadside were the men from small broken units, leaderless, and demoralized; the fighting men, somehow drawing energy from a latent source, marched in companies, with the Maoris the smartest of the lot.

But the bulk of the men were gunners without guns, tank crews without tanks, stevedores, postmen, cooks and butchers, workshop fitters, landing and maintenance units, labour groups, RASC, and Palestinian and Cypriot Pioneer Companies. Many among them still carried their rifles but many had found

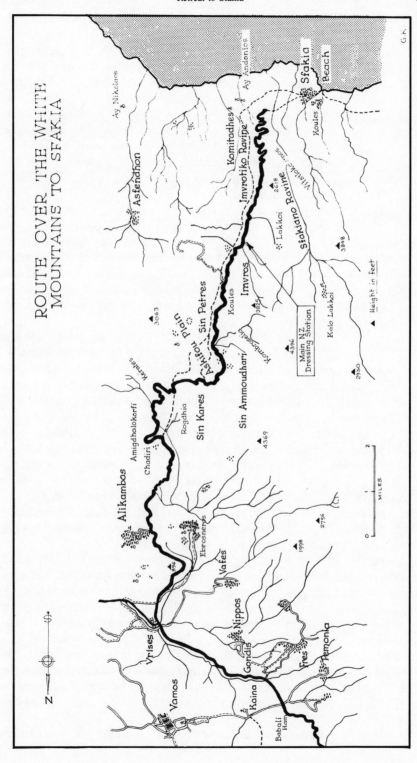

ROUTE OVER THE WHITE
MOUNTAINS TO SFAKIA

themselves in the middle of the land battle without the means to defend themselves.

Soon the mountain track to the south was littered with burnt-out vehicles, dead bodies, or the motionless forms of men too exhausted to rise to their feet again, while up and down the columns the vicious Messerschmitts strafed and bombed mercilessly. Many had dysentery and staggered onwards with faltering steps, weakened with pain and fever. Many were walking wounded, dragging their blood-soaked limbs among others, themselves too weary to give them aid. In their stinking clothes which they had worn day and night without the chance to wash their sweaty bodies, soldiers were breaking out in rashes. Many staggered on with their hands resting upon their heads for relief while others walked naked.

The shortage of water was acute. Forcing their unwilling feet up each progressively steeper incline the men hung on grimly to the hope that there would be a drink for them at the next village. But, usually, they found the village wells almost inaccessible to them, being without the means of drawing the water to the surface. Those with bottles on the end of lanyards waited impatiently while their comrades hauled up the precious liquid in small quantities in empty 'Bully' tins. Hour after hour of valuable time was lost by the parched crowds waiting their turn.

Great was the suffering of that long column of retreating troops and above all for our New Zealand friends of 5th Brigade who, with the Australians, were fighting rearguard actions all the way. No man among them had known sleep ever since 20th May. Now their officers and NCOs encouraged them onwards, pleading with them, making rash promises to them, lifting them over rise after rise. But some had reached the end of their endurance. Men collapsed and fell. No one had the strength to raise them again. And, more pitiful still, men by the roadside were crawling on their hands and knees, delirious for water.

The remainder staggered up the steep incline. It was near Vrises that some lunatic Royal Engineers blew up the road *in front* of the retreating troops. The men, holding on to what was left of their last resources of strength, waited until the rolling explosion had died away and then suddenly realised that to reach the water hole at the top of the pass they must now spend needless hours scaling up the stony, slippery scree-covered cliffs . . .

Several airmen were in that epic march. The six survivors from 'Port Detachment' moved off from Suda Bay in good spirits but, like the others, soon found the 'good' road had petered out into a rough mountain track. Scrambling up the steeper gradient they were forced to dive for shelter every few minutes by the Luftwaffe, flying to and fro along the retreating columns, bombing and strafing. Sometimes the erks lay in the open, unable to reach cover, and sweated as bullets and cannon shells puffed up the dust around them, raking the road in long lines. But soon the sharp stones underfoot were cutting into their shoes and when Wingrove stumbled forward he ripped one sole open so that it flapped and tripped him at every step until he was forced to cut it off with his knife.

By the afternoon the sun threw down its heat upon the hot rocks and they began to feel very thirsty; then, by a stroke of luck, they found some packets of iron ration biscuits in a derelict, bullet-riddled truck. But the biscuits only made their thirst more acute ... They were beginning to feel the effects of their sleepless nights out in the bay. A wave of weariness fell over them.

Towards the evening the bombers arrived as they approached a small village. They were near a tiny church. As the bombs whistled down the airmen vaulted a low wall and, being opportunists, piled into a newly-dug grave.

'If we all gets killed,' reflected Bill Taylor in his rich Bermondsey voice, 'someone will only 'ave to fill the grave in.'

There was water in the next village, but none of them had saved a water-bottle — they had hung on to their rifles instead. Nevertheless, they managed to quench their thirst although they could take none of the water along with them.

Then there were some soldiers walking with them. They possessed some tins of bully beef which they appeared willing to share with the airmen in return for some of their biscuits. They staggered wearily on together for some hours until extreme tiredness overtook them all and they flopped down along the track to snatch a few hours' sleep upon the rocks ...

Boot-nose Joe Wilkinson from Norwich, the first to awake, quickly aroused the others. It was daylight. They were alone. The soldiers had secretly decamped taking with them all their bully beef and the airmen's biscuits as well.

On the road again, refreshed by the sleep, they pushed ahead feeling very hungry and thirsty. But as the sun rose it became hot again and their weariness returned. Their cut and bleeding feet made every step agony. Then the aircraft were flying overhead once more and the hills and valleys echoed hollowly to the booming of exploding bombs and calico-ripping machine-gun fire. But, like the soldiers they passed in pathetic groups by the roadside, they were past caring. They took cover no longer but walked on and on mechanically. No one told them where they were heading for. No one knew. All they could hope for was that if they reached the south coast they would be rescued; they had all the time in the world to contemplate their chances. But, parched and light-headed as they were, nothing seemed to matter so much. Singly they would have fallen out long ago. Only because they were keeping together as a party could they help each other and forge ahead.

Then they started to descend. The long road wound like a snake around countless bends below them. Walking downhill seemed harder than climbing. In desperation they tried taking short cuts down the rugged mountainside which saved time and distance but sorely punished what was left of their footwear. Joe Wilkinson suffered agonies with his lacerated and badly blistered feet. To add to their troubles, Bill Taylor crocked his ankle. The time that they had gained was soon lost in the frequent halts now taken. Now they were staggering from rock to rock, forcing themselves onwards in near-despair. Then in the afternoon they turned a bend and saw the sea for the first time. Like Xenophon's warriors they croaked out shouts of joy:

'The sea! The sea!'

They knew that they would make it after that.

Meanwhile, on a hillside north of the high plateau of Askifou, LAC Dixie Dean, fighting pain and gasping for breath, slumped to the ground. For the wounded airman this was the end of the line. He could go no farther.

After the patients from the New Zealand 7th General had spent the night with their rescuers at 19th Battalion headquarters they had been moved to a series of caves on the seashore near the wrecked hospital. On one side of Dixie Dean was his wounded friend, the Aussie Vic Wyatt, on the other a young parachutist who did nothing but cry out continually, *Mutter! Mutter! Mein Gott!* Eventually a medical orderly approached with a morphine syringe. The German boy went into a panic, screaming *Nein!, Nein!* and made it impossible for the New Zealander to administer the drug. Later in the day, a conversation with a German-speaking Palestinian revealed that, before emplaning for Crete, the parachutists had been addressed by their commander. He urged them to fight to the death because, if wounded and captured, the British would kill them by injection. Yet another example of the spate of wartime rumours, circulated on both sides and widely believed at the time.

The other 33 Squadron airman, Albert Moore, had also been taken to the caves. In the bed next to him was a young paratrooper badly wounded in the stomach. Although critically ill himself, Albert did his best to smile at the German, trying to give him some small crumb of comfort.

Often in adversity the true character of a person is revealed. It was this cheerful optimism and concern for his fellow man which eventually not only saved the life of Albert Moore but gained him public recognition 38 years later . . .*

Outside, the war went on and there were sounds of fighting and heavy bombing nearby. The explosions shook the caves. The only food the New Zealanders brought were tins of bully beef and ship's biscuits. Water was plentiful but there was nothing to store it in. There was not a single water-bottle to be found.

On 25th May, after the heroic charge back into nearby Galatas by the New Zealanders, the patients were warned that the Germans might arrive at any moment. Only the brave action of the Kiwis was holding the enemy at bay, but they could not hold out much longer.

The stretcher cases were moved out in trucks and taken to Imvros where a main dressing station was established. Two walking wounded posts were set up and staffed by the field ambulances. Back at the hospital, those who could walk were told that the evacuation port was Sfakia over the White Mountains but where it was on the map no one was sure. They had to strike inland and fend for themselves. Each was given a tin of bully beef and some biscuits.

Under cover of darkness, the walking wounded set out in single file led by a New Zealand NCO. They struggled on through the New Zealand lines and across the Maleme–Canea road. Once in the olive groves they started to climb up a rough track which seemed to have no end. Over the uneven, rocky terrain the pain from their wounds was soon matched by the agony of their feet. Towards the end of the night they rested. For some, despair of ever being

*See 'After Crete', page 198.

rescued had already taken hold.

During the night the main German force under General Ringel, commander of the 5th Mountain Division, had occupied the deserted 7th General Hospital and moved to the outskirts of Canea. The next day Canea, the capital of Crete, had fallen. The evacuation of the wounded had not come one hour too soon!

Albert Moore, too ill to be moved, had been left behind in the caves unaware of the war outside until Germans suddenly burst in. The wounded paratrooper told them how well he had been treated by the New Zealanders and how the airman in the next bed had done his best to offer friendship. The mood of the Germans changed abruptly and, from then onwards, they showed him every kindness.

Meanwhile, the following day Dixie Dean and the little column of wounded plodded up their goat track southwards as best they could. They met no one. In the distance, from time to time, came the sounds of bombing and, on more than one occasion, low-flying Messerschmitt 109s caused them to take cover as targets, probably along the main retreat road, came under attack. They found a mountain stream of clear freezing water and at mid-day they rested again.

Then they were on the move again. Three miles south of Askifou, a pretty village like a 'Shangri La' hidden by mountains, lay Imvros and the main New Zealand dressing station. From here stretcher cases were being moved down towards Sfakia. Regretfully 30 seriously wounded had been left behind at Neon Khorion and all were captured.

For Vic Wyatt, the wound in his chest, needing attention, was becoming more painful at each step. He and his airman cobber staggered on until, after a rest on the mountainside, Dixie Dean, exhausted and breathless, gasped out, 'Vic, it's no good, old mate. I've had it. I'll just lay down here and wait to be picked up.' The LAC rigger, who only wanted to be left to do a good job servicing aircraft, had been through all this trauma before, at Dunkirk as well as at Nauplia. He had given up the struggle.

Forgetting the pain in his own wound, Vic Wyatt jumped up and stood over his newfound friend, shouting and raving at him. He called him a Pommy bastard in a dozen ways. He insulted him, his parents, the RAF ... for a long time.

Dixie was so mad that he forced himself to his feet and started to move along the track again. Wyatt's heavy-handed psychology had saved him.

For soldier Jim McNally, the Balkan war had started as soon as Germans had crossed the Yugoslav border in a swirling snow storm on 6th April. His unit had been one of the first to engage in those wild series of actions, often fighting at close quarters to try to stem the advance of the German Panzers.

Now, six weeks later, his unit depleted and scattered, he had been entrusted to lead ten men safely over the mountains. As they had no provisions, the water from a fountain in one mountain village gave them fresh heart, although they had to fight off some Aussies for it. There was a cave near at hand, already occupied but with plenty of room for his men to move around the sleeping bodies. Only as dawn broke did they realise that they had been sleeping with corpses, earlier casualties from a bombing attack.

When Coastal Defence Regiment driver Ted Telling arrived at night where the road petered out near Sfakia with a truck-load of Australians, he was told to push his vehicle over the cliff edge 'if he wanted to be first off the island'. This he chose not to do. Instead, he turned his vehicle around and drove back to Suda Bay for more troops. Once more reaching Sfakia safely after several air attacks he again refused offers of rescue. Somehow, by now exhausted, he reached Suda again where his officer and a sergeant had to force him out of his cab. He lay on the ground in a deep sleep. When he awoke, his truck had disappeared and he was in the middle of a dive-bombing attack. There was nothing for it but to travel his last heart-breaking journey over the White Mountains on foot . . .*

One 33 Squadron airman, 'Bandy' Farrell, would remember the retreat across the White Mountains more than most. When the invasion came he had been wearing a pair of worn out plimsoles. During the fighting he had tried binding them to his feet with string and, afterwards, reinforcing them with galoshers from a dead paratrooper (as I also had to do), but his improvised footwear soon fell apart and he was forced to cross the mountain barefooted!

At Sfakia, men had been arriving all through the following night with the few available trucks crammed full of stretcher cases. They picked their way cautiously among the boulders, like drunks, staggered down the ravine, and collapsed upon the wadi floor.

Only as morning came did we see the line of trucks along the top of the cliff with the sunlight flashing on their windscreens. It was too late. As on the day previous, a pair of Junkers were approaching from the sea. Everyone held their breath and watched them cross the top of the ravine. Next moment one of them pulled off course and swung down the rock face . . . The secret was out! The Germans now knew exactly where the troops were heading for along that long unfriendly coastline. Beneath a salvo of well-placed bombs the trucks disappeared. Fire started and a pile of ammunition crackled merrily in the flames.

We thought it prudent to move even farther down towards the sea. To our surprise the ravine now revealed another clearing of still more exotic splendour with lush green grasses among the rocks and a soft light-green carpet of moss covering the floor. Cathedral-like caves lined the western wall. Farther down still was a water point of which we had not been previously aware.

The caves were filled with New Zealanders, Marines, Cypriots, Australians, some wounded, all of them exhausted. A few of them had no nerves left. They started to scream and sob when the bombers came back to strafe the ridge above.

A tall young Cretan, dressed in traditional garb, looking every inch a buccaneer from his fringed cap to his high polished boots, stood aloof and smiling, leaning against a cave wall. The object of his amusement, a Greek pilot,

*See Appendix 5.

clad in white vest and underpants, stood completing his lengthy toilet by the stone water fountain, impervious to the German aircraft overhead and the shouts and curses of the bomb-happy soldiers.

That evening Mitchell had been warned to prepare his party for possible evacuation. The erks were more than glad. Most of them had spent the day taking water to the wounded and dead-beat soldiers but for some hours the burning dumps of ammunition on the ridge, still crackling away, had been having a bad effect upon some of the bomb-happy troops. Every now and then one or two of them would stumble about the ravine screaming that the Germans had arrived.

We waited impatiently as the shadows on the mountains softened and darkened until they formed a black wall behind us. Up there we knew that some of the fighting units were guarding the passes, tired and without water. In another ravine to the east of us, General Weston's Royal Marines waited to take over the final phase and for the ship which never came for them.

Then the indefatigable Sergeant Powell appeared.

'Follow me and not too much noise about it,' he said.

We tailed him up the wadi in single file. Picking our way through the boulders we arrived breathlessly above a large shoulder of rock separated from Sfakia village by yet another wider wadi. By now the thousands of soldiers around us had realised that their chances of being evacuated were slim and already some were trying to sneak in among the ranks of airmen.

Mitchell now met us again. Our rescue was conditional upon first bringing down all the walking wounded and stretcher cases.

Down the mountainside carpeted with thyme and sage, so strongly scented that it almost choked, we continued our trek and then descended sharply towards this second wadi. Junkers 88s still flew over Sfakia dropping bombs down below us. The hollow wadi magnified the noise of the explosions. A thick cloud of dust rose up and met us. Then the aircraft were gone. We were not journeying alone. Shadowy figures of Kiwis bearing stretchers loomed out of the darkness. Walking wounded hobbled along as best they could. The airmen took over the stretcher handles from the medical orderlies. They soon discovered how weak they were and how heavy a stretcher was. The going became worse down in the wadi. Water had worn away the rock in tiers making it impossible for all four bearers to walk on the same level. With the soles of their shoes flapping, the sharp stones cutting into their feet made agony of every step. Another aircraft flew over. A cluster of flares floated slowly down overhead, lighting up the men as they picked their way slowly through the rocks. Then there were more bombs and it was dark again. Some time later other hands took over my stretcher shafts. But my relief was to be short-lived.

'Lend a hand here, Dig.'

There was an orderly with a young soldier leaning upon his shoulder. For a long time the soldier and I staggered onwards towards the coast like a couple of drunks. I never discovered where he was wounded and I began to wonder whether he was only making sure of his passage to Egypt. Then, as I was

beginning to feel ashamed of my uncharitable thoughts, he took away his arm
and went on ahead under his own steam.

We reached the track leading to Sfakia village too weary to walk another
step. Here was Mitchell with a score of airmen. He said that there were still
four more stretchers to be fetched from the top of the slope. The prospect
of covering the same ground twice filled the erks with dismay, but, nevertheless, 16 airmen picked themselves up and set off back up the track.

The wadi, once bustling with shadowy forms, now appeared deserted. The
erks began to wonder if Mitchell had been mistaken. Perhaps they were for-
feiting their chances of evacuation? Then, out of the darkness, came the voice
of Jeffers. Next moment he could be seen coming towards us with three other
squadron men bearing a stretcher.

He said to us: 'This is the last of 'em.'

We clustered around to take up the poles thankfully. We all admired Jeffers
for that evening's work. Three times had he made the trip from the hills to
the beach.

At last the torture of the wadi ended. The airmen turned along the track
towards the village. Now the path was jammed with dozens of bandaged
wounded, sitting, lying, or standing in queues: the rows of stretchers on either
side like piles of discarded kit. Here were the rest of the squadron. Everyone
craved for water and there was none to be had. Stevenson, entrusted with a
little of the precious liquid for the four of us, had already given away our
bottle to a wounded Kiwi.

Half an hour later we moved off again, climbing inland once more. Other
soldiers lined the winding track: mostly Cypriots and Palestinians. Sometimes they attacked our line and tried to slip in among us and we had quite
a time fighting them off. There was a pause for a moment by a roadside well.
The water was too low to reach but Gummer, lowered down by his ankles,
was able to scoop some water into his tin hat. It tasted of rubber.

We passed a Calvary at one end of Sfakia village and then, suddenly, we
were on the beach. Crowds of troops stood in long lines with MPs holding
back the stragglers trying to queue-jump. Other soldiers stood by with orders
to fire upon them if they interfered with the programme.

Boatload after boatload of men chugged away into the blackness ahead but
there seemed little decrease in the numbers of soldiers awaiting their turn.
The boats stopped coming. Then — one by itself. Most of our party moved
forward, held back by the MPs, then eventually given a place. The boat disappeared into the night. There seemed to be no more boats. A small ship's
boat landed with supplies for those to be left behind. We helped to unload
with a sinking heart. Then an officer said: 'Pile in!' and we were over the
side and away. The rest was easy. Soon we were racing towards Alexandria
in HMS *Kelvin*, accompanied by three other destroyers. The time was three
o'clock on the morning of 29th May.

At about that time the 11 Squadron detachment was wearily climbing down
the last few hundred yards to the ravine beside Sfakia. The RAF still worked

a wireless in a hillside cave nearby and it was from the erks still there that Wingrove and his party heard that most of the RAF survivors had already left. After tucking into a handful of biscuits washed down with water, and having their feet attended to, they slept the day through until the afternoon when they were awakened by the sudden arrival of a large flight of diving Messerschmitts. Down below, devoid of cover, there was a long column of walking wounded winding down towards Sfakia. The aircraft were moving over to attack as the medical orderlies quickly displayed or waved their red-crosses, laying their stretcher cases in a wide circle. Immediately, the Messerschmitts dipped in salute and veered off to shoot up the hillside around the Wireless Transmitter and the neighbouring belt of pines. Another witness to this 'civilized' act was Sturgess, who at that moment was being moved towards the beach.

Similar incidents were reported throughout the battle for Crete, the first occurring on the morning after the invasion when the Casualty Post at Maleme had been threatened by Stukas. Here also the wounded, Allied and German, were laid out in a rough circle and everyone else took off their headgear. The Stukas came in low to look at them but waggled their wings and went off after other targets.

There still is left the inescapable fact that the Luftwaffe deliberately bombed the 7th General Hospital on two occasions before it was brutally assaulted by paratroops. Here reference must be made to the German maps of the time upon which the hospital is invariably shown as a 'tented camp'. It seems quite possible, therefore, that a genuine mistake had been made.

Some hours later, 'Port Detachment' was doing its last job in Crete. With a RAF padre, they had been sent to Sfakia village to guard the beach approaches and to hurry the men along. It was a thankless task. The men being helped and manhandled towards the rescue craft were too tired to appreciate the help they were receiving or the need for haste. The night all but turned blue with the continous under-current of soldiers' curses. The padre, dragging and encouraging them on down the narrow path, added a whole new page of oaths to his vocabulary — especially from the Aussies.

By 3.30am the convoy commander knew that the ships must go or be caught in Cretan waters by the increasingly active Luftwaffe. The airmen and the padre left in the last transport. As they left the beach, soldiers were still coming down from the hills — too late.

There was still hope for some of them for, despite the proximity of the German mountain troops, two more convoys were able to leave Sfakia and take off another 6,500 troops. But for the gallant defenders in the hills there could be no rescue — nor for the soldiers hiding up in the ravines nearby. Surrender took place on 1st June but already hundreds of men had taken to the mountains, some to be rescued later, some to make incredible individual escapes, but many to be later shot down in cold blood in ruthless manhunts by the occupation troops.

The Germans rounded up some 6,000 men and, after an evening of singing and drinking under the 'Old Pals Act' marched them back over the White

Mountains to Canea. To those soldiers who had forced their unwilling feet along that same heartbreaking track only the day before, to have their dreams of Egypt changed into a nightmare, this was the bitterest blow of all.

Altogether 13,000 troops had been rescued from Sfakia by the Royal Navy aided by a few merchant ships, but each passage to and from Alexandria was a chapter of excitement and heroism.

As soon as it was light, Junkers 88s had found our four destroyers and for a while aboard the *Kelvin* there was plenty of entertainment for the airmen who found themselves helping to feed shells up to the gun turrets. But after four of the attackers had been accounted for they had left us in peace.

On the following morning it was the turn of cruisers *Phoebe, Perth, Calcutta* and *Coventry*; Glen ship *Glengyle*; and destroyers *Jervis, Hasty* and *Janus*; carrying some 6,000 troops between them. The ships came under a severe bombardment soon after dawn inflicting many near misses. Aboard the *Perth* 'Bruiser' Northway, one of the 'Port Detachment', had a lucky escape when a bomb went down the funnel killing 13 soldiers and sailors.

The following two nights cost the Navy three damaged destroyers and the loss of the ack-ack cruiser *Calcutta*, but by far their worst losses had already occurred on 29th May attempting to evacuate the Heraklion garrison.

For the gallant little band of defenders at Rethymnon there had been nothing left but to surrender. Out of touch with the other sectors, no word could be got to them of the evacuation. A Hurricane sent with instructions for withdrawal had been shot down before it reached the area. Those airmen among the garrison were either killed or captured.

But at Heraklion arrangements had already been made for a mass evacuation by sea on the night of 28th/29th May. Unfortunately the news could not be imparted to a party of airmen already on their way to open up the obstacle-covered aerodrome at Pediada Kastelli and they were left to be headed off by the quick advance of the German infantry. Most were captured but a few took to the hills.*

That night Heraklion garrison together with the surviving members of 112 Squadron and 220 AMES put to sea. Every extra minute in Cretan waters increased their peril and they knew that there was the long northern coastline to negotiate before they could steer for Alexandria and safety.

The first mishap came within minutes of sailing when the previously damaged *Imperial* broke down. She lay helpless, steering out of action, wallowing in the waters outside the port. The Navy knew what they must do.

---

*In July 1943, at Cape Town, I met an LAC from this party who had escaped via Turkey. Despite the barbaric treatment meted out by the Germans to any locality known to have harboured a soldier on the run the good Cretans had hidden him and, later shipped him to Greece where he had lived under cover in Athens for a year. The Greeks fed him at a time when children lay about the streets of Athens — dying by the hundred from starvation. He was then smuggled by Greek patriots through the length of the country and across the Turkish border. Now, fresh from his interrogation in Cairo, he had been flown to South Africa — only to be given 14 days Jankers by the local authorities on the very day of his arrival for appearing in Cape Town without a hat.

Quickly moving alongside, the destroyer *Hotspur* took aboard the stranded troops and crew, opened fire and sank her. But minutes of precious time had been sacrificed to prevent the warship falling into enemy hands. Now, an hour and a half behind schedule, they sailed eastwards into the dawn.

The bombers found them at 6 a.m. and stayed with them all the way until the battered survivors were 100 miles from Alexandria. For nine long hours the ack-ack crews threw up everything they had against the attackers as they swarmed overhead to deliver attack after attack upon the overcrowded convoy. *Hereward*, first to be hit, lost speed and was soon left behind. As she drifted towards the shores of Crete, helpless and with heavy casualties, the Luftwaffe pounded her mercilessly. She sunk from another direct hit and went down with her guns still blazing defiance. Over 600 troops were killed or left to flounder in the water until picked up by Italian torpedo boats.*

RAF fighters, sent to give the fleet cover, failed to find the convoy — probably due to the upset time schedule; the Germans had it all their own way. Within an hour both the cruiser *Orion* and the destroyer *Decoy* had received heavy damage. The squadron was forced to reduce speed. Casualties now mounted at a fast rate. Within another five hours hardly a ship had escaped the onslaught. Troops were being struck down upon the packed decks. The *Orion*'s captain had been killed at the bridge when his ship had again been hit. *Dido* soon joined the ranks of crippled warships still fighting for their lives and for the lives of thousands of troops in their charge. And still the bombers followed the convoy, diving into the mouths of the guns, bombing, strafing, darting among the ships through a mesh of bursting pom-poms. The *Orion* was a mess. Fire swept down her decks from a gaping hell below. Dozens of soldiers died horribly as they fought to escape the flames. Holed below the waterline, the sea was pouring in for'ard. To save the ship, watertight doors had to be closed upon the struggling, screaming men, rescued from captivity only to die in this hideous fashion. Over 400 bodies were recovered from the *Orion* at Alexandria — for the game old ship kept afloat somehow and sailed on with emergency steering.

Not until another three hectic hours had passed did the savage onslaught cease. But the Royal Navy had won the victory. When the battered, bloody squadron steamed into Alexandria that evening, scarred, holed, minus several gun-turrets, and almost out of ammunition, they had rescued with impudence some 3,486 soldiers and airmen from certain captivity.

It was six months later. The second Allied offensive in the Western Desert was underway. There was a field-dressing station down a Libyan wadi where German Medical Corps troops had collected some 700 wounded New Zealanders, including many of our old friends from 5th Brigade. The Germans treated them well. Even Rommel called in to see them on one occasion.

It was apparent that there was considerable friction between the Germans and the Italians who, when they thought that they could get away with it, with-

*The Italians had by now decided that it was safe to aid their allies in the conquest of Crete.

drew their ack-ack positions until they were sheltered by the Red Cross, along the edge of the wadi. One day the friction developed into a brawl. The grinning Kiwis settled down to watch the free show but, just as the senior German officer had punched his Italian counterpart on the nose, something more exciting attracted everyone's attention.

From the east came the distant droning of many aircraft. Every eye scanned the horizon which had suddenly become packed with fighters . . . approaching at hundreds of miles an hour. Then they were overhead. In serried rows Hurricanes and Tomahawks swept low along the wadi. They flew into the ack-ack fire with machine-guns blazing. The Italians gave up firing after a few uncontrolled rounds and scattered for safety among the tents.

On their way down the slopes they ran into the Kiwis who had left their beds and were cheering wildly. Those who could stand forgot their wounds, brushed aside the German guards, and, still yelling, raced to the escarpment. Lining the wadi-edge the excited Maori boys stamped the ground, tore off their greatcoats and, waving them in big sweeps above their heads, shouted and cheered as the RAF roundels flashed by. They yelled until they were hoarse.

They were still talking about it when the Germans retreated and they were rescued by a British carrier patrol. For the first time in the Middle East the Royal Air Force was sweeping the Luftwaffe from the skies.

PART TWO

'On this occasion things had gone well with us, but it seemed almost a miracle that our great and hazardous enterprise had succeeded. How it did, I cannot say to this day. Success had suddenly come to us at a moment when ... we had ceased to believe in the possibility of success.'

Baron von der Heydte
Commander I Battalion, III Regiment.

1

Looking Back

The destroyer *Kelvin* landed us at Alexandria, Egypt, and we were taken to the RAF base camp at Aboukir. Here for seven days we fended for ourselves.

Crete had been the last straw, just one evacuation too many! In Britain and all over the world airmen had become targets for abuse, mainly from those who had never fired a shot in anger. Suddenly, for the RAF, the streets became unsafe. There were even free fights in the German POW camps.

For Churchill, the loss of Crete could hardly have been more ill-timed. Desperate to prove to a reluctant USA that the British had not lost their fighting spirit, he was beside himself with rage when he heard the news. Without questioning what had happened he instantly blamed the airmen at Maleme for causing the disaster by losing the vital airfield. He called for, 'Every airfield to become a stronghold of fighting air-groundsmen, and not the abode of uniformed civilians in the prime of life protected by detachments of soldiers.'

As a result, a few months later, the RAF Regiment was formed. The policy was excellent but his phraseology rang harshly after the fight put up by the airmen on Crete whose losses (half their number) were in the same proportion as army losses.

At Aboukir, Cretan survivors were held at arms' length and treated with disdain. It was as if the very sight of us was an unpleasant reminder to them that, although the war was in its second year and men had been fighting and dying for some time, this base camp still carried out the peacetime practice of working mornings only. Afternoons were reserved for relaxing . . . They held us responsible for the wave of anti-RAF feeling which they now encountered in the streets of Alexandria.

Some of our group had lost footwear on the mountain scree and had feet in urgent need of treatment. Nevertheless, no one was medically examined, given kit or even given a knife and fork.*

Some days later we were given a 'medical examination' which entailed removing our clothes and filing past the MO's open doorway. As each man appeared he shouted, 'Fit for Duty!', barely looking up from his desk.

However, after the 'medical' our fortunes began to change. We were then kitted out with some essential items of clothing and given seven days' leave. The pay parade was to be held the following morning.

This was indeed good news! No one had been paid for a long time. It was therefore unfortunate that a complication should have arisen. It appeared that our pay records had been kept safely in Egypt for all that while, only to be sent to Crete on 18th May, two days before the invasion!

Nevertheless, Aboukir Accounts were prepared to advance £7 to each of us, no doubt not realising in their generosity the cost of a bed in a back street Cairo hotel.

However, when they announced that they were prepared to trade in drachmas at pre-invasion rates, we had cause to bless that opportunist airman who, under fire from glider-troopers, had still managed to dive into the 'Shoot School' hut at Maleme! The wads of banknotes stuffed inside his shirt had been shared out on Kavkazia Hill. The result was amusing. After the third man the pay parade was forced to close down to await more funds.

In Cairo, airmen were targets for the army roughs. McKenna and I shared a hotel room and twice were hauled from our beds in the early hours by military policemen, ostensibly searching for weapons. Our only friends, despite their 'Rare As Fairies' banter, remained New Zealanders and Australians.

One night in the Bardia Cabaret, things were starting to look ugly. A newly-arrived crowd of soldiers had singled us out together with the two New Zealand friends we were with. Suddenly, Military Police framed every exit door . . . one of the Redcaps dropped a hand near his revolver.

As if a pre-arranged signal, half a dozen Maoris jumped up and joined us. Out from nowhere came Schmeisser automatic pistols.

The belly dancers, the tarbooshed waiters, the crowd of squaddies, all stared in disbelief. The silence lasted a long second, broken only when our Maori friends raised their weapons and blasted the ceiling lights. The Redcaps vanished. Then the Maoris bundled us out of the Bardia Cabaret and to safety.

The hurt and unfairness of the stigma so ignorantly applied to us has lasted

*'Bandy' Farrell, his feet cut and bleeding, went off in desperation to try to obtain shoes from the station clothing store. Instead he was soon pounced upon by a flight lieutenant and given a long blasting for being improperly dressed. The airman was so distressed by his treatment that he went to the station commander who, to give him his due, made the flight lieutenant seek him out and make a full apology.

throughout my life. From the time of that leave in Cairo 1941, I became determined that one day I would find out exactly what happened on Crete 50 years ago and the real story of why the island had fallen to the Germans.

The 1961 edition of *Operation Mercury* was one of the earlier accounts of the Crete invasion. To my knowledge, it is the *only* written record from notes made by someone who was actually on Kavkazia Hill (Hill 107), Maleme, throughout 20th May 1941.

Unfortunately, at the time of writing, much of the official invasion background was not then known to me, let alone made available for reference. Enigma (Top Secret Ultra) was still a secret. Air Historical Branch gave tea and biscuits but denied me a sight of squadron records. There was a reluctance to publish anything controversial and I detected a cover-up.

Since then a hundred or more books have been written. Most accept that Maleme was key to the whole operation but a variety of reasons are given as to how it fell into German hands.

As the news of the dreadful losses suffered by his élite troops reached Hitler he had been appalled. More Germans had been killed that morning at Maleme than in the previous 18 months of the war!

The German public did not receive a news bulletin until five days after the invasion. By this time, as each hour brought in fresh troops and equipment to Maleme, Goebbels, Hitler's propaganda minister, had become more confident in the result. Unable to admit that, initially, German troops suffered unacceptable losses for no gains and were only able to capture Maleme because the British made a silly mistake and vanished overnight, he was able to justify the casualties by falsely implying that the airborne forces had not been killed by the score while still in the air but had died driving the defenders away by hard fighting.

The theme that 'although the British fought bravely they were overwhelmed by the superior fighting quality of the Germans,' seemed to Goebbels the best explanation. However, not even Goebbels (whose maxim was that 'the bigger the lie, the more likely it will be believed') could have conceived that so many books would perpetuate his myth! British films and television programmes have also followed the German line that the Allies fought bravely but were overwhelmed.

Explanations for the loss of Maleme are varied and include:

'Due to the bombing, the Germans caught the defenders with their heads down.'

'There was an immense ball of red dust through which parachutists drifted to the ground ... The "fog of war" enveloped the battlefield.'

'They held their positions all that day, though more parachutists arrived, but under cover of darkness they were forced to retreat.'

'At midnight, with permission, Andrew withdrew 22nd Battalion to a line east of Pirgos, leaving the Maleme airfield open to the enemy.'

'By dusk the AA guns on the aerodrome were out of action. Worse still, the 22nd New Zealand Battalion had been driven back from its positions round the aerodrome.'

'By the end of the day the 22nd New Zealand Battalion had been forced off its position round the aerodrome and the enemy had scored his only dangerous success.'

Even today, with so much more conclusive information to refer to, the book *50th Anniversary Commemorative Edition, World War II** states: 'The capture of Maleme airfield was achieved by courageous pilots crash-landing 80 Ju52 aircraft on to the heavily shelled airfield itself, bringing in a regiment of mountain troops to seize the perimeter, under shellfire from British ships at sea.'

There is no mention that the perimeter was in German hands at the time! How Goebbels would have enjoyed reading that!

If that is what our own side say, imagine the stories concocted by the enemy! History is always in the hands of the victors.

German writers not only perpetrated, but embroidered upon the myth. The last thing they wanted was to admit that Crete had been a German disaster, not captured by German feat of arms but handed to them by mistake. When General Student, whose ego-trip this whole operation had been, spoke on the BBC after the war, he had apparently forgotten the despair he had experienced that fatal night of 20th May. He spoke with the confidence of hindsight and never admitted the truth.

However, the prize for the most ridiculous version of the Battle for Crete must surely go to an Italian film in the *World in Flames* series. In this account the ten days of fierce fighting that resulted in 3,500 Allied soldiers being killed or wounded and the winning of a Victoria Cross is dismissed in a sentence: 'The British gave only sporadic resistance and then surrendered.'

With the mass of fresh information made available since the publication of *Operation Mercury*, I have had the opportunity to examine afresh what *really* happened at Maleme.

It soon became obvious to me that the Battle for Crete was, in fact, two battles. In the first, the enemy were trying to consolidate some sort of fighting force out of the stray parachutist survivors reaching the Tavronitis in penny numbers and those Germans who fell in the safe area west of the village.

They were desperate for ammunition and the airdrops upon which they were wholly dependent were, at best, a haphazard affair and could not refurbish an army indefinitely.

Meanwhile, the defenders had everything their way. They occupied the high ground, their defences were well dug in, they had artillery, food and ammunition to spare and they had an un-tapped source of reserves. It was a situation, one would think, which must have ended in an Allied victory.

Even if seaborne troops had established a beach-head, the Germans had no back-up ships to maintain supplies. These fresh troops would also have had to depend upon the vagaries of airdrops.

---

*By Ivor Matanle, Colour Library Books Ltd.

With an aerodrome secure, the Germans were able to land ammunition, stores and reinforcements with *accuracy* in a never-ending shuttle-service. The whole battle situation was transformed and, within a short while, in the second of those battles, the initiative had been wrested from the Allies.

2
Maleme: 20th May 1941

Nearly 10,000 paratroops and 750 glider troops had fallen upon the Allied defenders of Crete. By 6 pm most were dead or wounded. Those who had survived had achieved no gains, captured no targets or even caused the defenders much concern.

The airfields at Heraklion and Rethymnon were in no danger of capture and the Allied forces there were jubilant. At Suda all Germans had been rounded up, at Kastelli every German killed or captured. In what was known as 'Prison Valley', Baron von der Heydte held on grimly with the remains of I Battalion, 3rd Regiment. He had suffered heavy losses and could hardly influence the battle.

Two miles from Maleme, on Vineyard Ridge, the 21st and 23rd New Zealand Infantry Battalions were in high spirits; they had killed the bulk of the 600-strong III Parachute Battalion which had dropped over their perimeters.

In Brigadier Hargest's 5th Brigade there were still reserves of men, such as the 28th Maori Battalion, fresh, confident and eager to get to grips with the invaders. It was only fitting that the defence of Maleme should have been given to Lieutenant-Colonel Andrew, and his 22nd Battalion. Andrew, 44 years old, a VC from the Great War, was as brave as a lion. A strict disciplinarian, several books relate his deafening parade-ground introductory shout to new recruits: 'My name is Andrew, not *Andrews*!'

However, it could be argued that what was needed to counter this unique enemy attack, the first mass paratroop assault in history, was not so much a rigid disciplinarian as a man with a more unorthodox approach and the ability to adapt to a changing situation.

Twenty or so years earlier he had shown plenty of this initiative when he took it upon himself to destroy three German machine-gun posts and a strong-point, but now he seemed to fail to appreciate the vital importance of the air-strip he was defending, let alone what could be achieved in a short time by a fleet of enemy transports should he let them capture it ...

It is true that, upon his own initiative, he had launched a counter-attack that afternoon, and perhaps such an improvised affair could have had more success than was the case. The Germans certainly panicked when they saw the 'Panzers' approaching. Yet it is surprising that the attack was launched without further efforts to contact the 'missing' company commanders. Despite what was said after the battle, they *were* accessible with little risk.

It is equally surprising that the crew of the second tank were not aware that they had the wrong ammunition for their gun *before* they went into bat-tle. It is almost unbelievable that, prior to the German arrival, some sort of reconnaissance had not been carried out so that the leading tank did not attempt to tackle the Tavronitis river-bed, with its soft gravel patches and man-size boulders, and so get bogged down and captured.

If, instead, the tank had turned in the direction of 'C' Company's western platoon area (the only small gain made initially that morning by glider-troops) this force of New Zealanders and Marines could have driven the Germans from this precarious toehold and back across the river-bed.

However, already two fresh companies, one from 23rd Battalion and the other from 28th Maori Battalion, were on their way to strengthen Andrew's position.

The men were confident. Reinforcements would be in place before dawn. Surely this must have been the prelude to the greatest Allied victory of the war and Germany's first great defeat! The Nazis were to be halted at last and the very cream of Goering's airmen killed or captured!

Outlined below is the sequence of events over those vital hours.

The First Battle for Crete

Communications with 5 New Zealand Brigade
10.55 am Colonel Andrew to Brigadier Hargest at Platanias:

> I HAVE NO COMMUNICATION WITH 'C', 'D', AND HQ COMPANIES AND AM
> BEING HEAVILY ATTACKED

Having wandered about the hill myself at that time it is difficult to compre-hend why he had no communication with at least 'C' and 'D' Companies. There were trees, shrubs and stone walls. Few parts of the hill were bare of cover. He could certainly have reached these two companies with persever-ance. 'C' and 'D' Companies were under constant attack, but, on the whole 'B' Company and 'A' Company, where Andrew held his headquarters, received the least attention from the Germans after the initial mass air-drop.

Andrew's main concern would have been light mortar fire from the far bank of the Tavronitis and, later on, from the RAF camp area. From our vantage point we watched the mortars being fired, heard the shells pant overhead and land. Not very pleasant and those which fell among us made big bangs.

Sporadic mortar fire to a seasoned soldier hardly constitutes the phrase 'Being heavily attacked'.

Of course there were isolated parachutists and small pockets of Germans hiding among the bushes in every direction but most of these were far more concerned with creeping undetected to the Tavronitis than in 'heavily attacking' 22nd Battalion.

11.55 am Colonel Leckie, 23rd Battalion, to Brigadier Hargest:

SITUATION ON MY AREA IN COMPLETE CONTROL. BATTALION IN HIGH SPIRITS.

Noon Colonel Andrew to Brigadier Hargest:

BATTALION BEING SUBJECTED TO ALMOST CONTINUOUS BOMBING.

This must refer to the Ju87B Stuka attack upon the summit of the hill. It was frightening and dreadful as anyone who has been victim of a Stuka attack must agree! The high-pitched scream of their dive, the sirens fixed to their under-carriages, the vamping sound of their Jumo engines, the continous explosions, is an experience which lives with me even now, fifty years after the event. But, with the exception of the mass pattern bombing which heralded the invasion, this was the one and only bombing attack that day! There were plenty of aircraft about and the odd machine-gun attack by Me110s but the Stuka episode was the first and only bombing at Maleme after paratroops had landed.

So what did Andrew mean? 'Subjected to *almost continuous* bombing?'

Throughout the campaign many troops appeared to be completely ignorant about aircraft.

A naivety is evident in many eye-witness accounts of the battle. Some reports of Ju52 troop-carriers over Maleme read more like quatrains from Nostradamus than modern descriptions. Regardless of shape and size, most other aircraft were labelled 'Stukas'.

Neither did they seem to be aware of the basic rules such as, when strafed it is usually better to run in the direction of the attacking aircraft than away from it, or, if an enemy bomber is overhead you are safe as houses. It's the man a mile away who should start worrying.

An army which does not appreciate how much or how little harm can come from aircraft overhead is always at a disadvantage. Airmen at Maleme were quickly aware of what was going on above them.

This may have been the reason that Colonel Andrew sent out that inaccurate communication.

2.25 pm Brigadier Hargest to Colonel Leckie, 23rd Battalion:

WILL NOT CALL UPON YOU FOR COUNTER-ATTACKING UNLESS POSITION VERY SERIOUS. SO FAR EVERYTHING IS IN HAND AND REPORTS FROM OTHER UNITS SATISFACTORY.

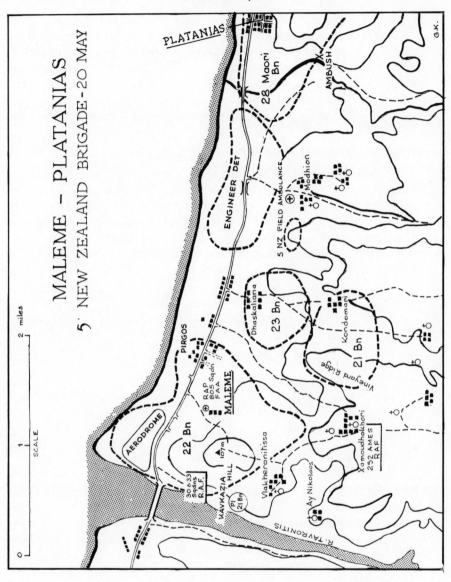

MALEME – PLATANIAS
5' NEW ZEALAND BRIGADE – 20 MAY

SCALE

0   1   2 miles

PLATANIAS

28 Maori Bn

AMBUSH

ENGINEER DET

Modhion

5 NZ FIELD AMBULANCE

Dhaskaliana

23 Bn

Kondomari

21 Bn

Vineyard Ridge

PIRGOS

RAP 805 Sqdn FAA

MALEME

AERODROME

22 Bn

Xamoudhokhari 252 AMES RAF

107m

Vlakheronitissa

30 & 33 Sqdns R.A.F.

KAVKAZIA HILL

Pl 21 Bn

Ay Nikolaos

R. TAVRONITIS

G.K.

By then it was over three hours since the Brigadier had received word from Andrew that he was in trouble and isolated from three of his companies. This had been followed by a further report that he was being 'subjected to almost continous bombing'. Hargest had taken no action then and his message to Colonel Leckie is inexplicable in the light of the anything but 'satisfactory' reports coming from the 22nd Battalion Commander.

2.55 pm Andrew to Hargest:

BATTALION HQ HAS BEEN PENETRATED.

It is difficult to understand what Colonel Andrew meant by this and from which direction the 'penetration' had taken place. We knew of the Germans in the undefended RAF camp but, after their abortive attempt to gain the slopes of the hill behind a screen of RAF prisoners, they had been contained and further attacks from this direction successfully repelled. On his southern flank, Stenzler's Germans advancing up the hill had also been halted and did not constitute a serious threat.

3.55 pm Andrew to Hargest:

LEFT FLANK HAS GIVEN WAY AND THE NEED FOR AT LEAST SOME REINFORCE-MENTS IS NOW URGENT.

Distress flares sent up by Andrew. They are not seen.

5.00 pm Andrew to Hargest:

WHEN CAN I EXPECT THE PRE-ARRANGED COUNTER-ATTACK?

5.15 pm Hargest to Andrew:

THE 23RD CANNOT CARRY OUT YOUR REQUEST BECAUSE IT IS ITSELF ENGAGED AGAINST PARATROOPS IN ITS OWN AREA.

It appears that Andrew was expecting the 23rd to move forward to give immediate support. But he received no such back-up from Hargest. There was no truth whatsoever in this statement from the Brigadier and it remains a mystery why it was sent.

5.15 pm Hargest to Division, but NOT to Andrew:

AM ORDERING REINFORCEMENTS TO MALEME.

5.15 pm Andrew launches his counter-attack using two tanks and 55 men; objective, the Iron Bridge. The attack fails with the loss of a tank and all bar three of the attackers killed or wounded. All over in 30 minutes.

Captain Johnson, 'C' Company, reported failure to Andrew. He told Andrew that he could hold out until dark but would like to be reinforced.

5.50 pm Andrew replied: 'Hold on at all costs!'

Captain Johnson then returned to his defences on the aerodrome perimeter and, after that, contact with Andrew seems to have been lost once more.

6.00 pm Andrew to Hargest:

I MUST WITHDRAW UNLESS REINFORCEMENTS REACH ME SOON.

At this point he had only local withdrawal in mind.

6.00 pm Hargest to Andrew:

IF YOU MUST, YOU MUST.

Andrew, confused and despondent, had turned to his Brigadier for support. Instead he had received this unhelpful message which once more underlined to the Colonel that he was on his own.

6.05 pm Hargest to Andrew:

AM SENDING YOU TWO COMPANIES, 'A' COMPANY 23RD BATTALION AND 'B' COMPANY 28TH (MAORI) BATTALION.

What to Andrew appeared to be a volte-face in Hargest's attitude was also a clear indicator that the Brigadier was, in fact, responding to his call for reinforcements, commencing with these two companies. Whatever his difficulties, real or imagined, he should now have held on to his position until help arrived.

9.00 pm Reinforcements not yet arrived.

9.00 pm (approx) Andrew to Hargest:

I WILL HAVE TO WITHDRAW TO 'B' COMPANY RIDGE.

The batteries of his old wireless set, his only means of communication, became weaker and then failed completely.

At some time during the early evening a soldier from 'D' Company arrived at Andrew's HQ claiming to be the only survivor. It is quite possible that Andrew took this probably self-extenuating statement at face value, thus adding to his belief that 'C', 'D' and HQ Companies were no longer a coherent force. But why did he assume this without further investigation? Just because telephonic communications had been destroyed by the bombing why should he have presumed that his men had been overwhelmed on such slight evidence?

9.30 pm Reinforcements from 23rd Battalion reach the top of Kavkazia hill and find Andrew with 'B' Company. There is some confusion as to what should have taken place. It appears that, on the assumption that the whole of 'D' Company defending the western boundary of the hill had been wiped out, the reinforcements should return to Andrew's old position on the summit and act as rear-guard for his withdrawal.

He provided one of his lieutenants as a guide. Unfortunately, upon arrival, a sudden burst of fire killed the guide and wounded several others.

By now Andrew had realised that his situation on 'B' Company ridge, without the other companies to back him, was one he could not defend. Without 'D', 'C', and HQ Company (at Pirgos) to secure Kavkazia Hill, he must retreat yet again. So, with roles reversed, the 23rd Battalion now had to supply a guide to escort Andrew's 'A' and 'B' Company back to the support positions on Vineyard Ridge.

Midnight: Andrew's forces complete their withdrawal, including the company from 23rd Battalion. The top of Kavkazia Hill, key to the battle of Crete, is empty of men and weapons!

At Platanias, five miles to the east, at the same time, Brigadier Hargest removed his uniform, put on his pyjamas and went to bed. It had been a great day! Success stories on every side! If it was true that his 22nd Battalion had been under some pressure, the arrival of two new companies at Maleme would have given Colonel Andrew fresh heart!

3
Maleme: 21st May 1941

Meanwhile, in the Hotel Grande Bretagne, Athens, General der Flieger Kurt Student, hero of earlier airborne assaults in Belgium, Holland and Norway, favourite of Goering and Hitler and beloved by his airforce troops, sat in absolute dejection.

Within the shuttered room with its huge map of Crete on the wall, it seemed such a short time ago that he had outlined his plans to the commanders of his paratroop regiments and battalions. They were his own, personal, plans, devised by him and worked out in every minute detail by him alone. Against opposition, mainly from the army, he had fought hard for them to be accepted. They became part of his life and he believed that nothing could prevent them succeeding.

He had told his commanders that there would be little opposition from handfuls of battle-weary defenders who had lost the will to fight. The Cretans would welcome the Germans as friends ...

Now it appeared that he had failed. From the very start the day had gone badly, for even before his first parachutist landed on Cretan soil, disaster had struck! General Wilhelm Suessmann, at 50, hero of Poland and of Norway, a recently transferred army officer chosen to become divisional commander and coordinate the actions around Canea, had been killed together with all his staff officers in an avoidable accident; an example of Teutonic stupidity.

The very best glider pilot, a qualified engineer named Lassen, had been detailed to fly the General and his staff to Crete. However, when it was discovered that Lassen was not even a sergeant, the Air Transport commander disapproved and called for a substitute with a rank more in keeping with the important officers he would be flying. As there were no officer glider pilots immediately available, a capable flyer, Lieutenant Doge, who was on another aerodrome, was sent for at once.

However, before he arrived, General Suessmann called the five glider pilots involved to his headquarters for briefing. As fate would have it, a sycophantic officer named Lieutenant Gruppe was present. He said that he would represent Doge and brief him later.

On the way to headquarters, Gruppe, distancing himself from the other pilots, had a long conversation with the senior officer who was escorting them. When they arrived, to everyone's amazement, it was announced that Gruppe would take the place of Lieutenant Doge. The pilots were then introduced to General Suessmann but no mention was made to him of the change of his pilot from Lassen, a superb glider expert, to Gruppe, a pilot with limited ability.

At 0500 hrs, 20th May, Lieutenant Gruppe had been delayed when, at the last minute, additional typewriters and bulky packages of stationery were bundled to the rear of his glider. A more experienced pilot would have refused the additional weight in the tail section as it was bound to affect stability.

Eventually tug and glider were airborne but, as they gained height, they flew into the slipstream of a distant Heinkel 111. The glider started to pitch and the over-correcting by the inexperienced Gruppe only made the movement more violent. Eventually both wings broke away and the flightless fuselage crashed upon the nearby island of Aegina.

And so for General Suessmann, the man who had survived the icy waters of Oslo Fjord when the *Blücher* had sunk, luck ran out. It could be argued that his end had probably only been advanced by a short time. Of the gliders in the Canea/Galatas area, none were to achieve their objectives and most of the glider-troops were destined not to survive.

To Student it appeared that, from that incident onwards, disaster followed disaster. His aircraft, flying over several 'key' targets throughout the morning reported no activity in those areas. He could only assume that lack of news must mean failure.

As the day progressed it seemed that the airborne assaults upon Rethymnon and Heraklion had fared no better. All that was left was Maleme and from here he was receiving no encouraging reports either. One battalion had completely disappeared. Instead of triumphant messages he heard nothing but failure. He realised that the bulk of his hand-picked parachutists were already dead, several thousands of them!

He had made no gains and had not captured one of the three airfields. Without an airfield, how could reinforcements be flown in? As if to underline the fact, on his desk lay the most recent report from the Assault Regiment at Maleme, 'Without reinforcements the attack on Crete cannot succeed.'

Student knew that the Assault Regiment commander, General Meindl, was badly wounded in the chest and he could well imagine the plight of the survivors. Five thousand Mountain Division troops were waiting to be flown in but there was no airfield to receive them. A further 7,000 seaborne troops were also awaiting the signal to sail but, even if not intercepted by the Royal Navy, their bridge-head landing could not be long supported by airdrops alone. In any case all the aircraft were only on loan for a few days. Within a short time they would be needed for Hitler's attack upon Russia!

Reconnaissance reported that, in spite of repeated dive bombing attacks, three cruisers and four destroyers still guarded Crete's western approaches. Earlier in the day Student had renewed his attempt to persuade the Italians to put their large fleet to sea to divert the Royal Navy, but, still smarting from the indignity of being themselves dive bombed in error on a couple of occasions, Rome refused his request.

He had virtually lost the battle. The army were pressing him and there seemed no other course to take than to abandon the operation.

Everything seemed to be going right for the British. They had responded to his airborne assault with remarkable ferocity. It was almost as if the Australians and New Zealanders had never heard of the superiority of the 'Master Race'! He could find little comfort in the fact that barely 600 out of 3,000 were still on their feet at Maleme! They would be battle-weary and short of food and ammunition.

All that remained of his airborne forces in Greece were a few hundred stragglers; two companies who should have dropped at Rethymnon and strays left behind due to engine failure and other mishaps. Altogether a further 600 men but, if 3,000 could not succeed, how could 600?

He divided this force into half, one group to fall in the 'safe' area west of the Tavronitis and the other 'undefended' territory to the east. German intelligence had still not made him aware that these troops would be dropping on top of the 28 Maori Battalion and most of them to certain death!

He knew Maleme airfield to be in Allied hands yet he asked one of his staff pilots, Hauptmann Kleye, to attempt a landing there. It would be a suicidal attempt by a very brave man.

Student signalled his intentions to the Assault Regiment at Maleme and, in so doing, committed his final blunder! His message was intercepted and a translation before General Freyberg a few hours later!

Besides giving advanced details of where the new drops were to be expected and their numbers, more importantly the message clearly revealed to the Allied Commander that these were the last of the reserves. There was no vast army of parachutists standing by in the wings. All Freyberg now had to do was to contain the Germans still on their feet and keep them away from the three airfields.

The First Battle for Crete: Maleme after midnight

Wednesday 21st May

1.00 am: The summit of Kavkazia hill, key to victory, now vacant *one hour.*

1.30 am   Maoris arrive at Vineyard Ridge, pick up a guide from 23rd Battalion and head for the hill. Unfortunately, they miss the left hand turning towards Xamoudhokhori and move on through Pirgos to the edge of the airfield. They do not see the HQ Company defenders.

(It has been suggested that they were indeed seen by some of HQ Company but, as they were all muttering in Maori tongue, they were mistaken for a force of Germans!)

After an exchange with some Germans near the aerodrome they reach the summit of Kavkazia hill and find it deserted. Eventually they locate Andrew. He tells them *they are not needed* and sends them on their way back to Platanias.

Disgruntled and spoiling for a fight, they hunt out pockets of Germans and kill some 40 or 50 of them . . .

2.00 am   Summit of Kavkazia hill now vacant *two hours*.

2.00 am   Colonel Andrew arrives on Vineyard Ridge.

2.00 am   Captain Campbell, 'D' Company, leaves his trench along the Tavronitis in search of water for his men. He makes preparations to evacuate his men.

Perhaps if he had gone to the summit half an hour earlier he may have met the Maoris full of fire and determination. They may have joined forces and remained defending the hill until the mystery of Andrew's disappearance had been sorted out.

2.30 am   Brigadier Hargest, aroused from his sleep, is told: 'We are officially off Maleme!'

He is taken by surprise and quite unprepared for this news. In fact, the information was incorrect, 'D' Company was still on the hill and HQ and 'C' Company were still holding their positions.

3.00 am   Kavkazia hill now vacant *three hours*.

3.00 am   Andrew holds conference with Lieutenant-Colonel Allen of 21st Battalion, Lieutenant-Colonel Leckie of 23rd Battalion and the 27th Battery Commander, Major Philp. They resolve 'To hold our positions next day!'

This was their *last chance* for a counter-attack under cover of night! The two fresh battalions could have covered the ground to the hill and annihilated the Germans before breakfast-time!

Instead, they decided against the prepared policy of *immediate counter-attack*, drummed into them by General Freyberg time after time, and reverted to 1914 trench-warfare thinking! When Brigadier Hargest was eventually consulted, he, too, agreed to staying put . . . This was the second vital decision that night which sealed the loss of Crete.

(D. M. Davin, Official historian for the New Zealand Forces in Crete, in his book *Crete* (Oxford University Press) states his views quite plainly. Present at the time and as 23rd Battalion's Intelligence Officer, he says that there was still time to get the two fresh battalions organised for a daylight attack if not before. They would have been strong enough 'to go forward and regain Point 107 (Kavkazia). 22nd Battalion could have taken over the rear.'

Many other accounts are of the same opinion. Even General Student, himself, wrote: 'If the enemy had made an organised counter-attack during the night ... he would probably have succeeded in routing the much battered and exhausted remnants of the Assault Regiment, especially as these were badly handicapped by shortage of ammunition.')*

3.00 am   Captain Campbell from 'D' Company, along with Marines and airmen from 33 Squadron, begins to move off the hill.

3.00 am   In Greece, Hauptmann Klete takes off for Maleme: his chances of survival with 'C' Company still holding the airfield perimeter, nil.

3.30 am   Some of HQ Company start to withdraw from Pirgos.

3.45 am   Captain Johnson of 'C' Company goes in search of Andrew and finds the summit deserted. He then starts to look for the other companies, a logical action which could have been pursued by the 22nd Battalion Commander.

4.00 am   Kavkazia hill now vacant *four hours.*

4.15 am   'C' Company vacate the aerodrome.

4.30 am   Hauptmann Kletye lands successfully by the western perimeter, is fired upon but takes off again with the wounded Meindl aboard; saved from disaster by only 15 minutes! A very lucky man.

5.00 am   Kavkazia hill now vacant *five hours.*

5.30 am   German probe towards Kavkazia hill. No opposition. Hill not occupied in force.

5.30 am   German probe along foot of the hill as far as the eastern perimeter of the aerodrome. Halted by rifle and machine-gun fire from the outskirts of Maleme village.

---

*Liddell Hart: *The Other Side of the Hill: Germany's Generals*, Cassell, 1953. This was Student's honest assessment before the propagandists took over and one must give praise to the courage of the paratroop survivors. As Dr Merk pointed out to me after the war, most of them were 18-year-olds, few had been under fire before and, for many, this was their first action. They were tired, hungry and well aware of the hopelessness of their situation. Word had already spread that III Battalion was completely destroyed which meant, beside the shock of the news, that no supporting attack upon the aerodrome was now to be expected from the east. They were on their own.

6.00 am   HQ Company moving towards Vineyard Ridge meet up with 'D' Company and RAF in wooded area. Fired upon from various directions. Eventually reach New Zealand lines. The New Zealand commanders are now aware that Andrew's 'lost' companies are safe after all.

On the strength of this good news it was now even more logical to Davin that preparations for a two-battalion counter-attack should be made at once. However, the need for immediate action appeared to have been missed by Hargest and others under his command. Instead, Hargest informed his divisional commander, Brigadier Puttick, of the situation. Puttick suggested a counter-attack by Maoris and others *after dark* the following evening. He put the suggestion to Major-General Freyberg VC, General Officer Commanding Crete. Freyberg did not consider the situation sufficiently important to warrant a personal visit. However, he suggested a *conference* at his HQ *that afternoon*!

Surely those brave soldiers deserved better support than this!

8.30 am   300 paratroops are dropped in the safe zone west of the aerodrome.

9.30 am   The parachute reinforcements group in the village and, as the bridge is still under sniping fire, are forced to cross the Tavronitis running from pier to pier. Eventually a lone New Zealander in the RAF camp, Sergeant John Woods, is captured. He had chosen to snipe at the enemy wherever he found them rather than retreat. He epitomized the aggressive spirit of those tough Anzac soldiers!

3.00 pm   Kavkazia still not occupied in force after *fifteen hours*!

3.00 pm   The whole of Vineyard Ridge, Maleme and Pirgos subjected to devastating Stuka attacks.

3.00 pm   Simultaneously, two companies of paratroops fall on top of the Maoris. Most are killed and only some 80 scattered stragglers survive.

4.00 pm   Germans probe around the foot of Kavkazia hill, capture Maleme village and discover the New Zealand First Aid Post.

Germans attack 23rd Battalion in strength. The New Zealanders stand firm and inflict many casualties. Germans withdraw leaving some 200 dead.

5.00 pm   Kavkazia hill is occupied in force by the Germans after *seventeen hours* of lost opportunities.

5.00 pm and onwards   Hundreds of Junkers commence landing at Maleme unloading thousands of reinforcements in spite of direct hits from British Artillery. With virtually unlimited reserves the Germans had commenced the *second battle for Crete*, a battle the Allies could never win.

Conclusion: A Personal View

Let it be said at once that in no theatre of war had Allied soldiers fought with more courage and determination. The fighting spirit of the New Zealanders at Maleme was matched by the Australian and British forces throughout the island! With proper leadership they could have beaten the Germans with one hand tied behind their backs!

There is criticism in one book that the RAF considered themselves as 'non-combatant'. It could not have been made by anyone at Maleme! In fact, it would have been very difficult to be non-combatant under such circumstances!

Following the Battle for Maleme, out of 229 officers and airmen, seven were eventually to receive awards: one OBE, two MMs, one MBE, two BEMs and one Mention in Dispatches.

Furthermore, out of those taken prisoner, one successfully escaped from Crete, one from Greece and a third from Poland. A further escape from Greece was achieved by an airman from 112 Squadron. Not bad for 'non-combatants'!

Let it not be forgotten that the brunt of the fighting that day was borne by 'D' and 'C' Companies and that, by evening, those surviving in the 'D' Company trenches nearest the enemy were 26 New Zealanders and no less than 60 Marines and 33 Squadron airmen!

It is difficult to be generous to those who appear responsible for the loss of Crete, although, in defence, it seems clear that, on the morning of 21st May, neither Brigadier Puttick, the divisional commander, nor Major-General Freyberg were given a clear picture of what really had happened. Their repeated instructions had been to *immediately counter-attack*.

I cannot believe that they were told the extent of Andrew's withdrawal or the circumstances. The Germans had not forced Andrew from the hill; it had been his decision to withdraw his men. If only Freyberg or Puttick had been on Vineyard Ridge that morning!

In defence of Lieutenant-Colonel Andrew, 20th May had been an unhappy day for him. In the previous war the enemy more or less stayed in one place. Now the enemy were in every direction and hostile aircraft roared above and around for most of the day! By an unlucky chance, it had been his headquarters that had been singled out for prolonged mortar attacks. Eventually this constant shelling had become unbearable and he had been forced to move his headquarters further south.

He had commenced the day with only half his complement of machine-guns and with few mortars. He had been short of officers and the 20 he started with had been soon reduced to 12. At the very beginning his few artillery batteries had been cut off from their forward observers and the early bombing had isolated him from three of his five companies for most of the day.

He must be given credit for attempting to carry out Freyberg's instuctions of 'immediate counter-attack' from the start. But his appeals to Brigadier Hargest for reinforcements appeared to have been ignored throughout the day.

Although he must have felt badly let down by the Brigadier, he still was intent upon carrying out an immediate counter-attack before the Germans could consolidate their small gains. In the afternoon he had sent two tanks and 55 men towards the enemy unwisely into an almost completely unknown situation.

Although by now well dug in north and south of the bridge, several young Germans did, in fact, turn tail and leave their positions when the tanks first appeared. If it hadn't have been for a handful of hard-line paratroops who remained firm and firing their three or four machine-guns, two lucky hits on the leading tank by mortar shells and the poor performance of the tank's two-pounder shells which, aimed at the Germans north of the bridge, twice missed their mark and hit trees, Andrew's counter-attack might even have succeeded in, at least, winning back 'C' company's western perimeter.

Tough disciplinarian he certainly was, but the loss of so many of his soldiers he had trained in New Zealand, in such a short time may well have depressed him further. Feeling let down in every way, there is little doubt that he really did think that his 'D' and HQ companies and probably most of the remainder of 'C' company had been overrun by the enemy.

The promised reinforcements were painfully slow in arriving and by the time he met the Maoris he was off the hill. It will never be explained why Hargest chose to send a company of Maoris on a five mile march through dangerous country when there were troops available near at hand from 23rd and 21st Battalions.

After the war Andrew stated: 'Looking back now and knowing more of the facts I am convinced that withdrawal at that time was the only possible action to take'.* However, taking all factors into consideration, accepting that Andrew had been shabbily treated by Hargest that day and that neither of the two supporting battalions had shown much individual initiative, I find it hard to accept that statement.

Was it really the only possible action to take to leave this key position whatever the provocation and while aware that two fresh companies were already on their way to strengthen the defences? Even had he thought, with the reinforcements taking so long to reach him, that something had gone wrong, his job was to hold on.

Was it really the only possible action to make no apparent attempt to inform his 'lost' soldiers of his intentions? And was it really correct to leave the hill before he had even made a reasonable assessment of the strength and disposition of the enemy?

Even although he had lost contact with three of his companies and he thought the situation really bad, soldiering was his profession. History books are crammed with heroic accounts of soldiers in adversity holding on grimly until relieved! It is what soldiers are supposed to do, especially soldiers who have been repeatedly told in advance that the hill and aerodrome were the enemy's prime objectives!

He had been told how vital it was to *stay put*! In any case, he must have reasoned that whereas air-drops were a wasteful, chancy business, with the gift of a landing-ground, ordinary soldiers, heavy weapons and supplies could

Greece and Crete 1941. Christopher Buckley. HMSO.

be shuttled in accurately without loss or limitation.

There were other mistakes made during the Battle for Crete but it was only this one incomprehensible decision by Colonel Andrew on 20th May which opened the back door and lost the island for the defenders. What is more, Crete was handed over to an enemy who, considering his own list of blunders, was a completely unworthy victor.

As for Winston Churchill's ignorantly implied comments that the airmen on Crete were 'uniformed civilians in the prime of life protected by detachments of soldiers', before the invasion and with no supervision, 33 Squadron airmen supported the Bofors guns with all the small-arms fire they could muster and, during that last afternoon of 19th May, when the Bofors guns were silent, only the two RAF machine-guns on the otherwise deserted landing-ground still fired defiance at the strafing Messerschmitts. The soldiers of the 5th New Zealand Brigade remained concealed during those hectic days and took no major part in the defence of the aerodrome.

On 20th May the airmen of 112 Squadron at Heraklion manned the defences alongside the soldiers and gave a good account of themselves while at Maleme 30 Squadron airmen joined 'A' company New Zealanders in holding the northeastern section of Kavkazia Hill against all comers. They lost 13 airmen, five corporals and two sergeants killed that day; a fifth of their number!

To the west of the hill facing the Tavronitis, 33 Squadron airmen, having suffered similar losses, were still defending Maleme for several hours *after* a large part of Churchill's 'detachment of soldiers', including their commanding officer, had vacated the area.

If Crete had not Fallen

It has been said that, logistically, Crete could never have been held. However, on this occasion, I am sure that every Australian, New Zealander and British defender would have paraphrased Henry Ford's statement and replied, 'Logistics is bunk!'

Certainly the island was at starvation level and delivering supplies to a victorious garrison would have stretched resources at a crucial time in the war. But the days of 'war on a shoestring' were, within a relatively short time, to be replaced by a new kind of soldiering fought with an abundance of men, aircraft, tanks and supplies. Those Generals who followed after Wavell and Auchinleck no longer needed their tactical skills when victory could be secured by an overwhelming superiority in numbers and supplies.

The value of holding this large island, so strategically placed, would have been far greater than, perhaps, was realised at the time.

While, at the end of 1940, the British pondered upon Hitler's next move they thought mainly of territorial gains, protecting Middle East oil and the fear that Turkey would, once again, throw in its lot with the Germans. The handful of RAF squadrons were sent to Greece as a sacrifice in an attempt to buy time while the Middle East was strengthened, but those airmen would have been surprised to have known how important their presence featured in the Fuhrer's thinking. For the German attitude was dominated not by territorial gains as such but by *oil*. Not having an Empire or a friendly American source, Hitler relied, almost solely, upon the oilfields at Ploesti in Roumania. If these wells were destroyed, the Nazi war would be halted in days.

His ambition had always been to annihilate Russia in 1941 but, whenever he studied the map, he realised that he could not proceed while Yugoslavia was an uncommitted neutral and the Royal Air Force were occupying Greek bases. With the advent of the larger British bombers now coming into service, these bases held the capacity for bombing Ploesti! It was a thought which, probably, had never occurred to the British.

For this reason, at a conference held in Berlin at the end of March 1941, Hitler announced that he was postponing the attack upon Russia in order that 'Yugoslavia could be liquidated, the British driven from the Balkans, and foundations laid for German air operations in the eastern Mediterranean.'

As a bonus he set in motion an ingenuous plan to grab the rich Iraqi oilfields at Mosul. To this end he released a flood of German 'tourists' (soldiers in mufti) from Turkey and the Lebanon to join forces with the Iraqi rebel, Sayid Rashid el Gailani, known to history as Rashid Ali. With this additional oil supply he thought that all his worries would be over.

Fortunately for the British, the plan in Iraq failed due in no small measure to the spirited resistance of the isolated RAF defenders at Habbaniyah who, with their old bi-plane trainers, knocked the stuffing out of their well-equipped besiegers, and to the re-capture of Rutbah by No 2 Company RAF Armoured Cars after a thousand-mile dash across the desert.

Hitler's capture of Mosul would now have to wait until after Russia had been captured in, say, another eight weeks time. Such was the crazed thinking of the Fuhrer in 1941. Wasting no time he set about neutralising Roumania, Bulgaria and Hungary and crushing Yugoslavia. He then turned to the British and Commonwealth defenders in Greece. Working on a tight schedule he had allowed seven days for the capture of Crete. With Crete in his hands the last threat to his oil supply would be removed and his troops could invade Russia and capture Moscow before the Bolsheviks' greatest ally, General Winter, took over.

As we now know, the unexpected resistance of the British and Anzac troops in the Balkans delayed the Fuhrer's Master Plan. He had lost so many paratroopers that he denied them a future airborne role. They served the rest of the war as infantrymen. The fleet of 700 Junkers 52s lent to Student for Crete and afterwards urgently needed for the Russian front was greatly depleted in numbers and many of those returned to him were in need of major repairs. But, due to his Balkan adventure, the greatest blow of all was his failure to capture Moscow in 1941. His soldiers, ill-equipped for the savage Russian winter, were to lie frozen in the snow on the outskirts of the capital.

If, however, instead of vacating Maleme we had stayed to mop up the remaining Germans and had held on to Crete, we would not have lost the many Allied lives; brave soldiers killed in the extensive rear-guard actions from Galatas to Sfakia; we would not have lost the many unsung brave airmen who gave their lives on individual suicide sorties from Egypt; the thousands of men taken prisoner would have been free to strengthen the island's garrison, the Royal Navy would have retained, at least, some of its eastern Mediterranean fleet, which was sacrificed during the evacuation, Rommel would never have reached Alamein, we would not have wasted British lives in the abortive operations around the Dodecanese islands and the Cretan population would not have been subjected to barbaric treatment and the murder of innocent civilians.

Within the year the vast high plateaus of the island could have been turned into heavy bomber bases with Ploesti well within their bombing capacity. They could also have dominated large areas under German occupation. It has been suggested that, by successfully raiding Ploesti oil, life-blood of Hitler's army, they could have shortened the European war by two years.

But, in addition to the military gains we would have achieved, the news of the first great defeat of the hated Nazis would have spread like a bush-fire all over the occupied territories from Norway to the Channel Islands and given fresh heart and hope to many who, in those dark days when Britain stood alone, had given up hope.

Fifty years on

I have re-visited Maleme, climbed Kavkazia Hill again and stood up the Iron Bridge over the Tavronitis once more. In the RAF tented camp the ruins of the old stone hut, in which 33 Squadron airmen played 'Shoot', still stands.

Appropriately wild poppies now grow among the olive trees where Ken Eaton, Tubby Dixon and many others met their death. Nearby, there is a small shrine and Cretans continue to lay fresh flowers beside it.

I saw an elderly lady, dressed in black, coming down the path. She talked about that dreadful day and wept. She told of the love Cretans will always feel for the young Englishmen who came to their aid and sacrificed their lives. I felt that the RAF would ever be present in that peaceful olive grove.

On the slopes of Suda Bay lies the British War Cemetery, a beautiful place of flowering shrubs and perfumed foliage, tended, with infinite care, by Cretans. Here lie the young men whose courage is forever recorded, New Zealanders, Australian and British. The RAF are there also; flyers lying in crews, comrades in life and death. No one could visit this hallowed place without shedding a tear for its exquisite beauty.

On the bald hill-top of Kavkazia stands the German Cemetery where no fewer than 6,000 Germans, mostly young, lie buried two to a grave. Row upon row of regimented slabs stretch to the horizon in every direction. There is a feeling of endlessness. No flowering shrubs here: only a small reddish ground-covering plant.

There could be no greater contrast than between the calm beauty of the British cemetery and the Teutonic correctness of these graves, forever on a hill, overlooking the aerodrome the Germans never captured.

After the war, when the Germans purchased the hill for their vast cemetery, the Greek Air Force still retained the aerodrome and surrounding areas. These included the olive grove along the river bank where, amongst the tents and slit trenches of 30 and 33 Squadrons, so much tragic history had been written.

In 1989, the Hellenic Air Force generously gave a plot of this land to a joint committee representing the two squadrons in order that they could 'erect a memorial as a tribute to honour those airmen who died bravely, fighting for Crete.'

Seventy-one airmen, mostly ground-crew, are known to have been killed in Crete. The true figure may never be known due to lost records and the fact that the invaders at that time were more concerned in tracing and burying so many of their own young men. Although at least 40 airmen from the two squadrons at Maleme were killed, only *one* known grave has ever been found.

Now, by donations from ex-Maleme airmen, relatives of those killed, and generous gifts from other sources, a simple monument bearing the known names of the dead has been designed to be erected in 1991. The site is by the new road, near the river bed, the old iron bridge and the ancient olive trees who remain the only witness to the events of that day, fifty years ago.

After Crete

Lieutenant-Colonel L. W. Andrew VC
Survived Crete and the war. Returned to New Zealand and peace time soldiering.

LAC H. F. Betts, ambulance driver, 30 Squadron
Died heroically during the fighting at Maleme while in the act of aiding a wounded man under fire. The posthumous award of the Military Medal for his actions on 18th May had been approved by Air Ministry, London, only to be withdrawn again prior to being Gazetted. See Appendix 4

Lieutenant J. W. C. Craig MC and bar, 22nd Battalion, New Zealand 5th Brigade
Captured with the wounded south of Kavkazia Hill on 20th May, he escaped from his POW camp two months later in July 1941. He then served with the M19 ('A' Force) in Greece.

He was recaptured January 1942. Taken to Italy, he escaped again in September 1943. From then onwards he served with distinction with the Italian partisans in the Ligurian Mountains, September 1943 to December 1944.

WO L. (Tubby) Cottingham DFC, B Flight, 33 Squadron
Accredited with 14 victories. Commissioned in the Desert. Survived the war and retired as Wing Commander 1971.

Tom Cullen MBE, FRCS 30 Squadron Medical Officer
On 20th May, although weak with dysentery, he attended the wounded on

the slopes of Kavkazia Hill and, when captured, in Tavronitis village, later to be joined by the New Zealand Medical Officer, Captain Longmore.

When the battle for Maleme was over the wounded were flown from Crete to Greece and taken to the POW hospital at Kokinia. Tom Cullen was eventually flown there also and placed in charge of one of the wards.

Towards the end of the year he was sent by Italian hospital ship to the transit camp in Salonika and from there on a 19-day rail journey to Stalag XXA at Torun in Poland. Here he remained until 29th February 1944 when, in company with QMS John Greig, he escaped.

They travelled to Sweden and by train, boat and plane were back in England by 19th March, one of the fastest escapes in WW2.

After the war he continued his medical career, first as a registrar and then as a senior registrar in surgery. In 1951 he was appointed Consultant Surgeon at Kettering General Hospital, a post he held until retirement.

LAC N. J. Darch MM, Medical Orderly, 30 Squadron
Hit in the back by cross-fire and taken prisoner on 20th May. In spite of his painful wounds he assisted Flying Officer Cullen in attending the British, German and Cretan casualties as they flooded into Tavronitis village until, with the doctor, he was flown to Eleusis by Junkers 52 on 3rd June. For the next four months he worked at the 5th Australian General Hospital at Kokinia in Greece.

Unbeknown to him, it was at Kokinia that Flying Officer Cullen, determined that Darch's outstanding conduct on 18th May and in the RAF camp during the invasion should be recognised, discussed the matter with the senior officer, Major Brooke Moore. They decided to make a recommendation which would be conveyed by the Red Cross representative on his next visit. As it turned out, a previous recommendation had already reached the Air Ministry (see Appendix 4). The eventual award of the Military Medal, which was Gazetted in November 1941 came as a complete surprise to Norman Darch.

He is a regular attender of 30 Squadron's RAF Association Dinners each year.

D. M. Davin, 23rd New Zealand Battalion Intelligence Officer
Wounded in Crete, he later served in the Western Desert and in Italy. He was awarded the MBE and three times mentioned in dispatches.

In 1945 he was New Zealand Intelligence Representative in the Allied Control Commission and, after the war, joined the Oxford University Press where, as Official Historian for the New Zealand Forces he wrote *Crete*, a most comprehensive and accurate report of the fighting in Crete.

Operation Mercury owes much to Mr Davin's facts, figures and maps and for his generosity in allowing me to use them.

Flight Lieutenant E. H. (Dixie) Dean DSO, DFC 'B' Flight Commander
Accredited with 14 victories. Became 274 Squadron Commanding Officer in the Western Desert.

LAC S. R. (Dixie) Dean, Rigger, 'B' Flight
After the war he and I joined the Prudential Assurance Company but it was
only in our retirement year, 34 years later, that we discovered each other's
existence! We now meet on 33 Squadron's 'Crete Day'. His friendship for the
Australian Vic Wyatt has lasted for 50 years.

LAC A. H. (Jack) Diamond, 'A' Flight
Having reached Egypt safely aboard the destroyer *Abdiel*, he was moved to
the Anzac hospital in the Italian College, Cairo, the only Englishman among
New Zealanders and Aussies. They ribbed him as a 'Rare As Fairy Pommy'
but showed every kindness and friendship. General Freyberg came one day
and shook him by the hand.

Four months later he rejoined 33 Squadron in the desert but they would
not let him stay long. They told him that now he could not run fast enough
when next the aerodrome was bombed and strafed and so they posted him
to 111 MU.

After services on various units he left the RAF and joined BEA which
became British Airways. Here he worked until his retirement.

Flying Officer C. H. (Deadstick) Dyson MBE, DFC and bar
Accredited with 9 victories. Survived the war. Retired as Wing Commander
1963. See Appendix 3.

AC1 Colin P. France, 33 Squadron telephonist
Captured twice, the only airman who was successful in escaping from Crete
after the German occupation (see Appendix 2, 'A Summer's Journey').

By the time he was rescued, his Greek was so proficient that Headquarters
RAF Middle East posted him to No 335 (Hellenic) Squadron. He stayed with
this Greek squadron for two years.

Since the war he has returned to Greece and Crete several times and, recently,
he has retraced his journeys along the length of that large, mountainous island.
He has met again those brave and loyal men and women who faced torture
and the firing squad to feed and shelter him.

Today, he is Secretary of the Leicester Branch of the UK Crete Veterans'
Association and, recently, he has returned to Crete, in a 30 Squadron Her-
cules aircraft with representatives from 30 and 33 Squadrons to present plaques
to the Museum of Cretan Resistance.

AC1 John (Jock) Fraser, 33 Squadron
One day when 33 Squadron were at Eleusis, Jock Fraser and Corporal Willy
Cann found themselves in a 'low dive' shooting gallery in Athens surrounded
by a villainous crowd of hostile riff-raff. Seemingly not imbued with the
friendly fervour of their compatriots, these unshaven roughs displayed open
animosity to the two airmen. The airmen brazened it out and queued for their
guns.

When their turn came, each was given a rifle and five rounds. The main
target was a bust of Mussolini, the aiming point one of his eyes. A direct
hit caused a small explosion and the Dictator's head would fall off.

Willy Cann fired first. There was an explosion and the head fell off. Fraser fired next, and the same thing happened. The Greeks stopped their noise. The airmen fired second shots and twice more the head hit the ground. By now, each success was met with a cheer. Ten times the airmen shot at Mussolini's eye and ten times the head blew off. The once 'hostile' Greeks cheered and cheered.

Some days later Jock Fraser paid a return visit. All the guns were in use, but not for long. The roughs grabbed a weapon forcibly from one of their members and gave it to Jock. They then took the protesting Greek, opened the door, and threw him into the street.

All his life John Fraser had held a respect for guns. Before the Invasion at Maleme he was so concerned that the sights of his rifle were out of line that he persuaded a Marine gunner to make the correct adjustments using his Bofors Gun Predictor.

During the battle his accurate firing became the talk of his colleagues. He survived Crete and, before he left the RAF his skill with guns earned him a place in the RAF Church Fenton Rifle Team to shoot at Bisley.

He is now retired and lives in Salisbury. We meet on 33 Squadron's Crete Day.

Major-General Bernard Freyberg, VC

Commander of the New Zealand Division and one of the world's greatest soldiers. Wounded no less than 30 times in the two world wars, his reputation for personal fearlessness was only equalled by his ability to inject this personal bravery into every man under his command.

Once, in the summer of 1941, I had the honour to meet him. Another airman and I had been dining at a famous Cairo hotel as guests of his officer cousin when we found General Fregberg standing on the balcony with his back to us gazing at the night sky. Before we could make a tactful retreat he turned and called us over. He did not question why airmen, not even of non-commissioned rank, were dining at an exclusive officers' hotel. Instead, he asked us about ourselves and we spoke of Crete.

I told him of some of my Maleme experiences with the Kiwis of 22nd Battalion and of my great respect for their fighting spirit. I told him also that I had sent an Airgraph home full of their praise and that this account had been passed to my uncle at the New Zealand Office. It had been well received and plans were being made to publish it.

There was a warm expression on his face as if to say 'We were all in that battle together'. We talked for a while longer and then he smiled, shook our hands and wished us luck. As we left him he returned once more to his former stance with hands resting on the balcony.

It had been a meeting charged with the electric personality of this brave and kindly man. I, too, would have followed him to Hell! A year later he was severely wounded at Mersa Matruh when Rommel cut off the New Zealand Division from their line of retreat. Nevertheless they were successful in withdrawing through the German lines.

While still a sick man he took part in the advance after the battle of El Alamein and he and his New Zealand Division fought with such distinction throughout North Africa and Italy that even Rommel gave them the highest praise.

He had few critics. He had extracted his men almost intact from an impossible position in Greece in the face of a German blitzkrieg advance. In some accounts he has been blamed for the loss of Crete but, in my opinion, quite unfairly. He had made the best distribution of his troops to defend the island, but the need to protect the secrecy about our possession of 'Ultra' weighed heavily upon him and denied him the chance to make any re-distribution of his forces. There is a criticism that he had limitations as a commander because his belief in the bayonet charge was an anachronism in WW2, yet, the bayonet was used on many occasions with success against paratroops. There is no doubt in my mind that if an advance with fixed bayonets had been made back to Maleme at any time during 21st May, the Germans would never have consolidated their victory.

Jacobus and Antigoni Giakovmakis (Kosta and Antigoni at the Tavronitis taverna)
Both children and their parents survived the fighting on 20th May.

After the war, Antigoni married and settled in Piraeus. Kosta (Jacobus) inherited the taverna from his parents. Now he serves German tourists because it is his business to do so. However, to mark his quiet contempt for those uninvited swashbucklers of 1941 he still keeps a German bucket helmet in his outside toilet.

As I knew him when he was a little boy, he calls me his 'very oldest friend'.

Sergeant G. E. C. (Chico) Genders AFC DFM
Accredited with 9 victories. Ended the war as Squadron Leader. Was killed at Hartley Wintney while testing the DH108, 1950.

Jg Walter Goltz, 9th Company III Battalion, Sturmregiment
Walter Goltz survived the fighting in Crete and four months later was in Leningrad with Stenzler and his II Battalion. After its almost total destruction his III Battalion was never re-formed.

In the fierce battle for Leningrad II Battalion suffered the same fate. It was totally destroyed by the Russian defenders. Almost every paratrooper was killed or wounded. Stenzler was killed in February 1942 and Goltz was wounded in the chest by shrapnel, a splinter of which is still in his lung. He was also shot in one leg and his shin shattered. He was evacuated and spent the next year in hospital in Brittany. He was then sent to Tunis and, once again, wounded. His Regimental Medical Officer said he would not be fit again for fighting duties. However, when he arrived in Naples the doctor there declared him fit for duty and sent him back to Tunis. He then served on the Western Front and was at Bereitstellung in Holland during the Ardennes Offensive.

Posted to East Germany to fight the Russians again he was transferred to

Lubeck in Schleswig Holstein just before the British mounted their offensive and here he was taken prisoner.

In 1945 he returned to Brandenburg and the next year did really marry the beautiful Lisalotte, his childhood sweetheart whom he had first met when only two years old.

Walter continued his trade as a locksmith but, in 1950/52 studied Mechanical Engineering and obtained a top job in a constuction firm.

When Walter and Lisalotte stayed for two weeks in England, their brand new BMW remained in my garage all the while. The hero of Maleme, Leningrad, Tunis and the Russian Front could not master driving on the left-hand-side.

Gerhard Hänel, 1st Battalion Sturmregiment, fell 2nd day
An enthusiastic member of the Hitler Youth Movement. Survived the fighting in Crete and was sent to guard Allied prisoners until the report of his 'crime' in Greece arrived. He had crashed a German army vehicle. From guarding prisoners he was, himself, made a prisoner, spending four weeks in the Greek prison in 'Prison Valley' — ironically the very area he had been sent to relieve during the fighting . . .

He was reported dead after the battle of Cassino in Italy and was eventually captured by American forces while driver for General Wilke, Commander 5th Parachute Division.

In England he was sent to a POW camp at Kineton but he never lost his sense of humour, prefering to recall the amusing incidents of war rather than the drama. He befriended a Scot named 'Rooky', recently repatriated from a German POW camp where he had been well treated.

Rooky had no rank but possessed a tunic with two Long Service stripes on the sleeve. One evening, Hänel dressed up in the Scotsman's uniform and, with Rooky in civilian clothes, walked out of the POW camp undetected. They went to Leamington Spa, had a few pints, picked up a couple of girls and then returned to the camp by taxi in the early hours, again undetected. No one ever questioned how the fresh-faced 22-year-old came to be wearing Long Service stripes on his tunic.

He remained in England and eventually married an English girl. He had always been a chef and soon found employment locally. In 1975 he bought the 'Nellie Dean' by the old Mill stream at Darley Abbey Mill on the Derwent near Derby. Three years later it was converted to the 'Rhinelander' a restaurant famed far and wide for its German food, wines and beers.

He has appeared on television with Colin France as it was once thought that he had been the actual guard on duty at the time of Colin's escape.

Brigadier J. Hargest
Farmer-politician-soldier. Survived Crete but was killed later on in the war.

'Lofty' Halstead, 11 Squadron, left behind at Almyros
Obtained his pilot's wings in Rhodesia in 1944. After being de-mobbed at the end of the war he re-joined the RAF and completed his full service. Retired to Cheltenham.

Squadron Leader Edward Howell OBE, DFC, commanding officer, 33 Squadron
Of all the many stories of courage, self-discipline and determination recorded
in the Balkan campaign, few can excel that of Edward Howell. His book *Escape
to Live* tells a remarkable story of his fight against death and total immobility
over many months upon an unchanged blood and pus-soaked mattress, his
escape from German captivity *without the use of his arms* and his many adventures which were to follow.

After the war he was selected to go to the Staff College but, upon grad-
uating, was given his first post-war Medical Board. He was told that the injury
to his arms were such that his flying career had ended and he was invalided
out of the RAF with the rank of Wing Commander after 14 momentous
years.

A follower of Frank Buchman's teaching, he was, for many post-war years
a full-time volunteer for Moral Re-Armament, spending much time in America.

However, he could not forget the many generous Greeks who had risked
their lives to give him help, food and shelter and he and his wife revisited
Greece shortly after the war and over subsequent visits managed to trace as
many of them as possible.

Charles and Ann House, American missionaries who had joined him in
captivity at Dulag 183, taught at the 'Farm School' near Salonika and here,
in a reciprocal gesture, they were able to educate some of the children of those
brave Greeks who aided his escape.

Wing Commander Howell has maintained these precious links with his old
friends in Greece and has returned there on several occasions. He and his
wife have helped at the Farm School. It is a unique gesture to a people, loyal
friends of the British since the days of Lord Byron, who still retained that
loyalty in a no-gain situation and at the risk of certain death at a time when
little hope of an ultimate British victory remained.

Edward Howell has also strong links with Crete and has attended several
ceremonies there together with his New Zealand friends. He featured in the
New Zealand film *Touch and Go*.

More recently he has spent some weeks in Greece with the BBC who have
made a TV/video of his remarkable escape.

'Lucky' Hudson, 11 Squadron pilot
Bill Hudson joined the RAAF 'by default' according to ex-XI Squadron pilot
Flight Lieutenant Harvey Besley MM in his book *Pilot-Prisoner-Survivor*. The
story goes that when the Empire Air Training Scheme commenced, Austra-
lia, on top of her existing training facilities, gave an additional 24 training
esablishments for British and Commonwealth aircrews. Bill Hudson, a reporter
on the *Sydney Sun*, was persuaded by a government minister to take a pilot's
course in order to write a series of propaganda articles about his experiences.
He was promised a discharge from the RAAF once he had gained his wings.
Unfortunately, the Minister was killed in an air crash before his secret plan
was put into effect. No one else would believe the story and Hudson found
himself in the Air Force for the duration.

He survived the Balkan Campaign and the Desert War. Harvey Besley writes of him as a Squadron Leader with XI Squadron on the Arakan front in Burma where he led many dangerous missions.

Besley, himself, eventually became a Japanese prisoner, not by enemy action but by a flying error over the target when a propeller of the Blenheim beneath him sliced up through his aircraft, killing his navigator and causing the machine to break into three sections. His rear-gunner could probably have saved his life but his parachute was in another section. Only the two pilots escaped.

After many privations, beatings and sub-human treatment meted out by his captors, over a long period in Rangoon prison, Besley recalls how Bill Hudson, now a Wing Commander, was brought in, badly wounded from a crash. Because of his higher rank, the Japanese gave him an even greater share of interrogation, kicking and punching etc. They repeatedly hit his wounds with rifle butts.

Meanwhile the Fourteenth British Army, the 'Forgotten Army', which had been fighting the Japanese for so long through monsoon rains, jungles and swamps, was about to become the only force in WW2 to defeat the Japanese Army in the field. They were now forging ahead towards Rangoon and the end of the Burma campaign. In friendly rivalry the Royal Navy was competing with them to reach Rangoon first.

The prisoners in the town were inspected by the Japanese to determine who would be capable of standing up to a retreat through the jungle. Finally some 450 men were selected. The remainder, including 'Lucky' Hudson, were left behind with a handful of guards.

Harvey Besley (who, himself, eventually escaped from the Japanese) records in his book how, each day, prisoners would collapse, unable to travel any further. Out of sight their guards would bayonet them. All were certain that their colleagues left behind had suffered the same fate. It really did appear as if, for Bill Hudson, luck had run out ...

But the handful of Japanese guards at Rangoon had other ideas. They were capable of inhuman and bestial cruelty while immune from retaliation but, with the Fourteenth Army close by, terrified of certain retribution, they fled to the jungle.

Immediately, weak as he was, Bill Hudson organised the prisoners. With other officers he went into the town and took over the Administration. As it turned out, Rangoon was not taken by Army or Navy but by an ex-XI Squadron pilot! To signal to the Allied aircraft flying over the town, he organised the prison roofs to be painted with whitewash, JAPS GONE and BRITISH PRISONERS HERE. To emphasise that this was no Japanese trap they also painted EXTRACT DIGIT, a phrase which only the Allies would understand.

He also organised gangs of Burmese coolies to fill up the holes and bomb craters on Rangoon airfield at Mingaladon. Many of the prisoners insisted upon helping also.

All this while, the Army were still organising a mass parachute drop and a Navy flotilla was steaming up the Irrawaddy both intent upon being first to capture Rangoon ...

Wing Commander Saunders in a Mosquito saw a large white marking painted by Hudson's men and landed on the airfield bursting a tyre. Hearing the good news but unable to take off again he took a sampan and sailed down the river to avert the seaborne invasion.

Soon a Dakota landed with supplies and to evacuate the prisoners, all of them emaciated skeletons in loin cloths. However, all but three, who were unable to stand, emphatically refused to be flown out until they had completed their task of repairing the airfield.

Corporal J. (Pat) Kimber, 11 Squadron
After Crete and the Western Desert he served in Ceylon (where XI suffered their great loss at the hands of the Japanese on Easter Sunday 1942, exactly 365 days from the German attack on Menidi on Easter Sunday 1941).

On one occasion he secretly connived with 'Lucky' Hudson to repair a twisted tail unit, damage caused by the Australian attempting to roll a Blenheim with a full bomb-load on board!

He left the squadron in Burma having completed more than four years with 'Legs Eleven' which had taken him from the Afghans on the North-West Frontier to Singapore, Aden, the Balkans, Libya, and the Far East once again.

For the past 18 years we have travelled together to the XI Squadron Reunion weekend, which for 26 years, has been at the kind invitation of the present Squadron.

LAC W. (Killer) Kishkey, MT driver, 11 Squadron
Like several other ground-crews from XI Squadron, Bill Kishkey was later trained as a pilot in Rhodesia. He won the dubious distinction of accidentally setting fire to the engines of four Avro Ansons in one day. After the war he became a schoolmaster.

General Eugen Meindl, commander Sturmregiment
Wounded in the chest while trying to cross beneath the Tavronitis bridge (by airmen like McKenna and Eaton?) he was successfully rescued by Hauptmann Klete and flown out of Maleme.

He recovered from his chest wound and commanded a division in Russia. Afterwards he commanded Parachute forces in Italy, Normandy, Holland and Germany. He was held in great affection and respect by his old soldiers. He died in 1951.

Dr Friedrich A. Merk, 9th Company, III Battalion, Sturmregiment
Survived Crete. Transferred to 1st Parachute Regiment as the III Battalion was never re-formed. Served in Russia around Smolensk and then Italy.

He was in Normandy for the D-Day landings and considers that the American film *The Longest Day* is a most accurate account of what actually took place from a German stand-point.

He survived the war and spent many years as a doctor in the United States. Upon retirement he purchased a large house at Wilhelmsfeld and obtained an interesting position in Industrial Medicine. A keen member of the Parachute Veterans Association he attends all their meetings and reunions.

Albert Moore BEM armourer, 33 Squadron
Severely wounded by shrapnel. After the fighting he was flown to Greece
and eventually moved to the POW hospital at Salonika.

After some months when Squadron Leader Howell was at last able to make
his first stumbling steps to recovery, he paid visits to the Maleme airmen in
other wards throughout the hospital. In his book *Escape to Live*, he describes
his first encounter with Albert Moore:

As I became more active I used to go and visit some of my airmen in other wards
through the hospital. One in particular was very badly wounded and had been hovering between life and death for many months. His name was Albert Moore and he
had been wounded with bomb splinters in Crete. He had more than 60 wounds on
him and his belly and back were lacerated and torn with shrapnel. A deep stomach
wound gave him great pain and discomfort and another splinter in the bone of his
pelvis had produced a lasting infection of the bone there. Yet with it all he was one
of the most cheerful men in the place. He always had a smile for every visitor and
his patience and courage were an inspiration to many. He wasted away to a skeleton,
but his will to live was undiminished and he fought through to partial recovery before
I left him.

When Squadron Leader Howell prepared for his escape from Salonika it was
Albert Moore who risked his own safety to hide the escape clothes under
his bed. On the night of his bid for freedom it was Albert Moore and a private from the Black Watch who escorted him to the outer door of the building.

During two and a half years as prisoner of war Albert had 30 operations
on his wounds but was so ill that he was repatriated on exchange via Sweden
in 1943. He was sent to the RAF hospital at Henlow and discharged as medically unfit. However, he was determined to live a full life. He married and
he obtained employment in the Ministry of Works (now Property Services
Department of the Environment) at Manchester. When he eventually retired
he was senior storeman.

Never out of pain and still with some shrapnel permanently lodged in his
body, he is an inspiration to all who meet him. Edward Howell, who still
keeps in touch, describes him as 'a walking miracle'. He soon became involved
in British Legion activities and, in 1969, became treasurer of the Middleton
Junction Branch where he is also a trustee.

When he retired he was presented with the Imperial Service Medal and,
to the delight of all who know him, his whole brave life, his courage as a
wounded POW, his part in Squadron Leader Howell's escape, and his cheer-
fulness and fortitude over many years was finally recognised. In the New Years
Honours List of 1979 he was awarded the British Empire Medal.

Pilot Officer 'Ping' Newton, 'B' Flight, 33 Squadron
Two years after Crete I went to Rhodesia to train as a pilot. As I carelessly
swung my kitbag from my shoulder outside the Elementary Flying Training School near Salisbury I accidentally knocked a Flight Lieutenant from
his bicycle ...

After the torrent of bad language had subsided, I realised that it was 'Ping'

Newton sitting on the ground. He immediately took me as his pupil and I soloed under his instructions. He was my pilot in Greece and my instructor in Rhodesia.

Warrant Officer F. (Chiefy) Salmon BEM, *33 Squadron*
Chiefy Salmon completed his excellent engineering service with the RAF between 1922 and 1948. He now lives in retirement in Kent. His technical skill and ability to improvise in the 'War on a shoestring' RAF of his time made his award of the British Empire Medal indeed well earned!

Lance-Corporal Max Schmelling, ex-World Heavyweight Boxing Champion
Perhaps the most unpopular paratrooper to fall on Crete was Max Schmelling, German hero of the 1930s.

From the days of early training at Wittstock/Dosse his colleagues had resented the special treatment he received. Not only was he excused all duties and given private quarters but, most evenings, he was wined, dined and feted by hero-worshipping Nazi officers.

When trained he was posted to the 3rd Parachute Regiment, No 4 Company, I Battalion, under Baron von der Heydte. He became part of a mortar section and was soon promoted lance corporal, not so much for his ability as for his strength. Not only had the leader the privilege of lying by the heavy base plate and signalling when to fire the mortar but, when on the move, he was expected to transport it on his back.

On the eve of departure to Crete he asked permission to drop out as he had diarrhoea. He was told to hoist up his jump-suit tighter and jump with the rest, he could report sick when he arrived in Crete.

At that time it was common knowledge among the defenders that Max Schmelling, the boxer, had jumped as a paratrooper. How we knew I know not.

Soon rumours started to spread from all directions, some of them remembered and believed even to this day.

It was Schmelling who was supposed to have led the assault on the New Zealand 7th General Hospital and shot the CO. At the same time he was seen at Maleme. He was seen wounded in various parts of Crete and, on 23rd May, was found wounded by the aerodrome after the New Zealand counter-attack. Aboard the destroyer *Nizam*, an Australian showed Tug Wilson a wrist watch, inscribed in French, apparently presented to Schmelling in Paris. The soldier said that it had been taken from the boxer who had been found wounded (50 miles away from where others had said they had seen him.) All these stories and many similar ones were nonsense; perhaps an excellent example of Dr Goebbel's propaganda machine.

The truth about Max Schmelling is that after landing in 'Prison Valley' with Baron von der Heydte's Ist Battalion, he took no further part in the fighting. The CO and his orderly, crawling around their position passed the mortar section and enquired where their leader was. The men laughed. He had collapsed and been taken to the main dressing station where he remained, suffering from fever and dysentery.

When the fighting was over and von der Heydte was making his recommendations he included Max Schmelling (our champion boxer) for the very lowest order of the Iron Cross. After all, he reasoned, he *had* jumped! To his annoyance he later read in the press that Schmelling had instead been awarded the Iron Cross, First Class for outstanding bravery and had been promoted on the field of battle!

Although displeased about this Baron von der Heydte could take no action. Only he and Reichsmarschall Goering had powers to alter the award and he naturally assumed that Goering had countermanded his recommendation. However some time later, when talking to the Reichsmarschall, it became apparent that he had not intervened. When told the whole story Goering was furious, 'I have been totally misinformed!' he said.

Max Schmelling, feted as a hero by the Nazis in Athens after the battle for Crete, was suddenly transfered from the paratroops and given a ground staff job.

He survived the war and retired to a village near Hamburg.

'Ginger' Stone

Killed Maleme, 20th May 1941. He was a loner; a quiet determined airman who, upon his own initiative, fitted up a 'Heath Robinson' airfield defence with two Browning machine-guns taken from a wreck. He fixed them to a low support, laid out belted ammunition and scooped out a shallow hole on the landing-ground so that, by lying prone, he could fire them. He used no sandbags, a trench or any other protection for himself.

On that last afternoon of 19th May the Bofors remained silent. We were the only airmen left on the aerodrome and ours were the only guns still firing. On one occasion a Messerschmitt flew low over us, slowly, as if throttled back. We could hardly miss it. Although not certain what finally happened, a long burst from Ginger certainly shot away a cowling which fell on the 'drome.

At about 5 pm Heinkel 111s dropped a stick of bombs, two of which fell very close to him and showered him with dust (see photograph).

That evening, when he and I returned to the RAF camp, we both agreed to rendezvous on the aerodrome early the next day. At the time we knew nothing of the afternoon invasion rehearsal and the arrangements to shelter the RAF within the safety of the New Zealand perimeter on the hill.

No one knows how or where he was killed but I wager heavily that it occurred in his shallow scooped-out hole behind his Brownings.

General Kurt Student, founder of German Airborne Forces

For Student his dreams had come true. He had, indeed, captured Crete but at what a terrible cost! Out of the 10,000 young men who had dropped out of the Cretan skies that day, 6,000 had been killed or wounded; most of these killed!

When he reported to Hitler in July he was dismayed to hear that 'The days of parachute troops are over. The parachute weapons depends upon surprise and that has now gone.' Never again were German paratroops to be used in aerial assault!

Student survived the war and retired to Southern Germany.

PWR (Pete) Wickham DSO, DFC and bar, 33 Squadron
Accredited score of 17 victories. Survived the Greek campaign and the war. Retired as Wing Commander.

Corporal W. F. J. (Tug) Wilson
After Crete and Auchinleck's Desert offensive Tug Wilson embarked upon a really remarkable career.

Returning to UK he worked with Wellingtons and Stirlings in Bomber Command and then became an instructor. He was then commissioned and sent to Negombo, Ceylon as Station Signals Officer. Joined the Radio Repair Squadron at Seletar, Singapore and, after returning to UK once more, he was sent on loan to the Malaysian Government for three years as Officer Commanding Electronics, Royal Malayan Air Force. When he returned to the UK again he became Senior Trade Test Officer, Air Electronics, Signalling and Photographic trades, at Cosford.

Once again he was sent to Malaya as Officer Commanding joint RAF/RMAF Communication Centre and then he returned to Cosford as Officer Commanding Aircraft Servicing Training. He was mainly responsible for the founding of the Aerospace Museum.

In 1971, as Squadron Leader, he left the RAF for a worthwhile retirement; Bursar to two schools and full investment with the Air Training Corps.

PO S. F. (Winnie) Winsland, 33 Squadron
One of the original Paramythia flight, he survived Greece.

Just after the 11 Squadron episode at LG 125, he and a South African, John Cloete, were attacking four CR42s when they were jumped by five more. Cloete, aircraft peppered like a sieve, made it home. Leading the Italians, Bernardino Serafini fired at close range and cut off Winsland's tail unit. He made a delayed parachute jump, landed in the middle of the Africa Corps ground battle, was fired on by the 5th Indian Division and was finally rescued by armoured car the next day.

After the war he became an airline pilot until his retirement. In 1984 he met Bernardino Serafini ('a nicer aristocrat of a man I couldn't have wished to have been shot down by!') and he and his wife became distinguished guests in the magnificent Serafini villa on the Adriatic. Three dinners were given in his honour, one with over 100 guests. Italian generals travelled from Turin and Rome to see 'the only RAF pilot to admit having been shot down by the Italians'.

The episode made the Italian newspapers for several days. Winnie appeared on Italian TV and various Italian organizations and individuals showered him with presents.

Flight Lieutenant V. C. Woodward DFC and bar, 'B' Flight, 33 Squadron
Second highest scorer for Canada in World War 2 with 21 victories. He survived the war and became a Hunter and then a Canberra pilot. Retired as wing commander, 1963. Emigrated to New Zealand.

Appendix I
British Forces in Crete

Disposition and Strength of RAF Crete, 20th May 1941

	Officers	Airmen	Total
Creforce			
HQ RAF and Signals	20	75	95
Heraklion			
220 AMES	1	50	51
112 Squadron and Airfield Det	16	125	141
Rethymnon			
Airfield Det	—	10	10
Suda Bay			
RAF Detail	3	33	36
Maleme			
252 AMES	2	54	56
30 and 33 Squadrons	19	210	229
Total	61	557	618

RAF Casualties

Killed	Wounded	Wounded and/or POW	Total
71	9	226	306+

+Davin

Strength of all British Forces in Crete, 20th May 1941

32,389

Total Casualties

Killed	Wounded	Wounded and/or POW	Total
1,751	1,738	12,254	15,743

Royal Navy Casualties

Killed	Wounded		Total
1,828	183		2,011

German Casualties

Killed	Wounded		Total
4,382	3,340		7,722

These figures must always be suspect. Over 6,000 young Germans lie buried in the cemetery at Maleme. Although some graves represent Germans who died during the occupation, these must have been few in comparison with those who lost their lives on 20th May. Several unaccounted for paratroops fell short of their target and drowned. Many were never discovered; the Cretans, understandably, ploughed over the sites and burial areas remain lost forever.

Above all else, the task of Goebbels was to minimise German losses as he had done with the Battle of Britain figures. In my opinion, the fact that Germans at the time admitted to the figures quoted above must imply that the true number was much higher.

Cretans Murdered by the Occupation Forces

Over 25,000

Appendix 2
A Summer's Journey

'Operation Mercury' covers the adventures of 33 Squadron airman, Colin France,
up to the time of his second capture by the Germans. Here below, in his own words,
is a modest account of his further adventures:

On 22nd May I commenced work on the 'drome removing crashed Ju52s. At times
Blenheims raided us and we were delighted to see Germans running from the airfield. We even saw the funny side of being bombed by our own aircraft.

The Austrians thought we prisoners were horses and made us carry heavy cases
of ammunition. Whenever we stopped for breath our 'masters' became annoyed. Later
I joined a grave-digging party, helping to bury some 80 Germans. They had been
dead for several days: we did not need to look, we 'smelled them out'. Then I got a
job after my own heart in a ration store. Another airman and three New Zealanders
were also chosen. The quartermaster, an Austrian, was quite a decent sort. We used
our position to steal every piece of food we could lay our hands on — even lager
beer! After nine days the store moved to Canea. We felt sorry as we marched to our
prison camp but could not help smiling. The kindly Austrian had given us each a
packet of ten cigarettes. He had not realised we had stolen over 900 during our
short stay.

I had often thought of escaping but lacked the courage to do so alone, but one
day an Australian and I overheard three New Zealanders planning. They let us join
them, so at 2 pm on 19th June we crept out of the Internment camp unnoticed. Sergeant Smythe was nominated leader; I was the interpreter as I had, by now, learnt
to speak Greek fairly well.

After an hour we hid until nightfall, then we were moving along a dried-up riverbed, passing the German garrison village with bated breath.

The villagers on the way were kind and gave us food and, when we reached Suya, it became our home for two days. There was a dinghy we decided to steal but were too late as it disappeared round the bay. We climbed the top of a mountain but never saw the boat again.

We were warned that a German patrol was expected and we left the village. By now the Australian's boots had worn out. Under the pretext that he was off to work in a bakery he said his farewells and left. Travelling over the mountains it was at Orthuni that an old man invited us to his home. Here we were treated as honoured guests for three days. Our first meal consisted of 20 eggs, two platefuls of chips, three tins of bully beef, cheese, tomatoes and plenty of wine. We could hardly walk to our beds! His niece offered to wash our clothes for us and her uncle supplied us with civilian suits until they were ready. It was the first chance I'd had to use my Greek and the old man, his three nieces and I conversed for many an hour into the night. Eventually, in dry clothes, we took our leave and made for Therisso.

Here, we had only stayed for a few days when the New Zealanders decided to move to Sfakia on the south coast. I remained in Therisso thinking them reckless as there was bound to be a German garrison there.

I soon made friends with a New Zealand cook, named 'Fatoutis' (toothless) by the Cretans, who had lived in Therisso for a month, and consequently knew everybody. I also made friends quickly. Different families fed me until the day I met Maria who persuaded her parents to take me in. Maria was an excellent cook and I ate at her house for five weeks.

One day I met Vernicos, a sea captain, and two English lieutenants, Miles and Parish. The captain spoke of rumours concerning radio transmitters and I immediately pricked up my ears. There was one in a village an hour's walk from Maleme aerodrome.

Telling Maria I was going away for a few days was difficult as she was concerned about my safety but, anyway, the next day I left for Lutraki and the transmitter.

At Lutraki I had difficulty in proving that I was not a spy but eventually drove away suspicion and departed the proud owner of a small German transmitter. Luck was with me. Just as I had left, a German patrol arrived . . . back at Therisso I was warned that another patrol was approaching!

Hiding the radio I set off at once into the mountains with a band of well-armed partisans. Proud and fierce-looking, I pitied any Germans they met.

When word reached us that the Germans had gone I returned to the village but two weeks later Fatoutis and I, much to Maria's sorrow, left these friendly people. She had become quite attached to me. She gave me food and, very much against my will, forced upon me some money. Before I left she kissed me on both cheeks. She had been crying too. We left that night. I carried the radio on my back.

Eventually we met an Australian captain we had seen in Maleme, followed him to a mountain summit and joined his large party of New Zealanders, Australians, Tommies and Greeks. From then on Fatoutis cooked their meals.

Trying to contact Egypt with my transmitter was a disaster! A Junkers 52 was coming in from the sea when I switched on. It was immediately changed course and headed for our hide-out. I switched off and it continued on its journey. Once more I switched on and, to our dismay, the 'plane returned and circled overhead. After that we decided against tinkering with German transmitters...

One day the two lieutenants arrived with the news that Captain Vernicos had obtained two boats! They hoped to reach Turkey. With every boat on Crete commandeered, some of us doubted this news.*

The Greek captain had given me a letter to take to the cafe proprietor in Cambi and, the following day, I set out. At Zouva an old woman cried: 'Run, the Germans are in the village!' I tore down the hill and dived into some bushes. No Germans followed so I headed as fast as I could for an olive grove in the valley.

Entering Therisso again I was told that Germans were expected. No time to see Maria, I bolted a hasty meal of snails and rice and departed for Dracona. One of the Cretans who had helped me obtain the transmitter was here and he had a tragic story. Shortly after I left him the Germans surrounded his village, killing a number of inhabitants including one of his sons.

Back in Therisso again the people were in a state of alarm. A German had been killed by a partisan and a patrol was already on its way to take reprisals...

For weeks I moved from village to village, always receiving a kindly welcome and food. I was hiding away from the village of Rustica and coming in at nights for a hot meal when three English soldiers walked down the street in daylight. Early next morning Germans surrounded the area and they were captured. I was lucky. A local policeman warned the family who had been feeding me ... and I hid in the orchard.

A submarine was expected on the south coast but, when I arrived, I found it be a false alarm.

Patrols were getting too frequent for comfort. I was actually in one village when the Germans entered and only the alertness and courage of the Cretans saved me. I joined forces with two New Zealanders, one named Roach from 22nd Battalion at Maleme and we headed off to a monastery near Frati on another submarine rumour. There were so many rumours that, after a while, we became 'submarine silly'.

Fifteen days later we had moved towards the Mesarra Plain and from a hill near Clima we could see the new aerodrome being built by the Germans. In the village we were fitted out with new clothes and given a good meal by a family who would not take 'No' for an answer and, by early morning, we were on the move again. A day later, in the darkness, we cautiously skirted the enemy airfield and reached our destination — a boat rumour. With Germans so near, our contact in the village moved us to a hut on the sea shore where we remained for some time, sharing our hermit's existence with an old shepherd.

Eventually the Kiwis became impatient and we journeyed to another monastery on the rumour that there were large trees there. They had intended building an outrigger canoe but found the trees too small. So we parted company. They moved on while I stayed at a place named Mournya where I practically became one of the inhabitants and was fed by different families each day.

Two weeks later the Kiwis returned with exciting news! On 23rd October a boat was arriving at Marithaki and I was told to follow them to Ashedria. Here I met two officers in transmitter contact with Egypt. Both had been captured, made prisoner, escaped to Egypt and volunteered to return to Crete. The third member was Nick Tsouris, an Egyptian Greek, wounded in Albania.

At Marithaki I was surprised to see a well-dressed girl in one of the houses shared with two Commandos, a Black Watch private and ten Cypriots. I later learned she was Poppy Lensdell, wife of one of the Commandos.

On 23rd October I saw a light out to sea and quickly told Nick. With his torch

*However, on 10 August, two captains, two lieutenants, a soldier and four Greeks, all emaciated, arrived in Egypt.

I flashed OK in morse as he directed. No signal followed.

At 2 am a Greek sounded the alarm — the Germans knew our whereabouts ! There had been so many such rumours that no notice was taken until 6 am when a rifle-shot echoed suddenly through the mountains. More shots followed and then a rat-tat-tat of a nearby machine-gun!

We rushed up the mountainside like a flock of frightened sheep! I climbed so far and reached a sheer cliff. Feeling very exposed I hid behind a bush before finding another route to the summit.

When the Germans had gone I joined two Cypriots and wandered from village to village, always following rumours. In one village by the coast I was fed for four days by Emmanuel Levendakis and his five red-headed daughters. They made me very welcome. Then I heard the frustrating news that a boat had indeed arrived at Marithaki and taken off Poppy, three Englishmen, five Cypriots and six Greeks! I decided to return at once. Emmanuel was very upset. He and his daughters kissed me on both cheeks and cried as if their hearts would break.

Eventually I joined a party of Kiwis, Cypriots and Greeks hiding in a cave near the monastery of Aghi Nikada. Two of the Greeks, Lulu and Marika were nurses fleeing the Germans. They had been caught helping the British to escape by dressing them up as women. Also wanted by the Germans were a mother and a daughter who continued feeding and hiding escaped prisoners even after her husand had been shot!

One day Germans discovered our whereabouts! Most of those in our cave fled, leaving four New Zealanders, Lulu and myself. At noon four armed Germans and a donkey came past us down the hill. Afterwards we saw smoke from the direction of the monastery. At 2 pm two more came down the track and halted opposite the cave, looked in our direction and then slowly climbed towards us ... My heart pounded ... Five yards from the cave entrance the soldiers cupped their hands to drink from a spring running down the rocks. I was so exhausted and overwrought I lost consciousness ...

I awoke to find the Germans had gone and the other escapers returned. The Cypriots joked about my falling to sleep.

We had been in another cave for a month when there were fresh rumours of a boat which had rescued some escapers from Tris Ecclesias monastery! Two Cypriots and I set off immediately. An hour later and we saw a *benzina* chugging along the coast. 'It's a German patrol boat,' said the Cypriots but I knew differently! Then we were running down the mountainside as fast as our legs could carry us! The boat stopped near our cave and those on board were already talking with our friends. The captain was an English officer dressed like a Cretan pirate complete with earring.

We were told to go to Marithaki again and would probably leave that night! I ran all the way! We had a good dinner; it rained but our spirits were not dampened. After a traumatic six months we were at last leaving this island prison — with its courageous and hospitable people.

That night, 26th November 1941, at 2030 hours we sailed for Egypt in the Greek submarine *Triton*.

Appendix 3
'Shot 6 Enemy Planes
Down in 15 Minutes'

'Egyptian Mail' report of the exploits of Flying Officer 'Dead-Stick' Dyson, December 1941.

A young flying officer of the Royal Air Force, piloting an eight-gun fighter aircraft, has set up a record in the Western Desert that will be hard to beat.

In a quarter of an hour he shot down six Italian CR 42s — five of the six pilots 'baled out' so there could be no question as to the ultimate fate of their aircraft — and he also attacked a seventh.

During his last attack he discovered, however, that his Glycol tank was perforated. Glycol sprayed over him and his cockpit quickly became filled with smoke and fumes. He carried on, and made a perfect forced landing in territory which had been occupied by our troops.

The pilot's adventures were not over, for he narrowly missed being blown up by a land-mine.

After being absent about two days he has just rejoined his squadron. He is now flying again.

The pilot, who was born at Jhansi, India, and who worn the DFC in Palestine has been with his squadron in the Desert since Italy came into the war. Here is his own account of his amazing fight:

'I was alone, 12,000 feet up, between Bardia and Sollum, when I saw a flight of six Breda 65s.

'I was going to attack the last three when, coming through the clouds, I saw two CR 42s in front of me and three more lower down. They were stepped up, escorting the Bredas. I at once attacked the two CR42s, giving each a burst, and both pilots, turning their aircraft on their backs, "baled out".

'I had dived to the attack and I carried on to the next three. With two bursts I got the leader and the starboard aircraft and each pilot "baled out". Three of the four aircraft had long trails of smoke coming from them when their pilots jumped. For a moment I lost sight of the last of the three CRs but when I rolled off the top of a loop, I saw him a considerable distance below me, and travelling in the same direction as myself.

'I dived at him and gave him a long burst. He too "baled out" — the fifth off the reel.'

As soon as he had disposed of this victim the British pilot was attacked by three more CR 42s.

'I put everything forward and touched 400 miles an hour, and I got away. My dive brought me down to 3,000 feet and I was over Sollum Bay. There I saw two more CRs making their way homeward. The leader saw me manoeuvring and they parted. Both the leader and I stall-turned and we faced each other head on. I don't think he had much ammunition left as I saw only small bursts of incendiaries pass me. I held my burst to a very short distance and just managed to clear him. Turning back I saw him going down vertically. I then managed to get in a quick burst at the other enemy aircraft and I believe my bullets went into him.'

Deciding to call it a day, the Flying Officer started for his base but was attacked by three more CR42s, who got on his tail. Then he realised that his Glycol tank was pierced. The Glycol poured into the cockpit.

'I opened the hood and hung my head outside. I carried on, still pursued, hoping that my aircraft would not catch fire. I did not know whether I was over enemy or friendly territory. Suddenly we were fired upon from the ground and I believe this saved me, for my pursuers broke off. Owing to the smoke and fumes I had been flying blind for three or four minutes, but I managed to put my aircraft down in a cross wind.'

British troops in reconnaissance trucks appeared and the pilot spent the night as the guest of a Brigadier General. Next day, from Tummar, where there was a big concentration of prisoners, he led a convoy of Italians across the desert, using only a small field compass. The truck on which he was riding passed over a land-mine, without harm, but a car following immediately behind, blew up.

The young pilot, having rejoined his squadron, was flying again the next day.

Appendix 4
The Remarkable Story of the Cancelled Military Medal

542821 Leading Aircraftman Norman John Darch, 30 Squadron

548425 Leading Aircraftman Henry Frederick Betts, 30 Squadron

During the attack on Maleme aerodrome by parachute troops, Leading Aircraftmen Betts and Darch drove the ambulance across the aerodrome in the face of very heavy fire in response to an urgent call to rescue wounded from the gun positions on the perimeter of the aerodrome. Leading Aircraftman Darch received two bullet wounds in the back but both airmen carried on and brought the wounded safely to the sick quarters. They showed a complete disregard for their own safety in carrying out their duties.

This is the report sent on 30th May 1941 to Air Ministry, London, from the Middle East. It is based upon the original report sent from Maleme on 18th May to Group Captain Beamish, Senior Air Officer in Crete, at Canea.

Whoever re-wrote the account seems to have confused the day the action took place, the day Darch was wounded, and, for good measure, added the words, 'by parachute troops'.

Unfortunately, no confirmation of the action could be obtained for verification. Darch was a POW and so was Flying Officer Cullen who knew the correct story. The gallant Betts was dead. Those 33 Squadron airmen on the aerodrome who witnessed the whole episode on 18th May were, naturally, never questioned afterwards.

A further account, outlining the action, was made by Pilot Officer R. K. Crowther, 30 Squadron, who, upon his escape to Egypt, wrote a full report of his and 30 Squadron's activities in Crete. He also placed the event as taking place during the invasion on 20th May.

Everyone who came in contact with Crowther on Kavkazia Hill found him a pillar of strength and an excellent commander to those airmen who came under his control. Unfortunately, he included in his report several incidents, widely believed at the time, but which simply did not take place and it is therefore difficult to place much reliance upon this second-hand version.

On 20th May, the whole of 'C' Company, 22nd Battalion, were around the aerodrome perimeter. There were also Marine gunners. In all, there must have been well over a hundred men. Yet in the detailed accounts of the fighting that day there is not one mention of another conspicuous dash across the open landing-ground by an RAF ambulance, similar to the ambulance dash which took place two days earlier. In any case, there would have been no ambulance manned at the Crash Centre on 20th May as the aerodrome had been made unoperational on 19th May. Norman Darch recalls that the action took place after a bombing and during a strafing attack and that the casualties had been Cretan civilians. He has never questioned the inaccuracies in the wording of the citation sent to Air Ministry, London, because, to this day, he has not seen it. All that was printed in the *London Gazette* was as follows:

> The King has been graciously pleased to approve the undermentioned award with effect from 30th May 1941, in recognition of gallant conduct: Military Medal: 542821 Leading Aircraftman Norman John Darch.

There was no heroic dash on 20th May but there certainly was two days earlier. Flying Officer Cullen confirms that the brave action of Darch and Betts took place on 18th May and also that on 20th May Norman Darch, far from manning an ambulance on the aerodrome, was working hard, assisting him with the wounded in the RAF camp. It was later that day when he received the bullet wounds while attempting to reach the New Zealand defences.

The date of the report was to become of paramount importance and the confusion, aided no doubt by Crowther's attempt to describe what was only known to him by hearsay, resulted, as the following correspondence reveals, in LAC Betts being deprived posthumously of the award he richly deserved.

> *Action Copy*
> *From*: AMCS Kingsway 15.8.41
> *to*: HQ RAF ME
> X6744 Secret
> What date were the recommendations for 542821 LAC N. J. Darch and 548425 LAC F. H. F. Betts first initiated?

> *Action Copy*
> Received AMCS Kingsway 0758 hours 17.8.41
> *From*: HQ RAF ME
> *To*: AM Kingsway P464 16.8 Secret
>
> Recommendations for 542821 LAC N. J. Darch and 548425 LAC F. H. F. Betts were initiated on 30.5.41 reference your X6744 dated 15.8 repeat 30.5.41.

This reply is incorrect. The recommendations were *initiated* on 18.5.41. It is only due to the unique situation in Crete involving both the initiator and the airmen themselves that this confusion occurred. The second, re-written, report was sent to the Air Ministry as soon as possible after Group Captain Beamish arrived back in Egypt.

To: Headquarters RAF Middle East
From: Air Ministry Kingsway 5548 20.8.41

Your P363 and 364 of 3/7. Award of Military Medal to 542821 LAC Norman John Darch and 548425 LAC Henry Frederick Betts approved, but publication withheld as they are reported missing. Request you also withhold publication in Middle East until a date to be notified to you later.
File A259288 refers.

*

Reference A259288/41

7th August 1942

Dear Vesey,

Your official letter 68/Gen/7337 (M.S.3.) of the 14th August last conveyed approval for seven Military Medals for Royal Air Force personnel. Five of these were Gazetted on the 19th August last, the remaining two (Darch and Betts) being withheld as they had been reported missing on the 31st May 1941.
2. Darch was found to be a prisoner of war and his Military medal was Gazetted on the 21st November last but the death of Betts, who was recommended for the Military Medal on the 30th May 1941 has now been presumed as from 20th May 1941 and we therefore propose to substitute a posthumous mention for the inadmissable Military Medal. May I trouble you to cancel the award in your register; I imagine you will be able to do this without resubmitting to the King.

Yours sincerely,
C.G. White

To: Major The Hon O. E. Vesey, CBE
The War Office (MS 3)

*

The War Office
London
11 August 1942

Ref 68/Gen/7337 (MS 3)

Dear White,

In reply to your letter A 259288/41 dated 7th August 1942, I write to say that as you had not announced the award of the Military Medal to the late Leading Aircraftman H. F. Betts in the London Gazette there will be no objection by the War Office to this award being changed to a posthumous Mention-in-Dispatches.

Under War Office procedure awards are only made to individuals reported killed, missing or prisoners of war if it is proved that the recommendation for the award was initiated before the individual became a casualty. In the cases of those reported missing or prisoners of war, if the recommendation was initiated after they became casualties, the awards and names are kept in Pool for consideration at the end of the war unless they rejoin in the meantime or unless they are reported later to have been killed or died in which case the only possible award is a posthumous Mention.

We shall be grateful, therefore, if you will advise us in all cases when putting forward your official requests for Military Crosses and Military Medals where the individuals are reported to be missing or prisoners of war and whether the recommendations were initiated before they became casualties.

Yours sincerely,
O. E. Vesey

To: C. G. White Esq
Dept Q. J.
Air Ministry

*

From: Air Ministry Kingsway
To: Headquarters RAF Middle East.
Your P364 of 3/7/41 and my X5548 of 20/8/41.
As the death of 548425 LAC H. F. Betts has officially been presumed to have occurred on 20.5.41 the award of the Military Medal is inadmissable since the recommendation was not initiated until 30.5.41 vide your P464 of 16.8.41.

Betts H. F. LAC RAF (548425)

Mention in Dispatches LG 1.1.43

Appendix 5
The Greek
Commemorative Medal

This was a commemorative award given by the Greek Government in 1979 to serv-
icemen who took part in the Crete campaign 'In recognition of their bravery and
sacrifice'.

All Australians and New Zealanders who served in Crete have been given this medal.
None of the British forces who served in Crete have received one. This unfortunate
situation is not due to any reticence on behalf of the Greek Government but rather
to roundabout and inconsistent reasoning by the Ministry of Defence and the Foreign Office. To the bystander it would appear to be yet another example of the British desire to give themselves a self inflicted wound! One might well ask, what other
country in the whole world would wish to deny their soldiers receiving such a sincere award from a foreign Government to mark their 'bravery and sacrifice'!

Her Majesty, Queen Elizabeth II, has confirmed that all Crete veterans should
receive this medal. However, the Foreign Office thinks differently. They have produced
a ruling which they insist proves that no foreign awards after a certain time can be
received. This rule, apparently, did not apply to the Russians when they decorated
British seamen who took part in the Arctic convoys or, yet again, to the French who
recently gave an award to a British airman for another war-time deed, etc, etc.

For some reason, only those who fought in Crete have been singled out for this
bureaucratic treatment. It has caused much bitterness and resentment among many
veterans and widows of those who gave the 'invincible' Germans their first licking
in the darkest hours of the war when we stood alone.

Ted Telling, a Crete veteran, who also fought at Cassino and Anzio and was twice
wounded, after a lifetime of suffering due to his war experiences, has carried his
campaign for this medal to the highest in the land. Due to the persistence of this

one stubborn man in a wheelchair, it now seems that, at last, his struggle is gathering momentum. Let us hope that, before long, Government red tape will be cut and veterans like Ted Telling, to whom this medal means so much, will receive their just recognition.

'It's not the medal as such,' he says. 'It is a symbol of recognition that we fought through one of the hardest, most terrible, campaigns of the war.'

Before the revised *Operation Mercury* was published in 1991, Ted Telling died. Disabled and in constant pain from his war wounds, he battled on fearlessly for recognition. He wrote to the Queen, the Foreign Office, the Home Secretary and several MPs with the courage and tenacity of one who refused to accept injustice. I am sure that he has inspired others in the UK Crete Veterans' Association to carry on the fight.

Appendix 6
Nos 11 and 33
Squadrons: Their Last
War-Time Encounter

When, on 18th November 1941, Sir Claud Auchinleck, the most inventive of all the wartime generals, launched his desert offensive he completely 'wrong-footed' Rommel. He had tanks by the coast road draped in canvas disguised as trucks. To the south he had old trucks disguised as tanks. There were also dummy aircraft and dummy aerodromes.*

Nos 33 Squadron and 113 Blenheim Squadron had quietly moved 140 miles southwards to Giarabub Oasis and, on the day of the 'Push', headed westwards into Libya escorted by the Rolls-Royces of No 2 Company, Royal Air Force Armoured Cars. At the same time, to ensure secrecy, 33 Squadron pilots, operating from Giarabub, strafed Benina airfield (with the loss of two Hurricanes).

Travelling light, with three blankets per man and no tents, they reached the edge of the Great Sand Sea and a dot on the map named LG125, 120 miles behind Rommel's lines. It was to this map reference that the army had been bravely crossing the Libyan border for some time, burying drums of oil and aircraft fuel in preparation for this bold plan.

No 33 Squadron's Hurricanes were indeed rare ones, fitted with 16 internal petrol tanks which gave an endurance of over five hours.

Their purpose was to maintain long patrols to bottle up the enemy land and air forces at Gialo and Augila to prevent them aiding the main German army on the coast.

The final results of these operations were to be a great success for 33 Squadron

*There was a stick and canvas dummy squadron of Maryland bombers at El Daba. Eventually a Ju88 attacked — and dropped a wooden bomb.

and, afterwards they received a special commendation but they were not achieved without problems.

The Germans soon discovered LG125 and, from then onwards, there was little peace. When under attack the airmen knew that they were the only target for more than a hundred miles. They had dug no trenches and they could not expect the Hurrcanes to stop their vital work and act as aerodrome defence.

Besides Savoia Marchetti 79s and Me110s, a strong force of Junkers 88s had arrived at Derna from Crete. To start with, these bombers had a field day. To inflict the greatest damage to the airmen they had dropped anti-personnel fragmentation bombs. Each had a rod attached to its nose to stick in the sand and explode in the air.

The 16-fuel-tank Hurricane easily developed air-locks and each aircraft took up to an hour to re-fuel. The petrol, painstakingly buried by the army, was never discovered. Instead they had to resort to the Bombay troop-carriers of 216 Squadron. They would land in the vague vicinity of the landing-ground and hastily throw out 8-gallon 'flimsy' cans of fuel. With enemy aircraft never far away, LG125 became so unhealthy that sometimes the Bombays did not even stop. They rolled their wheels along the ground, throwing out cans as they went ...

The Squadron water-bowser had been strafed and destroyed. Airmen and officers alike were forced to exist on the water in their bottles. When a 50 gallon fuel drum filled with water did arrive it was quickly condemned by the MO as it tasted strongly of 100 octane petrol.

It was upon 22nd November, five days after the 'Push' had commenced, that 33 and 11 met for the last time.

By LG125 standards, the day had commenced quietly enough with only a solitary Ju88 bombing and strafing. However, two hours later came a red rocket alert and six Hurricanes scrambled. Shortly afterwards nine Ju88s attacked with various sized bombs, diving out of gaps in the clouds. Several Hurricanes and Blenheims on the landing-ground were hit. The bombers then machine-gunned the area. They hit the squadron wireless van and charging plant with 20mm cannon fire, destroying both. However, they got more than they bargained for when they tried their luck against the RAF armoured cars. The cars damaged several and one Junkers crashed nearby. But for the Germans more bad luck was on its way for 33 Squadron's flight of Hurricanes had returned.

One young sergeant pilot from 'A' Flight found himself suddenly above and behind a formation of six bombers and dived to attack. Led by the American, Flight Lieutenant Lance Wade, the remaining fighters searched for other targets.*

Now within range, the sergeant pilot fired a long burst and he knew that his bullets were striking home on one of the bombers. At that same split second he realised that he was shooting down a Blenheim! The newly-arrived aircraft were 11 Squadron Blenheims returning from a raid! Such was the secrecy surrounding 33 Squadron's mission that no one in the RAF had been briefed. Although the existence of LG125 was known to the enemy it was unknown to the RAF!

Aghast at what he had done, the Sergeant went into shock. He dived his aircraft at the landing-ground without any attempt at flaps or undercarriage. Missing a group of airmen by inches and almost colliding with a parked Hurricane, he belly-landed at speed in a shower of dust and flying panels.

Unaware that there were battles taking place in the clouds around them or that

---

*Wing Commander Lance C. Wade DSO DFC and bar. Top scoring American pilot with the RAF with 25 kills to his credit. Killed 12.1.44 while flying an Auster.

a fresh formation of Junkers was rapidly approaching, the Blenheims of 11 Squadron landed to lodge a formal protest but barely had they rolled to a halt when the aerodrome was once more under attack. The new arrivals roared across the landing-ground, dropping bombs as they went. Most bombs, dropped too low, did not explode but simply bounced large craters in the sand. Unfortunately, one which did explode was a direct hit upon an 11 Squadron Blenheim. The pilot and his two crewmen were killed.

By the end of the day, four Junkers 88s had been destroyed and several more probables. Two were shot down by RAF armoured cars and two by Flight Lieutenant Wade. Wade also shot down a three-engined Savoia Marchetti 79 whose pilot, like 11 Squadron's pilots, had no idea that an RAF fighter squadron could possibly be operating so far behind Rommel's lines. The Italian pilot and four German aircrew were made prisoner.

This was to be the last meeting in wartime of these two famous squadrons. No 33 remained to take an important part in the desert battles, El Alamein and beyond. They returned to England in 1944 where, re-equipped with Spitfire IXs, they operated over Europe as escorts, dive-bombers or took part in shipping reconnaissance prior to 'D' Day. Re-equipped again, this time with Tempests they moved to Holland and then to Germany. When the war ended they were top fighter squadron in the RAF (if Squadron Leader Pattle's lost records in Greece are included). No 11 Squadron, on the other hand, left the Middle East for Ceylon and then Burma. Replacing their Blenheims with Hurricane IICs they gave support to the 'Forgotten' 14th Army in various capacities: escorting Vultee Vengeance dive-bombers and supply-dropping Dakotas as well as indulging in many low-level attacks upon the Japanese. Eventually reaching Singapore with Spitfire XIVs they then moved to Japan. Here the Spitfires were changed for FR18s which they flew on secret operations until 1948.

Both squadrons were formed in World War 1; 1915 (11 Squadron) and 1916 (33 Squadron). No XI Squadron (with their silver 'Legs Eleven' badges modelled on the legs of Ginger Rogers and with her warm approval) now fly Tornados from RAF Leeming.

No 33 Squadron, at RAF Odiham, now fly the Anglo-French Puma helicopter.

No XI Squadron (All Ranks) Reunion Association has met each year since 1950 and, after 1962, the present XI Squadron have always hosted a grand and generous Reunion weekend to its veterans, held at the RAF Station.

On 20th May each year, 33 Squadron celebrate 'Crete Day' with a fun day for everyone. There are amusements for the children, a Crete exhibition and a flying display.

Bibliography

Crete, D. M. Davin, Oxford University Press
Campaign in Greece, Army Board, Wellington
Royal Air Force 1939-1945 Vol 1., Denis Richards, HMSO
Wind of Freedom, Sir Compton Mackenzie, Chatto and Windus
Wings Over Olympus, T. E. Wisdom, Unwin Brothers
Escape to Live, Wing Commander Edward Howell, OBE, DFC, Longmans Green
    & Co Ltd.
50th Anniversary World War II, Ivor Matanle, Colour Library Books Ltd
Greece and Crete, Christopher Buckley, HMSO
The Fall of Crete, Alan Clark, Anthony Blond
Ten Days to Destiny, G. C. Kiriakopoulos, Franklin Watts
Daedalus Returned, Baron Frederich von der Heydte, Hutchinson
Airborne at War, Sir Napier Crookenden, Ian Allan Ltd
The Glider War, James E. Mrazek, Robert Hale
1941 Armageddon, Richard Collier, Hamish Hamilton
The Cretan Runner, George Pyschoundakis, John Murray
Record and Recall — A Cretan Memoir, James Britton, Lightfoot Publishing
Battle for Crete, John Hall Spencer, Heinmann
Pilot-Prisoner-Survivor, Harvey Besley, Darling Downs Institute Press

Other Sources

Middle East Review, RAF No 3 1943

Operations in Crete, No 30 Squadron, carried out by Ground Staff. Pilot Officer R. K. Crowther.
Squadron Diaries No 11 and No 33 Squadrons

Index